Constitutional Politics
in the States

Recent Titles in
Contributions in Legal Studies

Constitutional Politics in the States

Contemporary Controversies and Historical Patterns

Edited by G. ALAN TARR

Contributions in Legal Studies, *Number 81*

GREENWOOD PRESS
Westport, Connecticut • London

Library of Congress Cataloging-in-Publication Data

Tarr, G. Alan (George Alan)
　　Constitutional politics in the states : contemporary controversies
　and historical patterns / G. Alan Tarr.
　　　p. cm. — (Contributions in legal studies, ISSN 0147–1074 ;
　no. 81)
　　Includes bibliographical references and index.
　　ISBN 0–313–28523–3 (alk. paper)
　　　1. United States—Constitutional law, State. 2. Judicial review—
　United States. 3. Federal government—United States. I. Title.
　II. Series.
　KF4530.T35　　　　1996
　342.73'02—dc20　　95–37333
　[347.3022]

British Library Cataloguing in Publication Data is available.

Library of Congress Catalog Card Number: 95–37333
ISBN: 0–313–28523–3
ISSN: 0147–1074

First published in 1996

Greenwood Press, 88 Post Road West, Westport, CT 06881
An imprint of Greenwood Publishing Group, Inc.

Printed in the United States of America

The paper used in this book complies with the
Permanent Paper Standard issued by the National
Information Standards Organization (Z39.48–1984).

10　9　8　7　6　5　4　3　2　1

Copyright Acknowledgment

The editor and publisher gratefully acknowledge permission to reprint a revised
version of Donald Lutz, "Toward a Theory of Constitutional Amendment," *American
Political Science Review*, vol. 88, no. 2 (June 1994): 355–370.

For Mary Cornelia Porter,
scholar, collaborator, friend

Contents

I
Patterns in State Constitutional Politics

II
Case Studies:
Campaigns for Constitutional Change

III
Case Studies:
The Consequences of Constitutional Change

Illustrations

TABLES

FIGURE

Acknowledgments

For more than a decade I have conducted research on state constitutions and state courts. Throughout this period, I have learned from a number of colleagues who shared my interest, encouraged my research, and were generous with their time and wise in their advice. My thanks go to my longtime collaborator, Mary Cornelia Porter, to whom this volume is dedicated; to my distinguished colleague at Rutgers University, Robert Williams; to my unerring guide to the complexities of federalism, Daniel Elazar; and to the perceptive student of constitutionalism, Ellis Katz. Their contributions are reflected throughout this volume.

Thanks also to Elizabeth Murphy of Greenwood Press for her understanding and encouragement during the development of this volume and to Ellen Dorosh, who shepherded it through the production process. Finally, I thank my wife, Susan, and my sons, Robert and Andrew, for their loving support.

This research was supported in part by a grant from the Office of Research and Sponsored Programs at Rutgers University.

Introduction

The appointment in 1969 of Warren Burger to succeed Earl Warren as chief justice led civil-liberties litigants, distrustful of the reconstituted U.S. Supreme Court, to begin channeling cases into state courts, basing their constitutional claims on state declarations of rights rather than on the federal Bill of Rights. These litigants enjoyed some immediate successes, as a few pioneering state supreme courts afforded protections unavailable under the federal Constitution.[1] Over the next two decades, this "new judicial federalism" (as it came to be called) spread throughout the nation. Courts in almost every state announced rulings based on the rights guarantees of their state constitutions and began to develop a body of state civil-liberties law.[2] Some state courts even adopted the practice of addressing state constitutional claims first and considering federal constitutional claims only when a case could not be resolved on state grounds.[3] Legal scholars generally applauded this "rediscovery" of rights protections in state constitutions and produced a voluminous literature heralding the development of the new judicial federalism.[4]

This new judicial federalism, now over two decades old, certainly deserves credit for renewing interest in state constitutions. But the understanding of state constitutionalism and of state constitutional politics underlying the new judicial federalism — and the literature that it has spawned—is both incomplete and somewhat misleading. From the standpoint of state constitutional scholars, the most obvious problem with the new judicial federalism is that it focuses attention exclusively on the rights guarantees in state constitutions, ignoring other constitutional provisions equally worthy of analysis. After all, state constitutions do more than protect rights. They create a framework for state and local government, allocate powers, announce broad policy commitments, and, not infrequently, prescribe the means by which those commitments will be met. At the most fundamental level, they may embody the political identity and aspirations of the state's citizenry.[5]

In addition, by emphasizing civil-liberties litigation and state courts' development of legal doctrine concerning rights, proponents of the new judicial federalism have obscured important aspects of the role played by state courts in state constitutional politics. If a focus on state declarations of rights is unduly narrow, so too is a focus on civil-liberties litigation. State courts regularly announce important constitutional rulings on matters ranging from taxation to the separation of powers to the scope of local government powers. In fact, historically such issues — rather than civil-liberties questions — have dominated the constitutional agendas of state supreme courts.[6] Even today, new judicial federalism cases comprise only a small proportion of state courts' caseloads.

Even in discussing new judicial federalism cases, most commentators have adopted an unduly legalistic approach. During the 1960s and 1970s, when political scientists began to study systematically the impact of decisions of the U.S. Supreme Court, they found that judicial rulings did not always determine the outcome of constitutional disputes.[7] In some instances losers in the courts eventually prevailed in other arenas. In other instances target populations ignored or evaded judicial mandates. In still others the judicial rulings produced unanticipated social and political consequences. The few studies that have surveyed the impact of state rulings have reported similar findings.[8] Thus, to understand the effects of the new judicial federalism on public policy in the states, one must look beyond judicial opinions to the actual consequences of the state courts' rulings.

Finally, the literature on the new judicial federalism emphasizes litigation as the engine of state constitutional change. In doing so, it imposes on state constitutional politics the model of constitutional politics that has prevailed nationally. At the national level, constitutional amendment is infrequent and constitutional revision unheard of. Thus, constitutional development occurs for the most part through constitutional interpretation, particularly by the U.S. Supreme Court, and constitutional politics largely involves reactions to or efforts to influence judicial interpretations of the federal Constitution.

Within the states, however, constitutional change and constitutional politics have proceeded primarily through formal mechanisms for change, through constitutional amendment and constitutional revision, rather than through judicial interpretation. Far from viewing their constitutions as sacrosanct and above politics, the states have treated them as political documents to be changed in accordance with the shifting needs and opinions of their citizens. Indeed, when state judges have aggressively intervened in the state's constitutional politics, state electorates have sometimes removed the offending judges from office or amended their constitutions to overturn decisions with which they disagreed.[9]

These observations suggest that the new judicial federalism represents only one aspect of a much broader and richer state constitutional politics, which differs dramatically from constitutional politics at the national level. They also indicate the usefulness of a broader perspective on state constitutions and on state constitutional politics. The studies in this volume are designed to supply such a perspective. In exploring recent constitutional controversies in the states, the contributors to this book confirm the extraordinary diversity of contemporary state constitutional politics. They also show why groups may choose constitutional reform as a means for achieving their objectives and how they can succeed in their aims. In addition, these studies demonstrate the interplay between the judiciary and other branches of state government in state constitutional politics. In doing so, they reveal how state constitutions simultaneously structure and are embedded in the politics of their states.[10]

Like state politics more generally, state constitutional politics involves both issues peculiar to particular states and common concerns that arise time after time in state after state. In the initial chapter in this volume, I identify three recurring issues in state constitutional politics — the intrastate distribution of political power, the scope of state governmental authority, and the relation of the state government to economic activity — and trace the conflicts involving those issues over time. This history, in addition to its intrinsic interest, illustrates three important aspects of state constitutional politics. First, the recurrence of these issues in state after state encourages those seeking to resolve the issues to examine how sister states have solved them. Thus, constitutional developments in a single state may well have consequences beyond its borders. Second, the recurrence of these issues over time suggests that the resolutions of these issues are often provisional, subject to reexamination in the wake of changes in social conditions or in the relative strength of competing political forces. Finally, as the Supreme Court's reapportionment decisions and Congress's civil-rights legislation illustrate, national political changes, either constitutional or statutory, can profoundly affect state constitutional politics, empowering one set of disputants or even altogether withdrawing an issue from state constitutional politics.

One striking aspect of constitutional politics in the states is the extent to which constitutional change occurs through formal mechanisms for change (amendment or replacement of the constitution) rather than through informal mechanisms such as judicial interpretation. As of 1995, the American states had held over 230 constitutional conventions, adopted 146 constitutions, and amended their current constitutions (on average) over 120 times. In his chapter Donald S. Lutz attributes this greater propensity of the states to amend their constitutions to the greater length of those constitutions. Apparently, the longer the constitution, the more provisions that can serve as "targets" for constitutional change. In part, the greater length of state constitutions reflects the wider range of governmental functions at the state level. Lutz finds that this too affects the rate of state constitutional amendment: Fully 63 percent of all state amendments pertain to topics, such as local governmental structure and state and local debt, that have not been part of national constitutional concern. One might suspect that frequent amendment, by keeping state constitutions up-to-date, would discourage constitutional revision. Lutz's research, however, suggests the opposite: The longer a constitution is (and frequent amendment adds to length), the more quickly it is likely to be replaced. Thus, paradoxically, those participants in state constitutional politics who seek to achieve their objectives by constitutionalizing issues run the risk of jeopardizing their interests by promoting constitutional revision.

Complementing Lutz's study is Gerald Benjamin and Melissa Cusa's analysis of amendment politics in New York. Critics have charged that in the absence of the constitutional initiative or the periodic opportunity for the populace to call a constitutional convention, state legislators will be unlikely to initiate constitutional change, especially changes that would upset the political status quo. To some extent Benjamin and Cusa's findings contradict this claim. New York's system of legislative proposal of amendments produced a rate of amendment higher than that in all but seven states, with amendments addressing virtually every article of the state constitution. Moreover, the New York legislature proposed these amendments during a period in which partisan control of the legislature was typically divided, thus necessitating bipartisan support for amendments. Indeed, New York legislators were willing to introduce amendments far in excess of the number adopted, and some legislators became "constitutional-change entrepeneurs," proposing numerous amendments, particularly in their area of substantive expertise. Yet to some extent Benjamin and Cusa's findings also support the contention that the absence of opportunities for popular initiation of constitutional change will forestall changes that undermine the political status quo. They found that over half the amendment proposals were not "serious," involving efforts to reduce pressures from interest groups or to lay claim to political turf rather than to promote constitutional change. In addition, few amendments that were adopted instituted fundamental changes of the sort that might have emerged from a constitutional convention. Benjamin and Cusa therefore conclude that despite the high rate of amendment, the automatic convention call remains an important weapon ensuring responsiveness to the populace in state constitutional change.

The frequency of constitutional amendment in the states raises the question of how amendment proposals emerge and what determines their success or failure. In her case study of the adoption of Florida's amendment guaranteeing a state constitutional right to privacy, Rebecca Mae Salokar provides an interesting perspective on that question. What was striking about the ratification of the Florida privacy amendment in 1980 was that only two years earlier over 70 percent of Florida voters had rejected a similar amendment. Yet, as Salokar notes, this dramatic turnabout occurred without a major shift in either public opinion or the substance of the proposed amendment. In 1978 the privacy proposal was part of an omnibus package of amendments that failed to gain the support of political leaders, newspapers, and civic groups. It also suffered from spillover opposition, because it appeared on the ballot with an unpopular proposal for legalized gambling. In contrast, in 1980 the privacy proposal emerged from the legislature with strong bipartisan support, and it benefited from the presence of other popular proposals on the ballot. Salokar concludes that the difference in outcome in 1978 and 1980 shows how crucial process and political environment, factors extrinsic to the merits of a proposed amendment, can be to its adoption or rejection.

Among the most contentious constitutional issues in recent years has been the issue of term limitations, that is, restrictions on the consecutive terms that legislators can serve. The speed with which this reform has spread throughout the nation and the success it has enjoyed raises questions about how the movement for term limits emerged in so many states and whether there are connections among the groups championing the state constitutional amendments imposing such limits. John David

Rausch, Jr., addresses these questions through an in-depth analysis of the politics of term limitations in Oklahoma, Washington, Michigan, and Florida. His research documents a major shift in the politics of term limits. Initially, campaigns for term limits were indigenous political movements, led by state-level political entrepeneurs. However, as the success of their initial efforts spread the idea of term limits, national groups supporting term limitations became increasingly important as sources of technical assistance and funding. With the full maturation of the term limitation movement, Rausch found, these national groups assumed a dominant role. His research thus illustrates how state movements for constitutional change can be transformed into a form of national politics.

Another important aspect of state constitutional politics involves popular reaction against the constitutional rulings of state supreme courts. Nowhere has this reaction been more apparent than in California. In 1982 California voters adopted an amendment known as the "Victims' Bill of Rights," which effectively overturned various rulings of the California Supreme Court extending the rights of defendants. In 1986 the voters also ousted three members of the California Supreme Court, Chief Justice Rose Bird and Associate Justices Joseph Grodin and Cruz Reynoso, who were closely identified with the court's liberal rulings on criminal justice. Candace McCoy suggests in her chapter that the amendment's title was a misnomer because the amendment was not proposed by victims of crime and contained few provisions that directly benefited them. Rather, it was drafted and championed by conservative politicians angered by the Bird court's rulings and largely served to curtail the rights of defendants through limitations on the exclusionary rule, on plea bargaining, and the like. These political conservatives resorted to constitutional amendment through the ballot initiative because they could not gain support for their reforms in the California legislature. In that sense the initiative might be viewed as serving its intended purpose of providing an avenue for popular action when the legislature proves unresponsive. But McCoy argues that in fact moral entrepreneurs can use the initiative to achieve their ends by creating an issue and manipulating public opinion on it. She therefore concludes that the initiative empowers special interests rather than the general public.

Barry Latzer's study examines another aspect of the constitutional changes in California, namely, the aftermath of the replacement of Chief Justice Rose Bird and her two colleagues on the California Supreme Court. Those who campaigned against Bird expected that personnel changes on the court would reorient the state's constitutional law.

However, the limited success of presidential efforts to "pack" the U.S. Supreme Court cautions against assuming that such changes would automatically reorient the California Supreme Court. Nonetheless, Latzer's study of the criminal-justice rulings of the California Supreme Court suggests that the constitutional "counterrevolution" largely succeeded. Whereas the California court under Chief Justice Bird overturned death sentences in over 80 percent of the capital cases it heard, the reconstituted court has affirmed death sentences in over 80 percent of its capital cases. Whereas the Bird court imposed standards for search and seizure and for police interrogations more stringent than those of the U.S. Supreme Court, the reconstituted court rejected constitutional challenges to the Victims' Bill of Rights. Only when a subsequent constitutional initiative proposed to eliminate the judiciary's power to interpret state constitutional provisions independently did the California Supreme Court object. Thus, Latzer's study confirms that popular efforts to influence the course of constitutional law can succeed far more readily at the state level than at the national level.

State judges, like their federal counterparts, have at times sought to initiate social change through their rulings. Over the past two decades, perhaps the most dramatic effort has involved the reform of public school finance. From 1973 to 1994, supreme courts in twenty-two states heard state constitutional challenges to systems of school finance, and in ten states they invalidated those systems. Yet did these judicial interventions achieve their desired effects? In the final chapter in this volume, Russell S. Harrison and I consider the consequences of judicial efforts to reform school finance, focusing on New Jersey, a state with a long history of school-finance litigation. Our study reveals that the effects of the New Jersey court's initiatives were limited at best, a finding consistent with much of the literature examining the effectiveness of courts as social policymakers. The chapter also examines the usefulness for state courts and state constitutional litigation of Gerald Rosenberg's analysis of the circumstances in which judicial policy initiatives are likely to succeed. Although Rosenberg's model is helpful in explaining the consequences of federal judicial rulings, its applicability to state judicial initiatives is questionable. Many of the conditions favoring effective judicial action were present immediately following the New Jersey Supreme Court's invalidation of the state's system of school finance, and yet the ruling had only limited effects.

Taken altogether, the contributions to this volume testify to the striking diversity of state constitutional politics. The participants in state constitutional politics include not only judges and litigants but also legislatures, governors, and commissions, interest groups and social movements. The constitutional conflicts may involve the extraordinary politics of fundamental reform or the continuation of normal politics in a different arena. If the issues in state constitutional politics often include momentous concerns — such as the protection of fundamental rights, the effectuation of popular rule, and the division of power between state and locality — they almost as frequently reflect narrow partisan concerns or minor legal adjustments necessitated by unduly constraining constitutional language.

Yet despite this diversity, the contributions point to a single conclusion: constitutional politics is a central element of state politics, not an anomalous intrusion. To understand state politics, one must understand state constitutional politics, and the contributions to this volume are designed to advance that understanding.

NOTES

1.   See, for example, *Serrano v. Priest,* 487 P.2d 1241 (Cal. 1971); *Southern Burlington County N.A.A.C.P. v. Township of Mount Laurel,* 336 A.2d 713 (N.J. 1971); and *Ravin v. State,* 537 P.2d 494 (Alaska 1975). For an overview of early developments, see Stanley H. Friedelbaum, "Independent State Grounds: Contemporary Invitations to Judicial Activism," in *State Supreme Courts: Policymakers in the Federal System,* ed. Mary Cornelia Porter and G. Alan Tarr (Westport, Conn.: Greenwood Press, 1982), 23–53; and "Developments in the Law — The Interpretation of State Constitutional Rights," *Harvard Law Review* 95 (April 1982): 1324–1502.

2.   On the spread of the new judicial federalism, see Ronald K. L. Collins, Peter J. Galie, and John Kincaid, "State High Courts, State Constitutions, and Individual Rights Litigation since 1980: A Judicial Survey," *Publius: The Journal of Federalism* 16 (Summer 1986): 141–162. Annual surveys of state constitutional cases are found in the *Rutgers Law Journal.*

3.   These states include Oregon (*Sterling v. Cupp,* 625 P.2d 123 [Or. 1981]); Washington (*State v. Coe,* 679 P.2d 353 [Wash. 1984]); Maine (*State v. Cadman,* 476 A.2d 114 [Me. 1984]); and Vermont (*State v. Badger,* 450 A.2d 336 [Vt. 1982]). This approach was initially championed by Justice Hans E. Linde of the Oregon Supreme Court; see his "Without 'Due Process': Unconstitutional Law in Oregon," *Oregon Law Review* 49 (1970): 125–187.

4.   On the legal community's enthusiasm for the new judicial federalism, see G. Alan Tarr, "Constitutional Theory and State Constitutional Interpretation," *Rutgers Law Journal* 22 (Summer 1991): 843–850. For a useful bibliography of the literature on the new judicial federalism, see Earl M. Maltz, Robert F. Williams, and Michael Araten, "Selected Bibliography on State Constitutional Law, 1980–1989," *Rutgers Law Journal* 20 (Summer 1989): 1093–1113.

5.   See Daniel J. Elazar, "The Principles and Traditions Underlying American State Constitutions," *Publius: The Journal of Federalism* 12 (Winter 1982): 11–25; and

Donald S. Lutz, ed., *Documents of Political Foundation Written by Colonial Americans* (Philadelphia: Institute for the Study of Human Issues, 1986), 5–8.

    8.   See Robert A. Kagan, Bliss Cartwright, Lawrence M. Friedman, and Stanton Wheeler, "The Business of State Supreme Courts, 1870-1970," *Stanford Law Review* 30 (1977): 121–156. Even when state supreme courts confronted rights claims, they often have differed from those prevalent in federal courts. See Peter J. Galie, "State Courts and Economic Rights," *Annals of the American Academy of Political and Social Sciences* 496 (March 1988): 76–87; Susan P. Fino, "Judicial Federalism and Equality Guarantees in State Supreme Courts," *Publius: The Journal of Federalism* 17 (Winter 1987): 51–67; and G. Alan Tarr, "The Past and Future of the New Judicial Federalism," *Publius: The Journal of Federalism* 24 (Spring 1994): 63–79.

    7.   For an overview of the judicial-impact literature, see Charles A. Johnson and Bradley C. Canon, *Judicial Policies: Implementation and Impact* (Washington, D.C.: Congressional Quarterly Press, 1984). For a recent study emphasizing the limited effectiveness of judicial mandates, see Gerald Rosenberg, *The Hollow Hope: Can Courts Bring About Social Change?* (Chicago: University of Chicago Press, 1991).

    8.   See, for example, G. Alan Tarr and Russell S. Harrison, "Legitimacy and Capacity in State Supreme Court Policymaking: The New Jersey Court and Exclusionary Zoning," *Rutgers Law Journal* 15 (1984): 514–572; and Richard Lehne, *The Quest for Justice* (New York: Longman, 1978).

    9.   Three members of the California Supreme Court were removed in 1986, following a heated campaign focusing primarily on the court's death-penalty rulings. For a discussion of this campaign, see Candace McCoy, this volume, chap. 6.

    Constitutional amendments designed to overturn state judicial rulings include: California Constitution, art. 1, sec. 27, passed in response to *People v. Anderson*, 493 P.2d 880 (Cal. 1972); Massachusetts Constitution, pt. 1, art. 26, passed in response to *District Attorney v. Watson*, 411 N.E.2d 1274 (Mass. 1980); Florida Constitution, art. 1, sec. 12, passed in response to various search-and-seizure rulings of the Florida Supreme Court; and California Constitution, art. 1, sec. 28(d), passed in response to numerous criminal-justice rulings of the California Supreme Court.

    10.   James Dealey has noted, doubtless with some exaggeration: "One might almost say that the romance, the poetry, and even the drama of American politics are deeply embedded in the many state constitutions" (James Q. Dealey, *The Growth of American State Constitutions from 1776 to the End of the Year 1914* [Boston: Ginn & Co., 1915], 11).

I

PATTERNS IN STATE CONSTITUTIONAL POLITICS

1

State Constitutional Politics: An Historical Perspective

G. Alan Tarr

One of the most striking features of state constitutional politics is the tendency to pursue constitutional change through formal mechanisms of constitutional change, through amendment or replacement of the constitution, rather than through litigation. The contrast with federal constitutional politics, in which amendment is rare and revision unheard of, could hardly be sharper. As of January 1995 the American states had held over 230 constitutional conventions and adopted 146 constitutions.[1] They had also adopted over 6,000 statewide amendments to their current constitutions. This last figure, of course, substantially understates the frequency of state constitutional amendment, since it excludes both purely local amendments and amendments to the states' previous constitutions.[2]

The states' reliance on formal mechanisms of constitutional change means that an analysis of state constitutional provisions, as well as of how they emerged and changed over time, can offer considerable insight into state constitutional politics and into state politics more generally. Commentators such as James Bryce recognized this quite early, characterizing state constitutions as "a mine of instruction for the natural history of democratic communities."[3] Yet because constitutional change is so frequent, and there is so little apparent pattern to it, piecing together the story told by state constitutions remains a daunting task.

Like state politics more generally, state constitutional politics involves both issues peculiar to particular states and common concerns that arise time after time in state after state. In this chapter the most important recurring issues in state constitutional politics are examined: the intrastate distribution of political power, the scope of state governmental authority, and the relation of the state to economic activity. These issues are intrinsically important. In addition, analysis of the emergence, transformation, and — on occasion — resolution of these recurring issues helps clarify underlying patterns in state constitutional politics.

PERSPECTIVES ON STATE CONSTITUTIONAL POLITICS

My account builds upon, even as it at times diverges from, three earlier accounts of the dynamics of state constitutional politics and state constitutional change. Daniel Elazar has proposed a political-culture model, which describes a state's constitution as embodying the reigning political culture in the state because the predominant political forces tend to enshrine their basic values in the state constitution.[4] It follows that if states have different political cultures, the contrast should be reflected in the form and substance of their constitutions. Also, if the political culture of a state changes, so too should the state's constitution.

Other scholars have championed what might be labeled an historical-movement model. They argue that state constitutions reflect not distinctive state political cultures but rather the political forces prevailing nationally at the time they were adopted.[5] State constitutional politics is thus national politics writ small, or if one prefers, national politics is merely the aggregation of political conflicts within the various states. According to this account, one would expect a constitution adopted during the middle third of the nineteenth century to reflect the values of Jacksonian democracy and one adopted during the early twentieth century to embody the prescriptions of the Progressive movement.

Finally, some scholars have advanced what might be called an ordinary-politics model. They insist that constitutional politics in the states represents merely the continuation of ordinary state politics in a different arena.[6] According to this perspective, one should not expect a state constitution to embody a coherent design or overarching perspective on politics any more than one would expect it of a collection of the state's statutes. Rather, the constitution registers the result of group conflict within the state at the point at which various provisions were adopted.

The relationships among these models of state constitutional politics deserve particular attention. The political-culture and ordinary-politics models emphasize the importance of intrastate factors in state constitutional politics, whereas the historical-movement model views national factors as decisive. Yet because adjacent states often share a common political culture, both the political-culture and historical-movement models, in contrast with the ordinary-politics model, look for interstate similarities in constitutional politics and constitutional design. Finally, the political-culture model suggests that a state constitution typically manifests a coherence of perspective, whereas the historical-movement model expects coherence only among provisions adopted within a particular era and the ordinary-politics model expects none at all.

Despite their differences, these models overlap in significant respects. The indigenous political forces emphasized by the ordinary-politics model may well reflect the political culture of the state or mirror political cleavages found throughout the nation. Moreover, as we shall see, national political developments can influence the political culture of a state or affect the fortunes of political forces within it. Finally and most important, each model may accurately depict an aspect of state constitutional politics but need integration into a more comprehensive and yet more nuanced account.

RECURRING ISSUES IN STATE CONSTITUTIONAL POLITICS

The Intrastate Distribution of Political Power

One recurring constitutional dispute has involved the distribution of political power among groups and regions within the individual states. As various groups have gained political strength, they have pressed for constitutional recognition of their numbers and their interests. In some cases, recognition would have necessitated a modification of the system of representation in the state legislature; in others, the enfranchisement of previously excluded groups. Typically, groups that have benefited from the prevailing distribution of political power have opposed demands that it be redistributed.

Apportionment

During the early nineteenth century, population shifts within the original thirteen states fueled conflicts over representation in state legislatures. Several state constitutions prescribed representation for one or both houses of the state legislature based on political subdivisions, such as counties, without regard to population.[7] In many of the Southern states, constitutionally prescribed apportionment schemes ensured the dominance of coastal regions despite population growth in the interior. In New England, the transformation of some towns into cities — for example, Hartford and New Haven in Connecticut — and the decline of other rural towns produced grave inequalities. In other Northern states as well, urban-rural divisions quickly emerged.

Because state constitutions apportioned state legislatures, only constitutional reform could redress the grievances of those dissatisfied with the system of representation, and thus campaigns for constitutional conventions developed in several states. In some states, such as Virginia, the sitting legislators initially refused to call a convention but eventually bowed to the intense pressures for change. Yet often the representation at these conventions reflected the prevailing distribution of power in the states, and so the demands of underrepresented areas were seldom fully met. Thus, even though these areas secured somewhat greater representation in the councils of state government, the compromises did not resolve the issue. In other states, among them North Carolina, legislatures proposed constitutional amendments rather than risk a convention. In still other states, Connecticut, for example, conventions were convened but did nothing to remedy the existing disparities, which grew more severe over time.[8] Finally, in some states dissatisfied groups responded to legislative intransigence by convening extralegal constitutional conventions. For example, when the Rhode Island legislature adamantly refused even to sanction a convention, insurgent elements called one anyway, devised a constitution, and held elections under the new constitution, so that the state temporarily had two operating governments.[9]

The states' failure to deal successfully with legislative apportionment during the first half of the nineteenth century meant that the issue continued to fester, provoking periodic efforts to remedy inequities. Although at times these efforts succeeded, often the resistance of rural legislators increased with the disparities in population among legislative districts. For if the population disparities were substantial, remedying them would entail a major shift in political power. Beginning in the late nineteenth century, rural legislators found allies among Republican reformers, who claimed that republican government required that rural communities not be overwhelmed by the legislative power of urban areas dominated by (Democratic) party machines.[10] Often these coalitions made reapportionment impossible.[11]

Aggravating concerns about inequitable constitutional prescriptions was the failure of some state legislatures to follow constitutional mandates regarding apportionment. Tennessee provides an egregious example. Although the state constitution provided that representation in both houses of the state legislature be on the basis of population, the Tennessee Legislature for over sixty years ignored the constitutional requirement to reapportion every decade. Indeed, by the early 1960s Tennessee's most populous legislative district had over eighteen times the population of its least populous district. The failure of the Tennessee legislature to meet its constitutional responsibilities, together with the refusal of state courts to remedy the situation, paved the way for intervention by the U.S. Supreme Court.

The Supreme Court's intervention curtailed, but failed to foreclose, state constitutional disputes over the distribution of political power. In *Baker v. Carr* (1962) the Supreme Court ruled that legislative apportionment was not a "political question" and that federal courts could hear federal constitutional challenges to state apportionment schemes.[12] Two years later, in *Reynolds v. Sims* (1964), the Court held that the equal protection clause of the Fourteenth Amendment required that both houses of state legislatures be apportioned according to population. Subsequent rulings confirmed the Court's insistence on interdistrict equality in population.[13] Freed from the need to respect geographic or political boundaries by the Court's insistence on "one person, one vote," apportionment politics in the states shifted to a search for partisan advantage through the artful creation of legislative districts. However, the Supreme Court has indicated that this aspect of legislative apportionment too may be subject to federal constitutional scrutiny.[14]

The Court's rulings in *Baker v. Carr* and *Reynolds v. Sims* also removed a barrier to constitutional change in the states. Prior to the Court's rulings, rural legislators had sometimes opposed constitutional revision lest their own positions be jeopardized by reapportionment. For example, during the early twentieth century, efforts to devise a new constitution for New Jersey were stymied for three decades until constitutional reformers agreed to exclude reapportionment from the topics to be addressed at the constitutional convention.[15] The Supreme Court's resolution of the apportionment issue in effect freed rural legislators to support constitutional reform. Indeed, in the decade following the Court's rulings, several states either devised new constitutions or adopted constitutional amendments to bring their systems of legislative apportionment in line with the Court's requirements.

Political Participation

Constitutional disputes have also flared periodically over the size and composition of state electorates and over eligibility for public office.[16] The original state constitutions, reflecting republican traditions, encouraged broad participation but imposed some restrictions on the franchise and on officeholding.[17] Voters were expected to show a stake in the community, either by property holding or by payment of taxes, although local officials could sometimes waive such requirements. Property requirements for officeholding, especially for the upper house of the legislature, were typically more stringent. Donald Lutz has estimated that 65 to 75 percent of free white adult males were eligible to vote in state elections during the 1780s, and about half that number could serve in the upper house of state legislatures.[18]

From the 1820s to Reconstruction, these limitations on political participation came under sustained attack in constitutional conventions. Animated by the Jacksonian faith in the common man, radical delegates demolished the last barriers to white manhood suffrage, and even conservative delegates — fearful of being branded as opponents of popular rule — joined the assault.[19] In Wisconsin, Michigan, and other sparsely populated states, even aliens were enfranchised as soon as they indicated their intention to become citizens.[20] Yet the Jacksonian project involved more than granting the vote to the previously disenfranchised. Property qualifications for officeholding were abolished, and the number of offices subject to popular election and control were multiplied. The influential New York Constitution of 1846, for example, made even such technical offices as canal commissioner and prison inspector elective, and by 1861 twenty-four of the thirty-four states selected judges by election rather than by appointment.[21]

Once invoked in state constitutional politics, however, the doctrine of popular sovereignty proved difficult to contain. The same arguments used to enfranchise white males were appropriated by other groups — most notably, African Americans and women — seeking to participate in political life. Initially, the campaign for broader black participation met not only resistance but also concerted efforts to reduce black suffrage. The New York Constitution of 1846, for example, imposed different eligibility requirements on white and black voters, and other states altogether denied the franchise to free blacks.[22] After the Civil War, the Fifteenth Amendment outlawed the use of racial qualifications for voting. Yet, as is well known, this national effort to eliminate black suffrage as an issue in state constitutional politics failed. During the late nineteenth and early twentieth centuries in the aftermath of Reconstruction, the Southern states adopted literacy tests, poll taxes, and other constitutional barriers to black suffrage.[23] Even though some of these voting qualifications — for example, Oklahoma's "grandfather clause" — were ultimately declared unconstitutional by federal courts, it was not until the late 1960s, with the enactment of the Voting Rights Act of 1965, that full black suffrage returned to the South and racial qualifications for voting disappeared as a state constitutional issue.[24]

The quest for women's suffrage in the American states began in the mid-nineteenth century, and few constitutional conventions thereafter escaped consideration of the issue.[25] Initially, overwhelming majorities rejected women's suffrage, as in the New York convention of 1867 and the California convention of 1879.[26] By the late nineteenth century, however, the tide had turned, at least in the Western states. Colorado, Idaho, Utah, and Wyoming adopted women's suffrage in the last decade of the nineteenth century; in fact, the latter two states included women's suffrage in their original constitutions.[27] Between 1910 and 1914, seven more Western states followed suit.[28] The ratification of the Nineteenth Amendment eventually removed gender as a voting qualification from state constitutional politics.

The Scope of Government

Under standard constitutional theory, state governments possess plenary legislative powers — that is, their power to legislate is circumscribed only by the grants of power to the federal government and by limitations found in the federal constitution or in their own constitutions.[29] The state constitutional limitations include both guarantees in the declarations of rights and procedural and substantive restrictions found in the body of state constitutions. The number and substance of these limitations have changed dramatically over time, as the scope of state constitutional limitations (and hence of state legislative power) has periodically arisen as an issue in state constitutional politics.

Restrictions on Legislative Power

The initial state constitutions imposed few restrictions on state legislatures. Their "open-ended subject-matter authority" was unchecked by gubernatorial veto — few governors wielded a veto power, and most were elected by the legislature — or by anything other than the vigilance of the populace. Even the limitations on legislative authority found in the constitutions tended to be hortatory rather than legal. State declarations of rights provided statements of broad principles rather than legally enforceable rights. Massachusetts, for example, admonished its law-makers to make laws "for the common good" and "not for the profit, honor, or private interest of any one man, family, or class of men."[30]

Experience with this unfettered legislative power led to efforts to restrict it. Proponents of such restrictions charged that legislators had abused their authority for their own advantage and that of their friends. Moreover, in seeking economic development through internal improve-ments, they had underwritten ill-considered ventures with bonds that brought some states to default and others to the verge of insolvency. (These developments are discussed in detail below.) From the 1830s onward, constitution-makers responded by imposing procedural limits on legislative action — for example, requiring that all bills be read three times prior to passage and that their titles accurately describe their contents. From the 1850s onward, they added various substantive limits, forbidding the enactment of special or local laws in specified policy areas. Distrust of elected officials also led constitution-makers to insert detailed policy prescriptions into the constitutions themselves. In addi-tion, groups that had gained political power sought to give permanence to their policy views by constitutionalizing them. As a result, state constitutions "sprouted detail in their growth." These longer, more prescriptive and proscriptive constitutions imposed substantial limita-tions on legislative authority.[31]

During the twentieth century, however, these restrictions on legislative authority have come under increasing attack by constitutional reformers. Constitutions, these reformers insist, should be statements of funda-mental principle, not compendia of detailed and frequently obsolete policy prescriptions. Arguing that constitutional restrictions on legis-lative authority make effective response to contemporary problems impossible, groups such as the National Municipal League have campaigned tirelessly for the "modernization" of state constitutions. Their efforts have produced some noteworthy successes: from 1945 to 1970, six states revised their constitutions, and others undertook editorial revisions designed to remove unnecessary provisions and streamline their charters. However, not everyone embraced the reform prescription: During this same period voters in ten states defeated calls for conventions and in three states rejected the "modernized" constitutions that conventions had proposed. Moreover, voters in states with the constitutional initiative have often utilized this device for constitutional legislation prescribing policy or restricting legislative discretion.

Direct Popular Government

Paralleling the imposition of limitations on state legislative power have been experiments in substituting direct popular rule for institutionalized government. As a general rule, the states have not been nearly as convinced as the federal government of the advantages of representative democracy over direct democracy. During the heyday of constitutional conventions in the nineteenth century, some delegates claimed that the conventions displaced government and restored political power directly to the people. As an Illinois delegate enthused in 1847, "We are what the people of the State would be, if they were congregated here in one mass meeting."[32] Based on that theory, the South Carolina convention of 1860 did not relinquish its authority to the state legislature until a year and a half into the Civil War, and other conventions assumed the responsibilities of legislatures, imposing taxes and enacting laws.[33] During the Progressive Era, the attempt to constitutionalize direct popular rule took the form of the initiative and referendum. Between 1898 and 1918 thirteen states adopted the constitutional initiative under which voters could propose constitutional amendments and, in a few states, call a convention.[34] Nineteen states during the same period adopted the statutory initiative, permitting voters to propose and enact legislation, and twenty-two states adopted the referendum, which authorizes voters to accept or reject specific laws enacted by the legislature.[35] The antiinstitutional thrust of these provisions is illustrated by the Arizona Constitution, which defines the initiative as "the power reserved to the people to propose laws and amendments and to enact at polls independent of the legislature."[36] From 1968 to 1978, in another burst of enthusiasm for direct democracy, three states (Florida, Illinois, and Montana) adopted the constitutional initiative, one (Wyoming) the statutory initiative, and two (Illinois and Wyoming) the referendum.

State and Economy

At times, the divisions in state constitutional politics have followed religious lines, as when, for example, delegates to the Idaho constitutional convention rigged the state's apportionment scheme to reduce the influence of the Mormons.[37] At times, the divisions have reflected and promoted racial animosities — most obviously in the South, where constitution-makers sought to constitutionalize white supremacy in the aftermath of Reconstruction, but also in California, where the convention of 1878 was disfigured by virulent anti-Chinese prejudice and demagoguery.[38] Generally, though, state constitutional politics has supported James Madison's observation in Federalist No. 10 that the "most common and durable source of factions has been the verious and unequal distribution of property."[39]

That economic divisions have been the most durable source of constitutional conflicts does not mean that the lines of division have always remained the same. Class conflicts have spawned some constitutional disputes, but so have intrastate rivalries among groups such as miners and farmers. What is striking about economic conflicts in state constitutional politics, however, is the extent to which they have reflected an ambivalence about economic development and its prerequisites. On the one hand, the states have eagerly sought economic prosperity for their citizens. On the other hand, they have remained suspicious of groups and organizations whose economic success seemed to threaten the economic prospects of others or to rest on advantages not available to the general citizenry. Indeed, they have sought, with some trepidation, to rein in those whose success appeared to rest on unfair advantage, all the while fearful of the consequences of impeding economic development. My account of economic conflict and its regulation by state constitutions illustrates this ambivalence.

Antebellum America and the
Dual Perspective on Economic Activity

During the early nineteenth century, state governments employed a wide array of inducements to encourage economic development.[40] Southern states borrowed funds to enlarge banking facilities, issuing state bonds to supply working capital. Many Northern and Midwestern states constructed canals and other public works in order to facilitate the transportation of goods to major markets. These states also granted special charters to private corporations — such as turnpike corporations, bridge corporations, and railroad corporations — and enlisted them in developing transportation and communication links by dispensing benefits ranging from subsidies to outright grants of monopoly rights. The Jacksonian opposition to federal internal improvements, primarily because of constitutional concerns, helps explain the states' often reckless promotional efforts. So too does the prevailing mercantilist assumption that development depended on special protections for enterprises potentially unprofitable without them.[41] Corruption of state legislatures by potential recipients of state largesse undoubtedly played a role as well. But particularly influential were the hope of economic windfalls — what Marvin Meyers has called "the gaudy mid-thirties dream of sudden fortune" — promoted by the spectacular success of the Erie Canal, and the fear of being left behind, as other states courted prosperity with speculative ventures.[42] As J. Willard Hurst has noted, "All had in common a deep faith in the social benefits to flow from a rapid increase in productivity; all shared an impatience to get on with the job by whatever means functionally adapted to it, including the law."[43]

Coexisting in some tension with this enthusiasm for the release of productive forces, however, was a suspicion of special privilege. This suspicion existed in the states from the very outset: The Pennsylvania Constitution of 1776, for example, emphasized that "government is, or ought to be, instituted for the common benefit, protection and security of the people, nation or community; and not for the particular emolument or advantage of any single man, family, or set of men."[44] This provision, like analogous provisions in other state constitutions, was not an expression of class antagonisms. Rather, it reflected a judgment about the forms and sources of wealth. Historians have noted that the early Americans framed the distinction implicit in this judgment in various ways. Jacksonians typically contrasted the "real people," with their stable income resulting from honest, sober work with the "money power," whose wealth arose from financial manipulation and special privilege.[45] Antebellum economists distinguished "producers," who made and therefore deserved the fruit of all true wealth, from both laborers and, more important, from "capitalists," who used their privileged market position and legal position to create false paper-money wealth.[46] Yet whatever the formulation, the prevailing belief was that one's economic success should reflect one's contribution to the real wealth of the society.

Constitutional efforts to reconcile the release of economic energies with the avoidance of special privilege began early in the nineteenth century. In 1821 New York became concerned that the process of incorporation was too politicized and required a two-thirds vote of each house to create or renew a corporate charter.[47] Delaware in 1831 pioneered the use of reservation clauses to curtail imprudent grants to private entities. Several states adopted antimonopoly provisions or equality guarantees designed to safeguard the majority from minority privilege.[48] The main impetus for constitutional change, however, came from the economic collapse of 1837 when nine states defaulted on their debts. In its aftermath, state constitutions were revised or amended to curtail legislative promotion of economic development and remove public authority from allocation decisions. As a delegate to the Ohio convention of 1850–1851 plaintively put it, "I wish to see the State Government brought back to its simple and appropriate functions, [leaving] railroad, canal, turnpike and other corporate associations, to get along on their own credit, without any connection or partnership with the State whatever."[49] Similarly, the New York Constitution of 1846 forbade lending of the state's credit and required direct popular approval for new debt.[50] Most existing states adopted similar provisions, and every state entering the Union after 1845 wrote some sort of debt restriction into their constitutions. Many states also mandated general incorporation laws, either forbidding special incorporation laws (with their special privileges and incentives) or permitting them only, as in New York, when "the objects of the corporation cannot be attained under general laws."[51] Taken together, these provisions were designed to prevent corruption of the legislature by special interests seeking advantages through their privileged access to the seats of power.

Two aspects of these constitutional changes are particularly noteworthy. First, the constitutional reforms were not confined to those states that had suffered from overzealous efforts to promote economic development. To some extent, the experience in those states served a cautionary function, inducing other states to construct constitutional barriers to prevent such abuses from occurring within their borders. To some extent, also, the established practice of interstate borrowing in constitution-making encouraged the diffusion of restrictive provisions among the states. This process was facilitated at the constitutional conventions in some Western states by the experience of delegates who had previously served in constitutional conventions in other states.

Second, while twentieth-century reformers have attacked excessively long and detailed state constitutions, the history so far recounted suggests that to a considerable extent the length and detail of state constitutions represented a considered response to real problems.[52] State legislatures had proved unworthy of trust, and it was therefore deemed necessary to restrict their powers. Because state legislatures possessed plenary legislative power, successful restriction required prohibitions and limitations that were specific and detailed. Much of the constitutional legislation that swelled state constitutions during this period thus reflected not a lack of skill in constitution-making or a misunderstanding of constitutionalism but rather a determined attempt to restrict state legislative forays into economic boosterism and favoritism.

Late Nineteenth-Century America and the
Problem of Corporate Power

Americans in the aftermath of the Civil War recognized that they had entered a new era, one in which large corporations, such as railroads, wielded significant economic and political power. Not surprisingly, many Americans felt threatened by this change. Midwestern farmers and laborers, fearing that their interests were jeopardized by the rise of the new corporate giants, organized to combat their influence. Because farmer and labor groups distrusted state governments, which they believed (often correctly) were dominated or corrupted by corporate wealth, they looked to constitutional reform for relief, hoping to achieve their goals through constitutional revision. Illinois's "Granger constitution" of 1870, with its detailed provisions on grain elevators and its regulation of railroads, exemplifies their efforts.[53] During this same period, several Western states drafted their initial constitutions, seeking to enter the Union, or revised their early constitutions in light of the economic transitions they had experienced. Thus, the decades after the Civil War were an era of considerable constitutional change.

State constitution-makers during the late nineteenth and early twentieth centuries devised a wide variety of mechanisms to curtail the abuse of corporate power. First, they directly incorporated into their constitutions legislation regulating railroads and other corporations and protecting consumers and labor. The Idaho Constitution declared railroads to be public highways and subjected their rates to legislative regulation.[54] The Arizona, Montana, and Wyoming Constitutions abrogated the "fellow-servant" rule, a common-law doctrine that prevented workers from collecting for work-related injuries; and the Arizona and Wyoming charters also forbade labor contracts that released employers from liability for injuries suffered by workers.[55] Amendments to the California Constitution in 1911 not only eliminated the fellow-servant rule but also established a minimum wage and increased corporate taxes.[56]

Second, constitution-makers created institutions designed to monitor and, where necessary, curb illicit practices and abuses. Thus, the Idaho, North Dakota, and Washington Constitutions established labor commissions, the Wyoming Constitution an inspector of mines, and the Arizona Constitution a corporation commission.[57] Third, constitution-makers specifically withdrew legislative authority to enact various types of statutes, including those that might advantage corporate interests. Idaho, for instance, specifically forbade enactment of retroactive laws favorable to railroads.[58] The scope of these restrictions is suggested by the Missouri constitution of 1875, which included over three and one-half pages of substantive limitations on the legislature.[59] Fourth, constitution-makers in almost all states imposed various procedural requirements, such as the "single-subject" rule and the requirement that bills be referred to committee, in order to prevent duplicity and promote a more open and deliberative legislative process.[60] Finally, state constitution-makers attempted to prevent corruption of state officials by establishing elaborate constitutional limitations on the gifts and other benefits that those officials could accept from corporate interests.[61]

Yet convention records reveal that many delegates opposed stringent restrictions on corporations. This opposition to regulation was not confined to apologists for corporations. For if corporations were feared as a source of corruption and oppression, they were also recognized as a needed base of capital for economic development. Constitution-makers acknowledged, somewhat reluctantly, that the prosperity of their states was inextricably linked to the success of large "foreign" corporations and feared that excessive restrictions might drive those corporations from the state.

Western delegates in particular perceived this connection and, while imposing some restrictions, rejected more stringent ones and offered important concessions designed to attract corporations. One such concession, incorporated into the Colorado and Idaho Constitutions, permitted the taking of private property for private as well as public use, provided that just compensation was paid.[62] Such provisions supported the development of mining interests in those states, particularly large-scale, capital-intensive quartz mining.[63] Another significant concession was Nevada's elimination of taxation on mines. Opponents of the exemption argued that its beneficiaries would be "foreigners — aliens, who wish us no good."[64] However, its proponents successfully maintained that taxation of mines would drive away the "foreign" capital that was essential to developing the only resource the state possessed.

These same arguments were reiterated as conventions considered what constitutional restrictions to place on corporations. In Montana, for example, a proposal to make stockholders and corporation directors jointly liable for corporate debts was defeated after a delegate argued that it would "not only drive all foreign capital invested in the state away but would prevent all future inquiries."[65] In Colorado, another limitation was defeated after a delegate charged that if adopted, "not another mile of railroad [would] be built" in the state.[66]

CONCLUSIONS

This historical survey has documented that certain constitutional issues recur from state to state and from generation to generation. What are the implications of this for the prevailing models of state constitutional politics? For one thing, the simultaneous emergence of various issues in several states — for example, expansion of the suffrage in the mid-nineteenth century and promotion of direct democracy in the early twentieth century — confirms the impact of national political movements such as Jacksonian democracy and Progressivism on state constitutional politics. Yet it would be a mistake to conclude from this that state constitutional politics is merely national politics writ small. At least until the latter half of the twentieth century, the political forces raising these common issues were typically indigenous to the state, often having little contact with their counterparts in sister states. Moreover, the issues were usually perceived as state-specific problems rather than as part of a national agenda. The proliferation of restrictions on state legislative authority during the nineteenth century exemplifies the pattern of state-based but recurring issues.

The historical account also reveals that some recurring state constitutional issues have had important regional dimensions. For example, although the composition of the electorate excited political conflict throughout the nation, in the South attention focused on efforts to deny the franchise to African Americans and poor whites. Similarly, although the relation between government and the economy generated constitutional conflict in every state, in the West the debate centered on what constitutional restrictions to impose on large corporations. These examples show that neighboring states have at times viewed themselves as sharing common problems, distinct from those in other areas of the country. This sense of shared problems in turn explains why states have looked beyond their borders for solutions to those problems, freely borrowing from the constitutions of neighboring states. Because political culture in the United States is often viewed as coinciding with region, this pattern of distinct regional versions of recurring constitutional issues seems to offer some support for the political-culture model. However, because the meaning of "political culture" is often quite nebulous, one hesitates to rely on it too heavily in explaining state constitutional politics.

The present account also recognizes that state constitutional politics at times involves the continuation of "ordinary politics" in another arena. The disputes over the intrastate distribution of political power illustrate this. Presumably, had we examined constitutional issues peculiar to the various states rather than issues that have recurred over time and space, we would have discovered even more examples confirming the ordinary-politics model. Nonetheless, one should beware of reducing all state constitutional politics to this level. For, as the apportionment controversies and the efforts to restrict state legislatures reveal, it is often the failure of ordinary politics to resolve issues or prevent abuses that triggers efforts to institute constitutional change. Moreover, those involved in constitutional politics have frequently viewed themselves as engaged in a different enterprise and have been more likely to cast their appeals in terms of broad principle rather than narrow advantage.

Perhaps not surprising, no single model adequately encompasses the diversity of state constitutional politics. (In fairness, it must be added that the various proponents likely did not envision their models as comprehensive accounts of state constitutional politics.) However, a final point deserves mention. All three models underestimate the influence of federal law on state constitutional politics. This influence is reflected in the way long-standing state constitutional controversies have been eclipsed or transformed by federal action. Issues of voting rights and the distribution of political power through legislative apportionment are cases in point. The influence of federal law can also be seen in the effects of the constitutional division of responsibility between state and nation. The federal Constitution left it to the states to define the grounds of political participation, and thus this emerged as a major issue in the states. A federal Constitution of delegated and, at least temporarily, limited powers left to the states the responsibility of defining how much power would be exercised by the more powerful state governments, and this also became a major concern. Finally, the national government's reluctance during the nineteenth century to become involved in economic development and in the regulation of business left the states the responsibility to deal with fundamental questions of political economy. In sum, though the states set their own constitutional agendas, their agendas inevitably bear the imprint of legal developments beyond their borders.

NOTES

1.   Data on constitutional revision and constitutional amendment are drawn from Janice C. May, "State Constitutions and Constitutional Revision, 1992–93," in *The Book of the States, 1994–95* (Lexington, Ky.: Council of State Governments, 1994); Janice C. May, "Constitutional Amendment and Revision Revisited," *Publius:*

The Journal of Federalism 17 (Winter 1987): 153–179; and Albert L. Sturm, *Thirty Years of State Constitution-Making: 1938–1968* (New York: National Municipal League, 1970).

2.   Janice C. May notes that from 1984 to 1991 eighty-three local amendments were added to state constitutions. See May, "State Constitutions and Constitutional Revision, 1990–91," in *The Book of the States, 1992–93* (Lexington, Ky.: Council of State Governments, 1992), 6, table B.

3.   James Bryce, *The American Commonwealth*, vol. 1, 2d rev. ed. (New York: Macmillan, 1981), 434.

4.   Daniel J. Elazar, "The Principles and Traditions Underlying State Constitutions," *Publius: The Journal of Federalism* 12 (Winter 1982): 11–25.

5.   See Albert L. Sturm, "The Development of American State Constitutions," *Publius: The Journal of Federalism* 12 (Winter 1982): 57–98; and Kermit L. Hall, "Mostly Anchor and Little Sail: The Evolution of American State Constitutions," in *Toward a Usable Past: Liberty Under State Constitutions*, ed. Paul Finkelman and Stephen E. Gottleib (Athens: University of Georgia Press, 1991), 388–417.

6.   See, for example, Elmer E. Cornwell, Jr., Jay S. Goodman, and Wayne R. Swanson, *State Constitutional Conventions* (New York: Praeger, 1975); and Charles Press, "Assessing Policy and Operational Implications of State Constitutional Change," *Publius: The Journal of Federalism* 12 (Winter 1982): 99–111.

7.   See Robert G. Dixon, *Democratic Representation: Reapportionment in Law and Politics* (New York: Oxford University Press, 1968), 62–63, chart 1.

8.   A particularly useful account of the pressure for change in the Southern states is Fletcher M. Green, *Constitutional Development in the South Atlantic States, 1776–1860* (New York: W. W. Norton, 1966). For excerpts from the convention debates on the issue of representation in Virginia, Massachusetts, and New York, see Merrill D. Peterson, ed., *Democracy, Liberty, and Property: The State Constitutional Conventions of the 1820's* (Indianapolis, Ind.: Bobbs-Merrill, 1966). For a discussion of the representation issue in Connecticut, see Wesley W. Horton, *The Connecticut State Constitution: A Reference Guide* (Westport, Conn.: Greenwood Press, 1993), 11–14.

9.   See Marvin E. Gettleman, *The Dorr Rebellion: A Study in American Radicalism, 1833–1849* (New York: Random House, 1973).

10.   James A. Henretta, "The Rise and Decline of 'Democratic-Republicanism': Political Rights in New York and the Several States, 1800-1915," in *Toward a Usable Past*, ed. Paul Finkelman and Stephen E. Gottleib (Athens: University of Georgia Press, 1991), 50–90; and Richard L. McCormick, *From Realignment to Reform: Political Change in New York State, 1893–1910* (Ithaca, N.Y.: Cornell University Press, 1981).

11.   Delaware, for example, constitutionalized its system of malapportionment. Its 1897 Constitution specified legislative districts in detail, on an undemocratic basis, and made no provision for reapportionment. See James Q. Dealey, *Growth of American State Constitutions* (New York: DaCapo Press, 1972), 97.

12.   *Baker v. Carr*, 369 U.S. 186 (1962).

13.   *Reynolds v. Sims*, 377 U.S. 533 (1964). Subsequent rulings exemplifying the Court's approach include *Kirkpatrick v. Preisler*, 394 U.S. 526 (1969); and *Karcher v. Daggett*, 462 U.S. 725 (1983).

14.   *Davis v. Bandemer*, 478 U.S. 109 (1986); and *Shaw v. Reno*, 113 S. Ct. 2816 (1993).

15.   Robert F. Williams, *The New Jersey State Constitution: A Reference Guide* (Westport, Conn.: Greenwood Press, 1990), 13–16.

16.   Because of space limitations, our analysis excludes discussion of religious tests for office. Illustrative of such tests was North Carolina's, which excluded atheists, Roman Catholics, Jews, and Christian pacifists such as Quakers and Moravians. See John Orth, *The North Carolina State Constitution: A Reference Guide* (Westport, Conn.: Greenwood Press, 1993), 4.

17.   The analysis in this paragraph relies on Donald S. Lutz, *Popular Consent and Popular Control: Whig Political Theory in the Early State Constitutions* (Baton Rouge: Louisiana State University Press, 1980); and Donald S. Lutz, "Political Participation in Eighteenth-Century America," in *Toward a Usable Past*, ed. Paul Finkelman and Stephen E. Gottleib (Athens: University of Georgia Press, 1991), 19–49.

18.   Lutz, "Political Participation," 24–29.

19.   See the discussion in Daniel T. Rodgers, *Contested Truths: Keywords in American Politics since Independence* (New York: Basic Books, 1987), chap. 3; and Chilton Williamson, *American Suffrage: From Property to Democracy, 1760–1860* (Princeton, N.J.: Princeton University Press, 1960).

20.   See Don E. Fehrenbacher, "Constitutional History, 1848–1861," in *American Constitutional History*, ed. Leonard W. Levy (New York: Macmillan, 1986), 96; and Dealey, *Growth of American State Constitutions*, 150. Extension of the franchise to aliens was favored as a means of attracting inhabitants to population-starved areas.

21.   On the reforms in New York, see Morton Keller, "The Politics of State Constitutional Revision," in *The Constitutional Convention as an Amending Device*, ed. Kermit L. Hall, Harold M. Hyman, and Leon V. Sigal (Washington, D.C.: American Historical Association and American Political Science Association, 1981), 72. On the election of judges, see Philip L. Dubois, *From Ballot to Bench: Judicial Elections and the Quest for Accountability* (Austin: University of Texas Press, 1980), chap. 1; and Kermit L. Hall, "The Judiciary on Trial: Constitutional Reform and the Rise of an Elected Judiciary, 1846–1860," *Historian* 44 (May 1983): 337–354.

22.   See the discussions in Rodgers, *Contested Truths*, chap. 3; Henretta, "'Democratic-Republicanism,'" 50–90; and Eric Foner, "From Slavery to Citizenship: Blacks and the Right to Vote," in *Voting and the Spirit of American Democracy*, ed. Donald W. Rogers (Urbana: University of Illinois Press, 1990), 55–65.

23.   These devices may also have been used to disenfranchise poor whites. See J. Morgan Kousser, *The Shaping of Southern Politics: Suffrage Restrictions and the Establishment of the One-Party South, 1880–1910* (New Haven, Conn.: Yale University Press, 1974).

24.   The grandfather clause was contained in the Oklahoma Constitution, art. 3, sec. 4A. It was struck down by the U.S. Supreme Court in *Guinn v. United States*, 238 U.S. 347 (1915).

25.   Our account of the campaign for women's suffrage relies on Alan P. Grimes, *The Puritan Ethic and Woman Suffrage* (New York: Oxford University Press, 1967); Beverly Beeton, *Women Vote in the West: The Woman Suffrage Movement, 1869–1896* (New York: Garland, 1986); and Eleanor Flexner, *Century of Struggle: The Women's Rights Movement in the United States* (Cambridge, Mass.: Belknap Press, 1975).

26.   See Peter J. Galie, *The New York State Constitution: A Reference Guide* (Westport, Conn.: Greenwood Press, 1991), 15; and Joseph P. Grodin, Calvin R.

Massey, and Richard B. Cunningham, *The California State Constitution: A Reference Guide* (Westport, Conn.: Greenwood Press, 1993), 14.

27.   These developments are discussed in Gordon Morris Bakken, *Rocky Mountain Constitution Making, 1850–1912* (Westport, Conn.: Greenwood Press, 1987), chap. 8.

28.   These states included Washington (1910); California (1911); Oregon, Arizona, and Kansas (1912); and Nevada and Montana (1914).

29.   See the discussion in Robert F. Williams, *State Constitutional Law: Cases and Materials*, 2d ed. (Charlottesville, Va.: Michie, 1993), 316–317.

30.   The quotation is from the Massachusetts Constitution, art. 7. The analysis in this paragraph draws on James Willard Hurst, *The Growth of American Law: The Lawmakers* (Boston: Little, Brown, 1950), chap. 11; and Lutz, "Political Participation," esp. 21–22.

31.   Hurst, *The Growth of American Law*, 232. The analysis in this paragraph relies primarily on Hurst, *Law and Social Order in the United States* (Ithaca, N.Y.: Cornell University Press, 1977), 82–97; and A. James Heins, *Constitutional Restrictions Against State Debt* (Madison: University of Wisconsin Press, 1963).

32.   Quoted in Rodgers, *Contested Truths*, 98.

33.   Ibid., 92–101.

34.   The figures in this paragraph on the constitutional initiative are drawn from May, "Constitutional Amendment," 158.

35.   The data used in this paragraph are drawn from David B. Magleby, *Direct Legislation: Voting on Ballot Propositions in the United States* (Baltimore, Md.: Johns Hopkins University Press, 1984), 38–40, table 3.1.

36.   Arizona Constitution, art. 4, pt. 1, sec. 1. John D. Leshy has identified the tools of direct democracy as the "first and foremost" issue of the Arizona constitutional convention. See Leshy, *The Arizona State Constitution: A Reference Guide* (Westport, Conn.: Greenwood Press, 1993), 8.

37.   See Dennis C. Colson, *Idaho's Constitution: The Tie That Binds* (Moscow: University of Idaho Press, 1991), chap. 5.

38.   For a general account of Southern efforts to constitutionalize white supremacy, see Kousser, *The Shaping of Southern Politics*. For accounts of developments within individual states, see Orth, *The North Carolina State Constitution*, 17; Lee Hargrave, *The Louisiana State Constitution: A Reference Guide* (Westport, Conn.: Greenwood Press, 1991), 9–12; and Ralph Chipman McDaniel, *The Virginia Constitutional Convention of 1901–1902* (Baltimore, Md.: Johns Hopkins University Press, 1928). On anti-Chinese sentiment in the California constitutional convention, see David A. Johnson, *Founding the Far West: California, Oregon, and Nevada, 1840–1890* (Berkeley: University of California Press, 1992), 252–256.

39.   Alexander Hamilton, James Madison, and John Jay, *The Federalist Papers*, ed. Clinton Rossiter (New York: New American Library, 1961), 79.

40.   Our account of state economic boosterism relies primarily on Herbert Hovenkamp, *Enterprise and American Law, 1836–1937* (Cambridge, Mass.: Harvard University Press, 1991); Heins, *Constitutional Restrictions against State Debt*; and L. Roy Gunn, *The Decline of Authority: Public Economic Policy and Political Development in New York, 1800–1860* (Ithaca, N.Y.: Cornell University Press, 1988).

41.   Hovenkamp, *Enterprise and American Law*, 37–38.

42.   For data on the economic consequences of the completion of the Erie Canal, see Reginald McGrane, *Foreign Bondsholders and American State Debts* (New York: Macmillan, 1935), 5. The quotation is from Marvin Meyers, *The Jacksonian Persuasion: Politics and Belief* (Stanford, Calif.: Stanford University Press, 1957), 114.

43.   James Willard Hurst, *Law and the Conditions of Freedom in the Nineteenth-Century United States* (Madison: University of Wisconsin Press, 1956), 7.

44.   Pennsylvania Constitution of 1776, Declaration of Rights, art. 5. On the animating ideas of this constitution, see J. Paul Selsam, *The Pennsylvania Constitution of 1776: A Study in Revolutionary Democracy* (Philadelphia: University of Pennsylvania Press, 1936; New York: Da Capo Press, 1971).

45.   Meyers, *The Jacksonian Persuasion*, chaps. 2, 5.

46.   Tony A. Freyer, *Producers versus Capitalists: Constitutional Conflict in Antebellum America* (Charlottesville: University Press of Virginia, 1994).

47.   New York Constitution of 1821, art. 7, sec. 9.

48.   Robert F. Williams, "Equality Guarantees in State Constitutional Law," *Texas Law Review* 63 (March–April 1985): 1195–1224.

49.   Quoted in Kermit L. Hall, *The Magic Mirror: Law in American History* (New York: Oxford University Press, 1989), 103–104.

50.   New York Constitution of 1846, art. 7, sec. 9.

51.   New York Constitution of 1846, art. 3, sec. 18.

52.   This point is convincingly documented in Christian G. Fritz, "The American Constitutional Tradition Revisited: Preliminary Observations on State Constitution Making in the Nineteenth-Century West," paper delivered at the conference of the American Association of Law Schools, New Orleans, Louisiana, January 1995, 1–94.

53.   For a discussion of this constitution and its provisions protecting farmers, see Lawrence M. Friedman, *A History of American Law*, 2d ed. (New York: Simon & Schuster, 1985), 349–350.

54.   Idaho Constitution, art. 11, sec. 5. For discussion of the development of the corporations article of the Idaho Constitution, see Colson, *Idaho's Constitution*, chap. 7.

55.   John D. Hicks, *The Constitutions of the Northwest States* (Lincoln: University of Nebraska University Studies, 1923), 92–95; and Bakken, *Rocky Mountain Constitution Making*, 80, 85.

56.   Dealey, *Growth of American State Constitutions*, 107–108.

57.   Bakken, *Rocky Mountain Constitution Making*, chap. 7; Colson, *Idaho's Constitution*, 127–129; and Hicks, *Constitutions of the Northwest States*, 92–95.

58.   Idaho Constitution, art. 5, sec. 12. This provision is discussed in Colson, *Idaho's Constitution*, 125.

59.   Dealey, *Growth of American State Constitutions*, 78. This was not atypical. Lawrence Friedman notes that the Illinois Constitution of 1870 outlawed twenty-three types of "local or special" laws and that by 1889, in the North Dakota Constitution, the list had grown to thirty-five restrictions. See Friedman, *History of American Law*, 349–350.

60.   For an enlightening overview of such restrictions, see Robert F. Williams, "State Constitutional Limitations on Legislative Procedure: Legislative Compliance and Judicial Enforcement," *Publius: The Journal of Federalism* 17 (Winter 1987): 91–114.

61. See Hicks, *Constitutions of the Northwest States*, 56–63; and Friedman, *History of American Law*, 349–350.

62. Colorado Constitution, art. 2, sec. 14; and Idaho Constitution, art. 1, sec. 14.

63. Colson, *Idaho's Constitution*, 64–65.

64. Quoted in Johnson, *Founding the Far West*, 224.

65. Quoted in Bakken, *Rocky Mountain Constitution Making*, 78.

66. Bakken, *Rocky Mountain Constitution Making*, 177.

2

Patterns in the Amending of American State Constitutions

Donald S. Lutz

Americans have had more experience in the framing and operation of constitutions than any other people, and that experience has been overwhelmingly at the state level. Despite this considerable experience, and despite the certainty that Americans will continue to write new state constitutions on a regular basis, there has been curiously little attention paid to what our collective experience thus far might contribute to our understanding of how we should write constitutions in the future. This study is an initial attempt to identify some simple yet important patterns in constitutional design, to determine the implications of these patterns, and to devise a theory which will help us to explain these patterns. The results indicate that if one wishes to minimize the rate at which a state constitution is either amended or replaced, more careful attention must be paid to the length of the document. However, before we can examine the empirical results, we must first develop a coherent theory that will allow us to understand and interpret these results.

THE ORIGINAL PREMISES UNDERLYING THE AMENDMENT PROCESS

The modern written constitution, first developed in English–speaking North America, was grounded in a doctrine of popular sovereignty.[1]

Even though many in Britain were skeptical at best, Americans did not regard popular sovereignty as an experimental idea but rather as one that stood at the very heart of their shared political consensus.[2] American political writing had used the language of popular sovereignty before John Locke's *Second Treatise* was published, and the early state constitutions of the 1770s contained clear and firm statements that these documents rested upon popular consent.[3] Although the theory of popular sovereignty was well understood in America by 1776, the institutional implications of this innovative doctrine had to be worked out in constitutions adopted over the next decade. Gradually it was realized that a doctrine of popular sovereignty required that constitutions be written by a popularly selected convention rather than the legislature and then ratified through a process that elicited popular consent — ideally in a referendum. This double implication was established in the process used to frame and adopt the 1780 Massachusetts and 1784 New Hampshire Constitutions, although the referendum portion of the process did not become standard until the nineteenth century.

Americans moved quickly to the conclusion that if a constitution rested upon popular consent, then the people could also replace it with a new one. Locke had argued that the people could replace government but only when those entrusted with the powers of government had first disqualified themselves by endangering the happiness of the community to such a degree that civil society could be said to have reverted to a state of nature.[4] The Americans went well beyond Locke, and his chief interpreter William Blackstone, by institutionalizing constitutional change while still in civil society, which is to say whenever they wanted. It is of considerable importance that they included not only the replacement of a constitution but also its formal amendment.

The first new state constitution in 1776, that of New Jersey, contained an implicit notion of amendment, but the 1776 Pennsylvania document contained the first explicit amendment process — one that used a convention process and bypassed the legislature.[5] By 1780 almost half the states had an amendment procedure, and the principle that the fundamental law could be altered piecemeal by popular will was firmly in place.

In addition to popular sovereignty, the amendment process was based on three other premises central to the American consensus in the 1770s — an imperfect but educable human nature, the efficacy of a deliberative process, and the distinction between normal legislation and constitutional matters. The first premise held that humans are fallible but capable of learning through experience.[6] Americans had long considered each governmental institution and practice to be in the nature of an experiment. Since fallibility was part of human nature, provision had to be made for altering institutions after experience revealed their flaws and unintended consequences. Originally, therefore, the amendment process was predicated not only on the need to adapt to changing circumstances but also on the need to compensate for the limits of human understanding and virtue. In a sense the entire idea of a constitution rests on an assumption of human fallibility, since, if humans were angels, there would be no need to erect, direct, and limit government through a constitution.

A belief in the efficacy of a deliberative process was also part of the general American constitutional perspective. A constitution was viewed not as a means to arrive at collective decisions in the most efficient way possible but to arrive at the best possible decisions in pursuit of the common good under a condition of popular sovereignty. The common good is a more difficult standard to approximate than the good of one class or a part of the population, and the condition of popular sovereignty, even if operationalized as a system of representation, requires the involvement of many more people than forms of government based on other principles. This in turn requires a slow, deliberative process for any political decision, and the more important the decision, the more deliberative the process should be. Constitutional matters were considered more important in 1789 America than normal legislation, which led to a more highly deliberative process that distinguished constitutional and normal legislative matters. The codification of the distinction in constitutional articles of ratification and amendment resulted in American constitutions being viewed as a higher law that should limit and direct the content of normal legislation.

Popular sovereignty implies that all constitutional matters should be based upon some form of popular consent, which in turn implies a formal, public process. Human fallibility implies the need for some method of altering or revising the constitution. A distinction between legislative and constitutional matters implies that the latter requires a marked, highly deliberative process and thus points to the need for a more difficult procedure for constitutional amendment than that used for normal legislation.

Together these premises require that the procedure be neither too easy nor too difficult. A process that is too easy does not provide enough distinction between constitutional matters and normal legislation, thereby violates the assumption of the need for a high level of deliberation, and debases popular sovereignty; one that is too difficult interferes with the needed rectification of mistakes, thereby violates the assumption of human fallibility, and prevents the effective utilization of popular sovereignty.

The literature on constitutions at one time made a distinction between major and minor constitutional alterations by calling the former "revisions" and the latter "amendments." The distinction turned out in practice to be conceptually slippery, impossible to operationalize, and therefore generally useless.[7] It would be more useful to use "amendment" as a description of the *formal* process developed by the Americans and "revision" to describe processes that instead use the legislature or judiciary. Unless we maintain the distinction between formal amendment and revision, we will lose the ability to distinguish competing constitutional theories.

At the same time, a comparative study of amendment processes allows us to delve more deeply into the theory of constitutional amendment as a principle of constitutional design. For example, we might ask the following questions: What difference does it make when constitutions are formally amended through a political process that does not effectively distinguish constitutional matters from normal legislation? Why might we still want to draw a distinction between formal amendment and revision by normal politics as carefully and as strongly as possible?[8] One important answer is that the three prominent methods of constitutional alteration other than complete replacement — formal amendment, legislative revision, and judicial interpretation — reflect, in the order listed, a declining commitment to popular sovereignty; and the level of commitment to popular sovereignty may be a key attitude for defining the nature of the political system.

BASIC ASSUMPTIONS AND PROPOSITIONS

Every theory has to begin with a number of assumptions. We have seen how the original American version rested on the premises of popular sovereignty, an imperfect but educable human nature, the efficacy of a highly deliberative decisionmaking process, and the distinction between normal and constitutional law. While these help define the working assumptions of one theory of amendment, albeit the original one, they do not provide a complete basis for describing either the American theory or a general theory of amendment. We turn now to developing a theory that includes the American version and also provides the basis for analyzing any version of constitutional amendment. The intent of the analysis is to provide guidelines for constitutional design in any context — guidelines that will allow framers to securely link the design of a formal amendment process with desired outcomes.

Our first working assumption has to do with the expected change that is faced by every political system.

ASSUMPTION 1: Every political system needs to be altered over time as a result of some combination of: (1) changes in the environment within which the political system operates (including economics, technology, foreign relations, demographics, etc.); (2) changes in the value system distributed across the population; (3) unwanted or unexpected institutional effects; and (4) the cumulative effect of decisions made by the legislature, executive, and judiciary.

A second assumption concerns the nature of a constitution.

ASSUMPTION 2: In political systems that are constitutional, in which constitutions are taken seriously as limiting government and legitimating the decisionmaking process they describe, important alterations in the operation of the political system need to be reflected in the constitution.

If these two assumptions are used as premises in a deductive process, they imply a conclusion that stands as a further assumption.

ASSUMPTION 3: All constitutions require regular, periodic alteration, whether through amendment, revision, or replacement.

Revision, as noted earlier, refers to alterations in a constitution through judicial interpretation or legislative action. However, we are initially more concerned with the use of a formal amendment process. Amendment rate, a key concept, refers to the average number of formal amendments passed per year since the constitution came into effect. Many scholars criticize constitutions that are much amended.[9] However, constitutionalism and the logic of popular sovereignty are based on more than simplicity and tidiness. Any people who believe in constitutionalism will amend their constitution when needed, as opposed to using extraconstitutional means. Thus, a moderate amendment rate will indicate that the people living under it take their constitution seriously. The older a constitution is, under conditions of popular sovereignty, the more successful it has been and also the larger the number of amendments it will have. However, it is the *rate* of amendment that is important, not the total number of amendments.

A successful constitutional system would seem to be defined by a constitution of considerable age that has a total number of amendments that, when divided by the constitution's age in years represents a moderate amendment rate — one that is to be expected in the face of inevitable change. A less than successful constitutional system will have a high rate of constitutional replacement.

This raises the question of what constitutes a "moderate" rate of amendment. Because we hope to illuminate the question empirically rather than in an a priori manner, we must initially use a symbolic stand–in for "moderate rate of amendment." Because a moderate rate is likely to be a range of rates rather than a single one, the symbol will define boundaries such that any document with an amendment rate above or below its limits will have an increasing probability of being replaced or an increasing probability that some extraconstitutional means of constitutional evolution is being used. We shall use <#> to symbolically represent this moderate range of amendment rates.

The first proposition is frequently found in the literature, but it has neither been systematically verified nor its effect measured.

PROPOSITION 1: The longer a constitution, the higher its amendment rate; the shorter a constitution, the lower its amendment rate.

Commentators frequently note that the more provisions a constitution has, the more targets there are for amendment and the more likely the constitution will be targeted because it deals with too many details that are subject to change. While this seems intuitively correct, the data that are used usually raise the question of which comes first — the high amendment rate or the long constitution. This is because a constitution's length is usually given as of a particular year, not in terms of its original length. Is a constitution long because it had a high amendment rate, or did it have a high amendment rate because it was long to begin with?

Our second proposition is also a common one in the literature, although it too has never been systematically tested before.

PROPOSITION 2: The more difficult the amendment process, the lower the amendment rate; the easier the amendment process, the higher the amendment rate.

As obvious as this proposition is, it cannot be tested until one shifts from the number of amendments in a constitution to its amendment rate and until one develops an index for measuring the degree of difficulty associated with an amendment process. Such an index is presented in the next section as part of what is needed to develop a way of predicting the likely consequences of using one amendment process versus another.

The literature on American state constitutions generally argues that these documents are much longer than the national constitution because they must deal with more governmental functions. For example, if a constitution deals with matters like education, criminal law, local government, and finances, it is bound to be more detailed, longer, and thus have a higher amendment rate than one that does not address these matters. From this we can generalize to the following proposition.

PROPOSITION 3: The more governmental functions dealt with in a constitution, the longer it will be and the higher rate of amendment it will have.

Constitutions are usually replaced for one of three reasons. A change in regime may leave the values, institutions, or implications of the old constitution seriously at odds with those preferred by the people now in charge. Another reason for replacement is the failure of the constitution to keep up with the times. Finally, the old constitution may have been changed so many times that it is no longer clear what lies under the encrustations, and clarity demands a new beginning. A moderate amendment rate is an antidote to all three.

PROPOSITION 4: The farther the amendment rate is from the mean of <#>, either higher or lower, the greater the probability that the entire constitution will be replaced and thus the shorter its duration. Conversely, the closer an amendment rate is to the mean of <#>, the lower the probability the entire constitution will be replaced and thus the longer its duration.

A low rate of amendment in the face of needed change may lead to the development of some extraconstitutional means of revision, most likely judicial interpretation, to supplement the formal amendment process. We can now, on the basis of earlier discussion, generate several propositions that will prove useful toward the end of our discussion on the implications of the major competing forms of formal constitutional amendment.

PROPOSITION 5: A low amendment rate associated with a long average constitutional duration strongly implies the use of some alternative means of revision to supplement the formal amendment process.

PROPOSITION 6: In the absence of a high rate of constitutional replacement the lower the rate of formal amendment, the more likely the process of revision is dominated by a judicial body.

PROPOSITION 7: The higher the formal amendment rate, (1) the less likely the constitution is being viewed as a higher law, (2) the less likely a distinction is being drawn between constitutional matters and normal legislation, (3) the more likely the constitution is being viewed as a code, and (4) the more likely the formal amendment process is dominated by the legislature.

We will test propositions one through four using data from the American state constitutions. Propositions five through seven will not be tested directly using these data, but are listed here to indicate some of the broader implications of the theory being developed here.

AMENDMENT PATTERNS IN AMERICAN STATE CONSTITUTIONS, 1776–1991

Albert Sturm, one of the most able students of state constitutions, summarized the literature as seeing state constitutions burdened with (1) the effects of continuous expansion in state functions and responsibilities and the consequent growth of governmental machinery; (2) the primary responsibility for responding to the increasing pressure of major problems associated with rapid urbanization, technological development, population growth and mobility, economic change and development, and the fair treatment of minority groups; (3) the pressure of special interests for constitutional status; and (4) continuing popular distrust of the state legislature, based on past abuses, which result in detailed restrictions on governmental activity.[10] All these factors contribute to the length of state constitutions, and it is argued that not only do these pressures lead to many amendments, and thus greater length, but also that greater length itself leads to the accelerated need for amendment simply by providing so many targets for change. Thus, length becomes a surrogate measure for all of these other pressures to amend and is a key causal variable.

Table 2.1 shows that the average amendment rate is much higher for the state constitutions than it is for the national Constitution. Between 1789 and 1991 the U.S. Constitution was amended 26 times for a rate of .13 (26 amendments divided by 202 years equals .13 amendments per year). As of 1991, the 50 state constitutions had been in effect for an average of 95 years and had been amended a total of 5,845 times, or an average of 117 amendments per state. This produces an average

TABLE 2.1
Basic Data on State Constitutions, 1991

State	Number of Constitutions	Average Duration	Current Constitution Since	Number of Years in Effect	Original Length in Words	Number of Times Amended	Amendment Rate
Alabama	6	29	1901	90	65,400	726	8.07
Alaska	1	35	1959	32	11,800	22	.69
Arizona	1	80	1912	79	28,900	109	1.38
Arkansas	5	31	1874	117	24,100	76	.65
California	2	72	1879	112	21,400	471	4.21
Colorado	1	115	1876	115	22,000	115	1.00
Connecticut	4	54	1965	26	8,800	25	.96
Delaware	3	72	1897	94	19,000	119	1.27
Florida	6	25	1969	22	18,900	53	2.41
Georgia	10	21	1983	8	26,000	24	3.00
Hawaii	1	41	1959	32	16,800	82	2.56
Idaho	1	102	1890	101	18,800	107	1.06
Illinois	4	43	1971	20	12,900	6	.30
Indiana	2	88	1851	140	9,100	38	.27
Iowa	2	73	1857	134	9,700	48	.36
Kansas	1	132	1861	130	10,200	87	.67
Kentucky	4	50	1891	100	21,800	29	.29
Louisiana	11	16	1975	16	47,300	27	1.69
Maine	1	172	1820	171	10,100	157	.92
Maryland	4	54	1867	124	25,200	200	1.61

32

Massachusetts	1	211	1780	211	11,600	116	.55
Michigan	4	39	1964	27	18,600	16	.59
Minnesota	1	134	1858	133	8,500	112	.84
Mississippi	4	44	1890	101	20,100	102	1.01
Missouri	4	43	1945	46	39,300	74	1.61
Montana	2	51	1973	18	11,600	15	.83
Nebraska	2	63	1875	116	16,100	189	1.63
Nevada	1	127	1864	127	14,100	108	.85
New Hampshire	2	108	1784	207	8,000	142	.69
New Jersey	3	72	1948	43	16,400	39	.91
New Mexico	1	79	1912	79	22,000	120	1.52
New York	4	54	1895	96	26,800	207	2.16
North Carolina	3	72	1971	20	10,300	27	1.35
North Dakota	1	102	1889	102	18,100	125	1.23
Ohio	2	95	1851	140	14,200	145	1.04
Oklahoma	1	84	1907	84	58,200	133	1.58
Oregon	1	132	1859	132	11,200	188	1.42
Pennsylvania	5	43	1968	23	20,800	19	.83
Rhode Island	2	108	1843	148	7,400	53	.36
South Carolina	7	31	1896	95	21,900	463	4.87
South Dakota	1	102	1889	102	21,300	97	.95
Tennessee	3	65	1870	121	11,100	32	.26
Texas	5	29	1876	115	28,600	326	2.83
Utah	1	95	1896	95	13,900	77	.81
Vermont	3	71	1793	198	5,200	50	.25
Virginia	6	36	1971	20	18,100	20	1.00
Washington	1	102	1889	102	16,300	86	.84

Table 2.1, continued

State	Number of Constitutions	Average Duration	Current Constitution Since	Number of Years in Effect	Original Length in Words	Number of Times Amended	Amendment Rate
West Virginia	2	64	1872	119	15,900	62	.52
Wisconsin	1	143	1848	143	11,400	124	.87
Wyoming	1	101	1890	101	20,800	57	.56
MEAN	2.9	77	1896	95	19,300	117	1.23
U.S. Constitution	1	202	1789	202	4,300	26	.13

amendment rate of 1.23 for the states. The state rate of amendment (1.23) is thus about 9 1/2 times the national rate (.13).

The data in Table 2.1 allow us to begin our analysis of the propositions developed earlier. Proposition 1 hypothesized a positive relationship between the length of a constitution and its amendment rate — the longer a constitution when adopted, the higher its amendment rate. Table 2.2 strongly supports Proposition 1 with a correlation coefficient of .6249 that is significant at the .001 level. Furthermore, the relationship holds whether we use the original or the current amended length.

TABLE 2.2
The Length of a State Constitution and Its Amendment Rate as of 1991

Length in Words	Amendment Rate*	Amendment Rate**
5,000–10,000	.53	.52
	(7)	(6)
10,000–15,000	.81	.76
	(13)	(9)
15,000–20,000	1.27	1.06
	(11)	(6)
20,000–25,000	1.59	1.43
	(10)	(11)
25,000–30,000	2.20	1.64
	(5)	(7)
Over 30,000	2.99	2.20
	(4)	(11)

*Using the length of the constitution when it was adopted. The number of constitutions in each category is indicated within parentheses below the average amendment rate for that category.

**Using the length of the constitution including all amendments as of 1991.

The average length of state constitutions increases from about 19,300 words as originally written to about 24,300 as amended by 1991, which raises the interesting question of what difference it makes whether we use a constitution's original length or its current amended length. The surprising answer is that it makes no real difference. There is an extremely strong congruence between the curve of amendment rates using the original length of a constitution, with a slope of .58, and that of amendment rates using the amended length, with a slope of .62. There is thus good reason, when our propositions are being tested with foreign national constitutions, for using *either* the original or the amended length.

Also, the correlation coefficient between amended and unamended rates is .9936 (significant at the .001 level), which strongly implies that the rate of increase in amendment rate resulting from increasing a constitution's length is virtually constant across all lengths. Finally, since at any point in time the set of constitutions used to test our propositions will vary considerably in age, and thus be a mixture of documents ranging from slightly amended to highly amended, we should probably use a composite curve that reflects this inevitable mix. In the case of American state constitutions the obvious composite curve would be one that averaged .58 and .62. The resulting amendment rate curve with a slope of .60 indicates that for every 10,000-word increase in a constitution's length the amendment rate will increase by .60.

The relationship between the length of a constitution and its amendment rate is the strongest and most consistent one found in the analysis of data drawn from the American states. The strength of this relationship can be underscored by a partial listing of the variables examined that did not show any significant independent correlation with amendment rate. These variables include: geographical size, size of population, level of industrialization, per capita personal income, per capita state expenditures, size of legislature, partisan division in legislature, geographical region, geographical proximity, and the historical era in which the constitution was written. When we control for these other variables the importance of constitutional length remains, whereas when we control for constitutional length the few weak correlations with these other variables disappear.

State constitutions, on average, are significantly longer than the U.S. Constitution. Can we account for this difference? Proposition 3 suggests that the wider range of governmental functions at the state level results in significantly longer documents and thus, in line with Proposition 1, produces a higher amendment rate that makes them longer still.

Table 2.3 uses data from a recent decade to show the relative importance of different amendment categories.[11] Amendments dealing with local governmental structure (4.7 percent), state and local debt (4.3 percent), state functions (9.0 percent), taxation and finance (cash flow matters) (14.1 percent), amendment and revision (amending the process of amendment) (2.6 percent), and local issues (28 percent) comprise 63 percent of all state amendments and pertain to topics that have not been part of national constitutional concern.

TABLE 2.3
State Amendments by Category, 1970–1979

Category Topic	Total Proposed	Total Adopted	Percent Adopted	Percent of All Amendments
Bill of Rights	75	60	80	4.3
Suffrage and Elections	125	90	72	6.4
Legislative Branch	205	114	56	8.1
Executive Branch	145	102	70	7.3
Judicial Branch	131	106	81	7.5
Local Government	98	66	67	4.7
Taxation and Finance	308	198	64	14.1
State and Local Debt	122	60	49	4.3
State Functions	182	127	70	9.0
Amendment and Revision	53	37	70	2.6
General Revision Proposals	24	9	38	.6
Miscellaneous Proposals	53	43	81	3.1
Local Amendments	559	394	70	28.0
Totals	2,080	1,406	68	

If we exclude these categories of issues, we end up with an adjusted state rate of about .47. This figure is still a bit over 3-1/2 times the national amendment rate, but by eliminating the amendments peculiar to state constitutions we obtain a figure for comparison with the national rate of .13 using what amounts to the same base. The difference between .13 and .47 represents what we might term the "surplus rate," which still needs to be explained. An interesting question, one that seems never to be asked, is whether the state amendment rate is too high or the national amendment rate is too low.

The answer depends in part on your attitude toward judicial interpretation. Propositions 5 and 6 introduced earlier suggest that if you have reasons to prefer judicial interpretation as a means of modifying a constitution over a formal amendment process, then the amendment rate for the national document is not too low. However, if you have reasons to prefer a formal amendment process, such as an attachment to popular sovereignty, then the answer may well be that the amendment rate of the U.S. Constitution is too low and the amendment rate of the states is to be preferred.

Propositions 5 and 6 assume a low rate of amendment coupled with constitutional longevity. Proposition 4, on the other hand, posits a general relationship between the rate of amendment and constitutional longevity.

Dividing the number of constitutions a state has had into the number of years it has been a state produces the average duration of the state's constitutions — a measure of constitutional activity that controls for a state's age. Table 2.4 shows that a high amendment rate is associated with low average duration and thus high replacement rate ($r = -.3561$; significant at the .01 level).

TABLE 2.4
Average Duration of American State Constitutions and Amendment Rate, 1776–1991

Average Duration	Amendment Rate	Number of Constitutions in Category
1–25 years	2.37	3
26–50 years	1.95	13
51–75 years	1.26	13
76–100 years	1.10	6
101–125 years	.93	8
126–150 years	.84	5
151+ years	.64	2

However, Proposition 4 predicts that the rate at which constitutions are replaced will increase as the amendment rate moves up *or* down with respect to <#>. In Table 2.4 the amendment rate is the dependent variable. However, if we make it the independent variable instead, we can test directly for the bidirectional effect. Table 2.5 supports Proposition 4. The average duration of a state's constitution declines as the amendment rate goes above 1.00 and as it goes below .75. What this means is that for American state constitutions an amendment rate between .75 and 1.00 is associated with the longest–lived constitutions and thus with the lowest rate of constitutional replacement. This range, then, will be defined as <#>.

The thirteen constitutions with amendment rates within <#> as just defined average .89, which we will define as # within <#>.

TABLE 2.5
Amendment Rate and Average Duration of a State Constitution

Amendment Rate	Average Duration (in years)*	
0.00–0.50	71	(7)
0.51–0.75	90	(8)
0.76–1.00	100	(13)
1.01–1.25	86	(4)
1.26–1.50	79	(4)
1.51–1.75	57	(6)
1.76–2.00		(0)
2.00+	38	(8)

*Numbers in parentheses indicate the number of constitutions in that range of average duration.

AMENDMENT PATTERNS AND THE CHARACTERISTICS OF THE AMENDMENT PROCESS

In the American states the method of ratifying an amendment can essentially be held constant since every state but one now uses a popular referendum for approval. However, amendments may be initiated by the state's legislature, an initiative referendum, a constitutional convention, or a commission. It is generally held that the more difficult the process of initiation, the fewer amendments that are proposed and thus the fewer amendments passed. It is also believed that the initiative has made the process of proposing an amendment too easy and opened a floodgate of proposals that are then more readily adopted by the electorate that initiated them. Another widely held belief is that the stricter or more arduous the process a legislature must use to propose an amendment, the fewer amendments that are proposed.

First of all, as Table 2.6 shows, during a recent decade relatively few amendments were proposed by other than a legislature.[12] One third of the states use popular initiative as a method of proposing amendments, and yet in these states the legislative method was greatly preferred. The popular initiative has received a lot of attention, especially in California, but in fact it has had a minimal impact thus far.

What has been the relative success of these competing modes of proposing constitutions? Table 2.7 shows that the relatively few amendments proposed through popular initiative have a success rate

TABLE 2.6
Method of Initiation and State Amendment Rate, 1970–1979

Method of Initiating Amendment	Proposed by Legislative	Popular Initiative	Special Convention
Amendment Rate	1.24	1.38	1.26
Percent of Amendments Using This Method	91.5	2.2	6.3
Number of Constitutions in Category	50	17	5

roughly half that of the two prominent alternatives. The popular initiative is in fact more difficult to use than legislative initiative and results in proposals that are less well considered. Ironically, the supposedly easier method to use, legislative initiative, tends to produce a more well considered amendment proposal — one that is more likely to be accepted.

TABLE 2.7
Success Rate of Various Methods for Proposing
Amendments in the Fifty States, 1776–1979

	All Methods	Legislature	Initiative	Convention
Proposed	7,563	6,637	566	360
Adopted	4,704	4,268	182	254
Success Rate (in percent)	62	64	32	71

What about the varying methods for *legislative* initiation? States vary in how large a legislative majority is needed for a proposal to be put on the ballot, and some states require that the majority be sustained in two consecutive sessions. Table 2.8 summarizes what we find in this regard.

In this table we have normed the decline in the amendment rate produced by each type of legislative majority against that of the least difficult method. That is, since simple majority rule by the legislature results in the highest amendment rate, we ask what difference it makes to use a more difficult method for initiating amendments. The data indicate that in the American states, when the method of initiation is stiffened to require majority legislative approval twice, the amendment rate for that state's constitution goes down by 4 percent, which is the same as making

TABLE 2.8
Comparative Effect of Majority Size on Amendment
Rate in American State Constitutions

Required Legislative Majority	Ratio of Difficulty to Simple Majority	Number of Constitutions in Category
50% + 1	1.00	11
50% + 1 Twice	1.04	6
60%	1.26	9
67%	1.62	19
75%	1.83	1
67% Twice	3.56	4

the difficulty of amendment 4 percent higher. That is indicated here by the index of difficulty rising to 1.04. A requirement for a three–fifths legislative majority (60 percent) reduces a state's amendment rate by 26 percent compared with the amendment rate of states using a simple majority requirement, which is reflected here in an increase in the index of difficulty to 1.26.

We can derive the following conclusions from Table 2.9.

Generally speaking, the larger the legislative majority required for initiation, the fewer amendments proposed and the lower the amendment rate.

Requiring a legislature to pass a proposal twice does not significantly increase the difficulty of the amendment process if the decision rule is one half plus one.

The most effective way to increase the difficulty of amendment at the initiation stage is to require the approval of two consecutive legislatures using a two–thirds majority each time.

Beyond these three interesting proposals, it is also useful to discover that the variance in the degree of difficulty between alternative legislative majorities is sufficient to establish the core of an index of difficulty for any amendment process. An attempt at such an index is presented in Table 2.9. The index identifies more than seventy possible actions that could in some combination be used to initiate and approve a constitutional amendment and that together cover the combinations of virtually every amendment process in the world. The index score assigned to all but a few of these more than seventy possibilities in the index are derived from data on American states. Each score is a number

that represents a ratio of difficulty normed to a simple majority approval
in two legislative houses as used in Table 2.8.

TABLE 2.9
An Index for Estimating the Relative Difficulty of an Amendment Process

Constitutional Requirement		Increment
Initiation Requires:		
Action by an executive	Add	.25
Action by a special appointed body	Add	.50
Action by a special elected body	Add	.75
Action by a Unicameral Legislature:		
Legislative approval by a majority of 1/2 + 1	Add	.50
Legislative approval *twice* using 1/2 + 1	Add	.50
Legislative approval by an absolute majority	Add	.65
Legislative approval *twice* by absolute majority	Add	.65
Legislative approval by a 3/5 majority	Add	.65
Legislative approval *twice* by 3/5 majority	Add	.65
Legislative approval by a 2/3 majority	Add	.80
Legislative approval by a 3/4 majority	Add	.90
Legislative approval *twice* by a 2/3 majority	Add	1.75
If an election is required between two votes	Add	.25
Action by a bicameral legislature:		
Legislative approval by a majority of 1/2 + 1	Add	1.00
Legislative approval *twice* using 1/2 + 1	Add	1.00
Legislative approval by an absolute majority	Add	1.25
Legislative approval *twice* by absolute majority	Add	1.25
Legislative approval by a 3/5 majority	Add	1.25
Legislative approval *twice* by 3/5 majority	Add	1.25
Legislative approval by a 2/3 majority	Add	1.60
Legislative approval by a 3/4 majority	Add	1.80
Legislative approval *twice* by a 2/3 majority	Add	3.55
If an election is required between two votes	Add	.50
A petition of 0–250,000 voters	Add	3.00
A petition of 250,000–500,000 voters	Add	3.50
A petition by more than 500,000 voters	Add	4.00
Multiple state legislatures, 1/2 + 1	Add	2.00
Multiple state conventions, 1/2 + 1	Add	2.00
Multiple state legislatures or conventions, 2/3	Add	3.00
Multiple state legislatures or conventions, 3/4	Add	3.50
Approval Requires:		
Action by an executive	Add	.50
Approval by a special body, 1/3 or less	Add	.25
Approval by a special body, 1/2 + 1	Add	.50

Constitutional Requirement	Increment	
Approval by a special body, absolute majority	Add	.65
Approval by a special body, 3/5 majority	Add	.65
Approval by a special body, 2/3 majority	Add	.80
Approval by a special body, 3/4 majority	Add	.90
If any of the above acts a second time	Add	.50
Action by a Unicameral Legislature:		
Legislative approval, 1/3 majority or less	Add	.25
Legislative approval, 1/2 + 1	Add	.50
Legislative approval, *twice* by 1/2 + 1	Add	.50
Legislative approval, absolute majority	Add	.65
Legislative approval, *twice* by absolute majority	Add	.65
Legislative approval, 3/5 majority	Add	.65
Legislative approval, *twice* by 3/5 majority	Add	.65
Legislative approval, 2/3 majority	Add	.80
Legislative approval, 3/4 majority	Add	.90
If an election is required between two votes	Add	.25
Legislative approval, *twice* by a 2/3 majority	Add	1.75
Action by a bicameral legislature:		
Legislative approval, 1/3 majority or less	Add	.50
Legislative approval, 1/2 + 1	Add	1.00
Legislative approval, absolute majority	Add	1.25
Legislative approval, *twice* by absolute majority	Add	1.25
Legislative approval, 3/5 majority	Add	1.25
Legislative approval, *twice* by 3/5 majority	Add	1.25
Legislative approval, 2/3 majority	Add	1.60
Legislative approval, 3/4 majority	Add	1.80
Legislative approval, *twice* by 2/3 majority	Add	3.55
If an election is required between two votes	Add	.50
A popular referendum, 1/2 + 1	Add	1.50
A popular referendum, absolute majority	Add	1.75
A popular referendum, 3/5 or more	Add	2.00
Multiple state legislatures, 1/2 + 1	Add	2.00
Multiple state conventions, 1/2 + 1	Add	2.00
Multiple state legislatures or conventions, 2/3	Add	3.00
Multiple state legislatures or conventions, 3/4	Add	3.50
Majority of voters *and* majority of state	Add	3.75
Unanimous approval by state governments	Add	4.00

For example, we know from Table 2.8 that amendment proposals made by popular initiative have almost exactly one–half the success rate of those initiated by the legislature in American states and are thus twice as difficult to pass as those initiated by the legislature. Nineteen states use a two–thirds legislative majority and seventeen use a simple majority. The score for the popular initiative will be twice the weighted score for the legislative method. This combined weighted score for legislative initiative in all fifty states turns out to be almost exactly 1.50, and thus the index score for a popular initiative is 3.00.

Also, we know from examining state data going back to 1776 that the amendment approval rate after the adoption of popular referenda as the means of approval has remained virtually the same as it was when the primary agent of approval was the state legislature. We can thus say that a popular referendum used as the means for approving a proposed amendment, as opposed to initiating one, is about as difficult as having the state legislature approve it. As just noted, the average degree of difficulty for state legislative action, weighted for the relative frequency of using one type of majority versus another, is 1.50. We thus assign a weight of 1.50 to approval by a majority popular referendum.

The index score assigned to a given amendment process is generated by adding together the numbers assigned by the index to every step required by that process. How the index works can be illustrated by using it with the amendment process described in Article 5 of the U.S. Constitution. There is more than one path to amendment, and each must be evaluated. A two-thirds vote by Congress, since it requires two houses to initiate the process, is worth 1.60, whereas initiation by two thirds of the state legislatures is worth 2.25. The latter path leads to a national convention, which uses majority rule in advancing a proposal, thus adding .75 — under the assumption that the special initiating body is elected. The first path still totals 1.60, and the other now totals 3.00. Ratification by three–fourths of the states through either their legislatures or elected conventions adds 3.50. The path beginning with Congress now totals 5.20, while the path beginning with the state legislatures and using a national convention totals 6.50. Even though the second path has never been successful, and one can see more clearly now why it has not, it is still a valid option. For the total amendment process we can use the lower figure unless or until the more difficult procedure is ever used. That is, because the 6.50 path has never been used, a weighted composite score would be 5.10, which is what we will use here.

If we perform the same calculation for the American states, we find that the average index score is 2.92 with very little variance. The highest state score is 3.60 (Delaware), and twenty–six states are tied for the lowest score at 2.75. Another sixteen states have a score of 3.10. Thus, while we were able to detect variance between select subsets of states, in general the range of variance is very small compared with that found in the constitutions of other nations.

CONCLUSION

The amendment patterns uncovered here are simple and the implications are straightforward. Since there is so little variance in the difficulty of the amendment process across the fifty states, this constitutional variable contributes little to our understanding of why one state averages only one amendment every three years and another averages more than eight per year. Other traditionally used variables add little more to our understanding of these patterns. Instead, the length of the document seems to be crucial both for amendment rate and for constitutional longevity. This, in turn, implies that there is merit to the view that ordinary legislative matters not needed to establish a constitutional framework should be kept out of the constitution. Ironically, the attempt to "settle" difficult political matters by constitutionalizing them may have the opposite effect.

Constitutionalizing an issue either at the time a constitution is written, or later by piling needless amendments onto it, not only increases the length of a constitution but also undercuts its status as a higher law. The longer a constitution is, the more quickly it is likely to be replaced. When a constitution is replaced, *everything* is once again up for grabs — a situation in which the constitutional safeguards that "settled" any given matter are at least temporarily overturned, and many other interests of each political actor are also put at risk. A rational actor with a long–range view should thus seek to keep a constitution short in order to safeguard his or her constitutional interests. However, once one nonconstitutional policy issue is allowed in, any policy issue can be constitutionalized, so a short–range strategy of constitutionalizing a particular policy issue leads to a kind of tragedy of the constitutional commons whereby the security of everyone's long–range interests is reduced. Thus, the concept of a reasonable rate of amendment, along with an initially short constitution, is in accord with long–term rationality.

NOTES

1.   The two best books on the role of popular sovereignty in American political thought are Edmund S. Morgan, *Inventing the People: The Rise of Popular Sovereignty in England and America* (New York: W. W. Norton, 1988); and Willi Paul Adams, *The First American Constitutions* (Chapel Hill: University of North Carolina Press, 1980), esp. chap. 6.

2.   Donald S. Lutz, *The Origins of American Constitutionalism* (Baton Rouge: Louisiana State University Press, 1988), esp. chap. 7.

3.   This position is developed further in Donald S. Lutz, *Popular Consent and Popular Control: Whig Political Theory in the Early State Constitutions* (Baton Rouge:

Louisiana State University Press, 1980), 218–225.

4. Willi Paul Adams argues this interpretation in his *First American Constitutions*, 139. However, many political theorists probably interpret Locke as saying that the constitution may be changed when those in power have put *themselves* in a state of nature vis-à-vis civil society. Under this interpretation civil society has not ended, since the social compact is still operative — that is, the people continue to give their consent to be bound by the majority in the selection of government. Since those in government no longer follow majority will, they have implicitly withdrawn their consent and have moved outside the civil society into a state of nature. This is closer to the interpretation used by Americans during the founding era.

5. While this was the first explicit amendment process in a state constitution, the first explicit use of an amendment process anywhere was in William Penn's 1678 *Frame of Government*, which may well explain why the 1776 Pennsylvania Constitution was first among the post–independence state documents. See John R. Vile, *The Constitutional Amending Process in American Political Thought* (New York: Praeger, 1992), 11–12.

6. For the phrasing and theoretical importance of this assumption, I am indebted to Vincent Ostrom, *The Political Theory of a Compound Republic: Designing the American Experiment*, 2d. ed. (Lincoln: University of Nebraska Press, 1987).

7. On this point see Albert L. Sturm, *Thirty Years of State Constitution–Making: 1938–1968* (New York: National Municipal League, 1970), 18.

8. For an interesting discussion of this surprisingly complex question see Sanford Levinson, "Accounting for Constitutional Change," *Constitutional Commentary* 8 (Summer 1991): 409–431.

9. For an overview of the standard criticisms about the shortcomings of state constitutions in this and other respects, see Albert L. Sturm, *Thirty Years of State Constitution–Making*, esp. 1–17.

10. The data in Table 2.1 are based on information in Albert L. Sturm, *Thirty Years of State Constitution–Making*; H. W. Stanley and R. G. Niemi, *Vital Statistics on American Politics*, 3d, ed. (Washington, D.C.: C.Q. Press, 1992); James Q. Dealey, *Growth of American State Constitutions* (New York: Da Capo Press, 1972); Walter F. Dodd, *The Revision and Amendment of State Constitutions* (New York: Da Capo Press, 1970); Daniel J. Elazar, *American Federalism: A View from the States*, 2d. ed. (New York: Thomas Y. Crowell Co., 1972); Fletcher M. Green, *Constitutional Development in the South Atlantic States, 1776–1860* (New York: Da Capo Press, 1971); and Ellis Paxson Oberholtzer, *The Referendum in America* (New York: Da Capo Press, 1971).

11. Table 2.3 is based on a table from Albert L. Sturm, "The Development of American State Constitutions," *Publius: The Journal of Federalism* 12 (Winter 1982): 90.

12. Table 2.6 is based on data from Albert L. Sturm, "Development of American State Constitutions," 78–79. Total of all methods will exceed fifty since many states specify the possibility of more than one method of proposing amendments. During the 1970s the initiative method of proposing amendments added about five amendments per year nationwide beyond what we would expect if the legislative method were the only one available.

3

Constitutional Amendment through the Legislature in New York

Gerald Benjamin and Melissa Cusa

"Shall there be a convention to revise the constitution and amend the same?" In accord with the state constitutional requirement that it be submitted to the people every twenty years, this question will be on the ballot in New York in 1997. With a referendum a certainty, the merits of calling a state constitutional convention were already being debated in 1994.

Modern democratic governing institutions are defined in written constitutions and altered, if necessary, by constitutional amendment. The amending process is therefore crucial to any set of constitutional arrangements. "A good amending process," James Madison wrote in the *Federalist Papers*, "should guard against the extreme facility which would render the Constitution too mutable, and on the other hand . . . guard against the extreme difficulty which might perpetuate its discovered faults."[1] A more recent formulation suggests that a commitment to constitutionalism is reflected in amending processes that incorporate popular sovereignty, provide a highly deliberative decisionmaking environment, and include a distinction between statutory and constitutional provisions.[2]

In recent years, the constitutional convention as a method for constitutional change has been in disfavor. Automatic questions calling conventions have usually been answered "no" by voters in the states. In Michigan in 1994, for example, opponents argued that "the statewide property tax school finance ballot question demonstrated, [that] individual elements of the Constitution — even the most important ones — can be changed by elected officials and citizens without an open-ended effort at overall constitutional revision." They also cited as reasons for their opposition the considerable taxpayer costs and the "real danger [of] single–issue zealots . . . seizing control of the convention process."[3]

Of course, even without conventions major changes in the structure of state government are still occurring. Consider for example the wide-spread adoption of term limitation in the initiative and referendum states. The result, one analyst argues, is "an odd juxtaposition of popular dis-content and enormous *yet* selective institutional change, with the nearly complete absence of deliberate and comprehensive reform."[4] Another observes that the decline of the convention and the use of legislative amendment processes and judicial interpretation to change state constitutions "reflect . . . declining [degrees of] commitment to popular sovereignty" and adds that "the level of commitment to popular sover-eignty may be a key attitude for defining the nature of the political system."[5]

Skeptics in New York, like those in other states where convention opportunities have recently been rejected, are concerned about the convention as a means for constitutional change. A major basis for this concern is that, once called, the potential scope of a constitutional convention in the state is unlimited. (This is the case because such a convention is the direct agent of the sovereign people, convened not to govern but to create the government.) Therefore, it is argued, calling a constitutional convention would involve political risks — the loss of current protections for some groups or interests, the adoption of new, controversial provisions not widely supported in the state — that are out of proportion to the potential gains.

Moreover, if structural change in state government is truly needed, it is argued, a more focused means to this end is available. New York does not have a popular initiative process, but like all states can alter its constitution through the state legislature. In fact, in twenty-four states, the only way the constitution may be changed is through specific action of the legislature or through a convention process that must be started in it.

The legislative route to constitutional change is desirable, its pro-ponents suggest, for at least three reasons. First, as noted, it may be limited in focus. Second, it assures deliberateness and deliberation. Finally, they argue, there is a concentration of expertise in the legislature on the actual operation of constitutionally defined institutions.

But legislative processes for constitutional change are by their nature controlled by politicians who have succeeded in the present system, who likely wish to continue to do so, and who therefore may have a stake in "perpetuating discovered faults." This is why one political scientist describes constitutionally defined democratic institutions as "bargains among self interested politicians."[6]

This chapter focuses on experience with the legislative route to constitutional change in one state, New York, where the automatic convention question is used. Its purpose is to explore whether this route is indeed a viable alternative for achieving serious structural reform in state government, especially in circumstances in which legislators are self-interested and where there is no constitutional initiative process to spur them on.

To provide a comparative context for the detailed look at New York that follows, we first consider a summary analysis of methods now used in the states to make constitutional change.

THE COMPARATIVE CONTEXT

The norm in the American states is for constitutions to be amended through specially defined legislative processes. Between 1986 and 1993, almost nine of every ten constitutional amendments proposed in the states were initiated in state legislatures. Additionally, amendments that came through this route remained the ones most likely to be approved by the voters at the polls.[7]

But three other methods are currently in use (see Table 3.1). The best known of these is the constitutional initiative, which permits voters to petition to put amendments to a vote of the citizenry. A second approach, used only in Florida, provides for periodic automatic creation of a commission that may propose constitutional amendments directly to the voters. The constitutional convention, relatively frequently used in the states but never since the founding at the national level, provides a final alternative but only in those states where the convention call does not rely on legislative action.[8]

TABLE 3.1
State Methods for Constitutional Change outside the Legislature

	Initiative and Referendum	
	Yes	No
Convention — Yes	*Convention & Initiative & Referendum* Illinois Michigan Montana Mississippi Ohio Oklahoma	*Convention Only* Rhode Island Maryland Connecticut Alaska Hawaii Iowa New Hampshire New York
Convention — No	*Initiative & Referendum Only* Massachusetts Colorado Nebraska Arkansas Arizona Nevada California South Dakota Florida* Oregon Missouri	*Neither Convention nor Initiative & Referendum* Wyoming North Dakota Utah Washington Alabama Louisiana Delaware Minnesota Georgia New Jersey Indiana New Mexico Kansas North Carolina Kentucky Pennsylvania South Carolina Vermont Tennessee Virginia Texas West Virginia Wisconsin Idaho Maine

*Additionally, Florida employs a commission system that can place questions directly on the ballot.

Constitutional Initiative

Constitutional initiative and referendum procedures in seventeen states allow voters to petition to put constitutional amendments on the ballot and bring them to a vote. According to one account, in 1994 citizen proposals limiting government and politicians reached their highest level since 1932.[9] In a recent paper political scientist Caroline Tolbert concluded that the "use of the initiative is a predominant explanation of the adoption of legislative term limits and constraints on governmental taxation and spending."[10]

The merits of these changes, and of initiative and referendum generally, remain the subject of lively debate. But that is not the concern here. What is crucial is that despite their often being directly at odds with the self-interest of those governing, these changes could and did occur. That is, initiative and referendum worked just as intended by Progressive Era reformers concerned about entrenched politicians blocking constitutional change when their own prerogatives or power were at stake.

In addition to their actual use to bypass the legislature, the presence of initiative and referendum procedures for constitutional amendment in state constitutions may encourage change by the legislative route. Confronted by likely outcomes that they oppose brought forward by initiative, legislators may devise "less bad" options for consideration of the voters. In California in the 1970s, for example, the legislature proposed a ballot alternative to Proposition 13, rolling back the property tax.[11] In Florida in 1992 a term-limits proposal less stringent than the one proposed by petition was passed in one house of the legislature.[12]

In fact, a legislative role may be built into the popular initiative process for constitutional change through the "indirect initiative" procedure. Under such a procedure the legislature is given a chance to consider the substance of a popular initiative before it is put to a vote by the citizenry at–large. Thus the Massachusetts Constitution requires that an amendment proposed by initiative gain the support of at least one quarter of each legislative house in two sessions before it is offered at the polls. In fact, however, rules of procedure in the Massachusetts legislature have been used to undermine the intent of this process, effectively requiring a majority of each house for action on constitutional amendment initiatives.[13]

Clearly, the combined effects of different modes of constitutional amendment, as well as their separate effects, must be considered when determining their impact in a political system.

Constitutional Commission with Ballot Access

The Florida commission approach, first adopted in 1968, has had mixed success. Its far-reaching examination of state constitutional issues in 1977–1978 led to serious proposals for change. These were first rejected at the polls but shaped the agenda for further constitutional revision in that state for years to come. A constitutionally based tax and budget reform commission, created by Florida voters in 1988 on the model of the revision commission with similar direct access to the voters, was more successful. Its proposal for budget reform was adopted in 1992. In accord with the twenty-year cycle set out in the Florida

Constitution, a new constitutional revision commission will come into being in 1997.[14]

The Automatic Convention Question

A constitutional convention process, not one through the legislature, was used in the first formal amending process included in a state constitution, that of Pennsylvania in 1776.[15] As indicated in Table 3.1, there are thirteen states in addition to New York where the question of whether to hold a constitutional convention is periodically placed on the ballot automatically, and a convention is held if the voters say "yes." For New York and seven others, those without initiative and referendum, the automatic convention question is the only way of bypassing those in power to make constitutional change.

ALTERNATIVE METHODS OF AMENDMENT THROUGH THE LEGISLATURE

The New York Constitution currently requires a majority vote of those elected to each house of two separately elected legislatures in order to offer a constitutional amendment to the public at referendum. The constitution includes no limit on the number of amendments that may be made in a year, the number of articles that may be affected, or the content of amendments. Requirements for proposing constitutional amendments through the legislature and their popular ratification differ from state to state.[16]

Proposal

In accord with the status of constitutions as "higher law," initiation of amendments through the legislature in most states is purposely made more difficult than is the passage of ordinary legislation by one or more of three means:

1. requiring the maximum denominator for the recording of a majority (all members elected to the body rather than those present or those voting);
2. requiring extraordinary majorities (three fifths, two thirds, or three quarters);
3. and/or requiring passage more than once, often by separately elected majorities.

Additionally, constitutional amendment is made more difficult in some states by limiting the number of proposals that may be offered in any one year, by limiting the number of articles of the constitution that may be changed in any year, and by limiting the substance of an amendment to a single purpose (though more than one article may be affected).

New York's requirements for proposing amendments, detailed above and similar to those of ten other states, are more difficult than single passage by extraordinary majority of those elected, the approach used in half the states.[17]

Ratification

As the original source of their constitutions in democratic theory, the sovereign people must agree to changes in these basic documents. This is why all constitutional change processes in the American states (except that of Delaware) require popular ratification of constitutional amendments however they are initiated. In most states, including New York, ratification of legislatively initiated constitutional changes is by simple majority cast on the amendment question. In a small number of states, minimum majorities or dual majorities are specified. There appear to be three reasons for this: experience with "voter fall–off" on constitutional amendments and other referendum questions; the particular geographic impact of some state constitutional provisions; and a perceived special need to protect particular constitutional arrangements from change.

New York's standard for passage of a constitutional amendment proposed through the legislature is the one most commonly used and offers the lowest threshold for a positive outcome.

THE VALUE OF THE NEW YORK CASE

The relative frequency of constitutional change in New York, despite its relative difficulty, makes the state an interesting one in which to examine the change process. New York's current constitution was amended 207 times between its adoption in 1895 and 1991. One comparison found that the annual rate of amendment in New York was higher than that for all but seven states.[18] A relatively high rate of formal amendment is not unusual for a document of the length of the New York Constitution, but is uncommon for one of its age. According to Donald Lutz, such a rate may be indicative of an insufficiently deliberative process for constitutional change or the inclusion of "statutory matter" in a constitution. It is also suggestive of a constitution more likely to be replaced entirely.[19]

A Focus on Process

Empirical studies of constitutional amendment have reached conclusions about the change process by focusing not on the process but on its products, amendments once they are proposed. There has been substantive categorization of amendments brought to referendum in the states but no assessment of the relative capacity of proposals for structural change to survive the legislative gauntlet, compared with proposals in which current decisionmakers may be less self–interested.[20]

This analysis seeks to go beyond these by looking at the process itself. It examines the political origin of ideas for constitutional change in New York since 1967, when the last convention was held, and seeks to assess why and how some ideas advance while others do not. Constitutional-change ideas are treated as similar to, but different from, ideas for legislative change, floating in a "policy primeval soup . . . [where] . . . some survive and prosper."[21] As with proposals for legislative change, a number of factors will determine the outcome of the much more demanding "natural selection" process for ideas for constitutional change, for example: the presence of "entrepreneurs" well placed in the process, aware of and interested in constitutional change; a general political environment receptive to amendment ideas as "solutions"; the presence of compelling arguments for constitutional change, as opposed to statutory or other approaches; and the persistent congruence of change proposals with values and interests of key decisionmakers. Persistence is crucial because the dual passage requirement in New York requires that "windows of opportunity" for constitutional amendment, the times in which ideas may couple with circumstances that allow change, must be kept opened longer than is the case for ordinary legislation.[22]

The Legislature in New York

The specific nature of the legislative institution itself is crucial for determining any constitutional-change agenda. The New York state legislature is highly partisan, disciplined, and leadership dominated.[23] The assembly has 150 members. Democrats controlled it for the 1967–1993 period, with the exception of six years between 1969 and 1974. The senate, Republican for the entire study period, has sixty-one members. The persistence of divided partisan control has meant that, as with ordinary legislation, constitutional change through the legislature in New York has required bipartisan support. Where this support has not been achieved — one example is disputes between the parties about the design of new multicounty judicial districts, used for the nomination and election of state judges — reform has been effectively blocked for years.

The speaker in the assembly and the majority leader in the senate control committee chairmanships and assignments, dominate the flow of business, and control a vast array of formal and informal resources, both political and governmental. Responsive to the leadership, committee chairs hold broad sway within their specified areas of responsibility. To succeed, proposals for constitutional change in each house must gain the support of the leadership of the body and the committee, and the imprimatur of the majority party in each house, given in its conference. The nature of sponsorship — the leadership status of the sponsor, his or her party, the sponsor's committee assignment — is thus indicative of the relative seriousness of any proposed change.

Initially in any legislative session, members are not limited in the number of bills they may introduce, and professional assistance for drafting is freely available. Barriers to the introduction of constitutional changes are thus very low. Legislators may thus easily propose amendments to please constituents, gain publicity or stake out an area of interest, even if they do not plan to "push" them during the session. After a date specified in the rules, however, all bills must be filed by leadership-dominated Rules Committees.

THE LEGISLATIVE ROUTE TO CONSTITUTIONAL AMENDMENT IN NEW YORK

From 1967 to 1993 there were 4,437 constitutional amendments filed in New York State, an average of 171 per year (Table 3.2). The peak year was 1970, when 417 ideas for constitutional change were submitted in the legislature; a low of 80 proposed amendments was reached in 1988. There has, on average, been more activity in odd- than in even-numbered years, reflecting the need to reintroduce measures after the election of a new legislature to keep them alive.

In 1915 and 1967 constitutions proposed by conventions in New York were rejected by the voters at the polls. Nevertheless it is commonly observed in the state that the convention event and record in these years generate ideas for change by the legislative route. Confirming this, the number of amendments offered in the several years following the 1967 convention was consistently higher than the average for all years during

TABLE 3.2
Number of Bills to Amend the New York Constitution, 1967–1993

	Article									
	1	*2*	*3*	*4*	*5*	*6*	*7*	*8*	*9*	*10*
1967	11	19	5	5	4	3	8	10	5	1
1968	30	24	1	7	14	10	29	2	1	5
1969	36	28	32	10	34	61	40	59	19	6
1970	37	50	25	9	20	37	29	27	5	1
1971	34	17	42	11	24	37	29	35	3	0
1972	18	12	32	12	17	29	16	17	6	1
1973	24	11	28	13	12	47	34	17	7	0
1974	18	4	24	9	9	33	26	19	2	0
1975	22	3	37	9	20	50	35	18	5	0
1976	10	3	25	10	16	34	33	5	1	3
1977	6	10	22	12	11	60	25	13	5	7
1978	20	5	9	3	11	13	9	3	3	3
1979	11	9	14	1	13	17	11	13	2	2
1980	27	1	5	0	9	20	6	3	2	1
1981	15	5	7	3	20	31	14	9	2	4
1982	19	3	12	1	12	21	8	5	4	5
1983	17	5	6	2	16	38	12	8	3	4
1984	20	4	6	4	15	6	15	6	1	2
1985	15	4	5	13	15	28	16	8	2	4
1986	14	2	7	4	11	23	6	3	1	1
1987	13	4	12	12	12	26	11	3	1	1
1988	11	2	8	6	7	19	7	0	0	0
1989	12	5	4	11	6	21	28	2	1	2
1990	11	3	5	6	9	22	11	6	2	5
1991	12	5	7	8	8	37	27	3	2	2
1992	11	3	16	7	9	14	29	6	2	0
1993	11	2	17	11	14	24	20	6	5	1
Sum	485	243	414	199	368	761	534	306	92	61

					Article					
11	*12*	*13*	*14*	*15*	*16*	*17*	*18*	*19*	*20*	*Total*
1	0	11	6	1	3	1	1	9	0	104
13	1	0	13	5	8	4	8	11	1	187
22	0	10	6	2	15	13	16	8	0	417
12	0	9	2	1	7	5	14	4	0	294
8	0	66	6	3	14	8	13	6	0	296
3	0	3	3	3	8	4	8	4	1	197
1	0	9	5	7	8	5	9	5	2	244
0	0	8	6	2	4	0	1	7	5	177
1	0	12	3	1	5	2	2	6	9	240
2	0	11	5	0	5	2	1	8	7	181
3	0	7	3	1	9	0	1	3	11	209
0	0	7	2	2	7	3	1	5	12	118
1	0	4	4	3	14	1	0	3	15	138
0	0	1	2	2	2	1	0	3	13	98
1	0	2	5	1	10	0	0	2	11	142
1	0	2	4	2	8	0	0	1	6	114
1	0	3	6	1	8	1	0	2	6	139
2	0	1	3	0	7	0	1	1	5	99
1	0	1	6	0	7	3	1	2	5	137
1	0	2	7	0	4	0	2	1	3	92
3	0	3	6	0	3	0	4	0	5	119
1	0	3	6	0	3	0	2	0	5	80
2	0	2	4	7	0	0	5	0	6	118
2	0	2	1	3	2	0	1	0	6	97
5	0	2	4	5	1	0	2	0	10	140
5	0	3	5	0	1	0	1	2	9	123
4	0	2	4	0	1	1	1	5	8	137
96	1	126	127	52	164	54	95	98	161	

57

this period, and several amendments sent by the legislature to the voters in the late 1960s and early 1970s were part of the draft 1967 constitution. In fact 1977, the year of the last mandatory convention question vote, seems to be a watershed, with all years following below and all years preceding above the average.

Where the mandatory constitutional convention question is used, its scheduled date is known far in advance. One possible strategy for convention opponents is to try to preempt the event by advancing key changes through the legislature in the years just before the scheduled vote. There is, however, no clear indication in New York that the prospect of a vote on the mandatory question resulted in such a preemptive strategy in 1977.

Constitutional-change Entrepreneurs

Relatively few New York state legislators demonstrated an awareness of and special interest in the state constitution and state constitutional change. The scope of their activity suggests that they are "constitutional change-entrepreneurs" (see Table 3.3).

TABLE 3.3
Member Status and Proposals to Amend, 1983–1993

Status	Number of Proposals	Percentage of Total
Leaders	18	1.9
Chair of Committee	111	11.4
Committee Member	265	27.3
Other Members	577	59.4
Total	971	100.0

For the period 1983 to 1993 nine assembly members (6 percent of the house) and five senators (8 percent of the house) proposed fifteen or more constitutional amendments. Their submissions totaled 275, more than one in four of the 941 amendments filed during the period (28.7 percent).

Of the assembly members, five were in the Democratic majority and four in the Republican minority. Of the senators, in contrast, all were in the Republican majority.

The efforts of some of these constitutional-change entrepreneurs were quite focused and linked to their legislative roles. For example, Assemblyperson Oliver Koppell, chair of the Judiciary Committee, filed twenty–five amendments concerning the judiciary article during this period. In similar fashion, Senator Tarky Lombardi offered eighteen amendments to the state and local finance articles. He was chair of the Senate Finance Committee.

Other members, however, manifest a general interest in constitutional change. During the ten years under study, Assemblyperson Doug Prescott (R.-Queens) proposed amendments to six different articles, and Assemblyperson Robin Schimmiger (D.-Buffalo) to five. In the other house, Senator Ron Stafford (R.-North Country) offered amendments to seven different articles and John Marchi (R.-Staten Island) to eight.

Seriousness of Change Proposals

Patterns of sponsorship of constitutional amendments over the ten-year period indicate that between two-fifths and one-half of these introduced in New York reflect some serious political effort beyond the act of introduction itself (see Table 3.4). Two measures of the seriousness of a constitutional-change proposal in the New York state legislature are the role of its sponsor or sponsors and whether it can attract majority party sponsorship in each house. Sponsorship of a proposal by a well-placed member in each house — a leader, committee chair, or committee member — is indicative not only of that person's interest but of the likely

TABLE 3.4
Proposals with Sponsorship in Both Houses

Chamber		Number of Proposals	Percentage of Total
Senate	Assembly		
Republican Majority	Democrat Majority	216	55
Republican Majority	Republican Minority	141	36
Democrat Minority	Democrat Majority	32	8
Republican Minority	Democrat Minority	7	2
Total		396	100

Note: Four hundred six proposals received sponsorship in both houses; however the origins of only 396 could be identified from the data.

presence of significant political effort on the matter. Majority sponsorship in each house — Democrats in the assembly, Republicans in the senate — means that the initial steps toward the bipartisan coalition necessary to move the amendment have been taken. In contrast, a single house or single party proposal, or one opposed by the leadership, has no serious prospects in New York.

As noted earlier it is important to understand that a proposal may be put in the legislative hopper with little expectation that it will pass or even get serious consideration. Members who have no intention of expending political capital on an amendment may introduce it to take interest group or constituent pressure off themselves or to take credit for its introduction while campaigning. It is also possible that they may simply be seeking to start a debate, with an understanding that their proposal may come to be taken seriously years later after it gains visibility or when the political environment changes. Staking out of political and policy turf is also involved. By putting an amendment in early, a legislator effectively "claims" it as his or her issue for the future. The relatively low barriers to preparing and proposing constitutional amendments and the variety of available incentives to do so, both noted above, encourage individual legislators to introduce proposals in which they may be only marginally interested.

Sponsorship and Bicameral Effort

During the decade under study, constitutional change was rarely proposed (less than 2 percent of the time) by those in leadership roles in the legislature, the assembly speaker and the majority and minority leaders in each house. About one-fifth (19 percent) were sponsored by committee chairs of the relevant policy area, while another one-third (34 percent) were advanced by members of these committees. The rest, more than two-fifths (44 percent) of proposed amendments, were put in by members acting outside of the substantive areas of their legislative concentration (see Table 3.3).

Additionally, only about two-fifths (41 percent) of proposals received sponsorship in both houses. Of these, about one-half (55 percent) had majority sponsorship in both houses — Democrat in the assembly, Republican in the senate — an added sign of seriousness of purpose. An additional one-third (35 percent) were Republican, sponsored by the majority in the assembly and the minority in the senate, while about one-tenth (8 percent) were Democratic. A curious 2% of these amendments were sponsored by minority members in both houses, a strange combination indeed in New York State (see Table 3.4)!

Dual sponsorship appeared most often on amendments to Article 6, reflecting major efforts to gain court reform by the governor and leaders of the court system for the entire period under study. Often other proposals that received dual sponsorship concerned matters that had reached a significant level of visibility in the public-policy debate. Examples include institution of the death penalty by amendment after repeated gubernatorial vetoes of statutory efforts; reform of the budget process in reaction to years of failure to adopt a timely budget; and removal of constitutional restrictions on gambling.

Strategic Behavior: The Assembly Republican Minority

It is interesting that the Republicans, the party out of power in the executive, were much more active in advancing constitutional-change ideas that found support from members of their party in both houses than were legislators of the governor's party. Sometimes there was a geographic basis for this cooperation. For example, almost all of Assemblyperson Doug Prescott's constitutional-amendment proposals were introduced in the senate by his copartisan from Queens, Frank Padavan. The Republican minority in the assembly was more aggressive in the constitutional-change arena than the Democratic minority in the senate, and Republicans in the senate more supportive than Democrats in the assembly of these sorts of actions. One notable example concerns initiative and referendum, a subject for which minority assembly Republicans were able to find majority senate Republican sponsors despite the opposition of senate Republican leadership and the obvious threat such a change poses for those in power in the legislature.

THE SUBSTANCE OF AMENDMENTS: WHAT IS PROPOSED? WHAT PASSES?

The presentation in Table 3.2 of the frequency with which specific articles of the state constitution have been targeted for change since 1967, and the substance of these proposals, does not separate the more serious proposals from the less serious, nor can it distinguish wide-reaching ideas from those that are more narrowly focused. It is useful, however, for understanding those areas in which legislators felt some impulse, however small, to put a matter on the legislature's agenda and to take the responsibility of sponsorship in doing so.

Frequency of Proposals

Some articles of the state constitution have been the focal points for frequent amendment efforts for most years over the entire quarter century. These include the state bill of rights (Article 1); the judicial article (Article 6); state finance provisions, including the budgetary process (Article 7); the provision concerning the number, management, and staffing of state departments (Article 5); the legislative article (Article 3); and the local finance article (Article 8).

A second group is made up of articles that on average attracted moderate levels of amendment activity, largely but not entirely in the decade or so immediately following the last constitutional convention. These include the provisions on suffrage (Article 2), the executive (Article 4), public officers (Article 13), conservation (Article 14), and taxation (Article 16). (Article 20 is included in this category because various entirely new provisions have been proposed by legislators with this number.)

A third category includes articles that show low levels but relatively persistent change effort: These are the articles on home rule (Article 9), education (Article 11), and housing (Article 18).

The final group of constitutional articles appears to be relatively settled. Some have attracted virtually no interest at all. For others, attempts to amend them have been infrequent in recent years, though a few have experienced brief bursts of activity. These are the articles on corporations (Article 10), defense (Article 12), canals (Article 15), social welfare (Article 17), and amendment of the constitution itself (Article 19).

Subject of Proposals

When it comes to constitutional change, five major subjects have been on New York State's "mind" in recent years. These are: (1) state and local relations, (2) distribution of power between the executive and legislative branches, (3) rights, (4) structure and scope of government, and (5) judicial reform.

State and Local Relations

Proposed constitutional amendments in this area sought enhanced local discretion in decisionmaking, increased state capacity to support local economic development efforts, and barriers to the transference of costs to localities by the state. In the 1967–1977 period, suggested amendments to articles on state finance, local finance, public corporations, and taxation (Articles 7, 8, 10, and 16) addressed increased local control of total spending, the incurring of debt, and allowable tax exemptions. Proponents sought increases in state liability for financing local improvements and public corporations, expansion of projects for which bonds might be issued, greater flexibility in bond type and repayment schedules, increase in both exclusions to debt and tax limits, and greater allowable percentages of revenue that might be raised by taxes. These reflect an interest in expanding New York State's ability to work for economic development and an interest in allowing a greater flexibility to localities, especially the largest ones, in financing their own operations.

During the late 1970s and early 1980s, the legislative agenda for constitutional change continued to suggest an interest in greater fiscal discretion for local governments and a desire for redistribution of power from the state to the localities. Typical proposed amendments sought to require the printing of local fiscal impact on bills (on the assumption that greater visibility would be a disincentive to unfunded mandates), increase local control over land use, increase local options in debt and tax management, restrict legislative authority to create or dissolve counties, and enhance local authority to create laws and perform duties not directly prohibited by the constitution.

Matters specific to social welfare (Article 17) also describe the home rule constitutional agenda. The consistent concern is to achieve state takeover of public assistance and Medicaid programs.

Distribution of Power between Branches

The last several decades are commonly regarded as ones of legislative resurgence in New York. It is thus not surprising that struggles to strengthen legislative authority vis-à-vis the executive have been part of the legislature's agenda for constitutional change. For all years studied, proposed changes to the executive (Article 4) have been restrictive of the executive while expansive of the legislative branch, or have linked changes desired by the executive to proposals strengthening the legislature. (Exceptions were a few efforts in the early 1970s to increase the governor's authority to reorganize the executive branch and other state departments.) For example, proposed increases in the time allowed to the governor to act on legislation, offered in the early 1970s, were tied with concomitant proposals submitted to increase legislative power to convene itself, act on its own agenda, and override the executive veto. Other constitutional changes proposed by the legislature have sought to limit gubernatorial reeligibility to two terms while increasing the length of legislative terms (now two years for both houses); grant the legislature appointment power for the office of the lieutenant governor; allow legislative discretion in offering succession to executive offices; and create limitations of executive authority to grant reprieves, commutation, and pardons. Additionally, attempts to remove the need for a message of necessity from the governor to overcome the three-day constitutional waiting period for legislation, in the legislative (Article 3), would enhance legislative and restrict executive power.

Another avenue for increasing legislative authority or restricting the executive is alteration of the constitutional provisions relating to officers and civil departments and public officers (Articles 5 and 13). Some proposed amendments sought legislative control over appointment and removal of the heads of state departments, for example for the Education Department and the Public Service Commission. Alternatively, other proposals called for the election of the heads of these departments.

In the last decade studied (1983–1993), efforts to restrict legislative authority became more common, reflecting the antigovernmental environment of the era. Some proposals sought to limit the length of legislative sessions. The prime examples, however, are efforts to institute term limitations for legislators and authorization of initiative and referendum (Articles 19 and 20).

Rights

Proposed amendments concerning rights have involved both rights-enhancing and rights-constraining proposals.[24] Within the traditional notion of constitutionally defined rights — limits on government capacity to regulate the behavior of individuals — rights-enhancing proposals included expansion of the freedom of speech and extension of rights to privacy, private property, abortion choice, and gender equality. These were most prevalent during the first period of study. In contrast, rights-constraining proposals, more evident during the latter portion of the period, included defining "family" to exclude homosexual and alternative family structures, eliminating the right to abortion, and establishing English as the "official" language of the state.

Due-process proposals are somewhat harder to classify. Waiving the right to a grand jury in criminal proceedings and the protection of witnesses from intimidation appear to be restrictive of the rights of the accused. However, some believe grand juries in practice have little effect on verdicts and that removal of these from the constitution may be an attempt to facilitate court proceedings.

Amendments concerning rights were also advanced in other parts of the constitution. For example, proposed changes to the suffrage article (Article 2) would facilitate voting by establishing less restrictive registration procedures. Attempts to increase enfranchisement to diverse populations through the repeal of certain discriminatory age and literacy requirements were also introduced by members.

Scholars have noted the special place of "positive rights" in state constitutions.[25] These are obligations placed on the state to meet social or human needs of its citizens. Amendments to the New York Constitution have been offered over the last quarter century that would advance positive rights to quality and equal education, a healthful environment, and a decent place to live.

Structure and Scope of Government

As frustration with governmental gridlock has grown over the past decade, and as government at all levels has increasingly come to be regarded as part of the problem rather than part of the solution, ideas for altering the structure of government and limiting its scope have gained. Term limitation and initiative and referendum have already been mentioned. Additional ideas have included a proposal for a unicameral legislature and a range of suggestions for the reform of the budget process to force timely action. Proposals to limit government have also included caps or restrictions on spending, taxing, and borrowing.

Judicial Reform

The judicial article (Article 6) comprises about one-fourth of the New York Constitution. It therefore may be expected that it would be the focus of a large portion of the proposals addressing constitutional amendment. Topics of interest to some legislators concerning the judiciary article include: the manner of nomination, selection, and determination of qualifications; the supervision of individual judges (conduct) and the system; the scope of duties and jurisdiction of courts; the structure of the system; and financial administration and responsibility. It has been argued that the detail in the constitution regarding the third branch is attributable to the judiciary's interest in establishing its independent authority over itself. The courts are, after all, the final arbiters of the constitution. The irony, however, is that to have this final say the leaders of the judiciary trade ease of change, even when they come to regard change in their institutional interest. The difficulty of achieving judicial reform has led recently to calls by judges for a constitutional convention.[26]

AMENDMENTS PASSED BY THE LEGISLATURE AND THE PEOPLE

During the 1967–1993 period, sixty-one constitutional amendments were placed on the ballot and forty-one passed at referendum (see Table 3.5). Voters were most skeptical of legislative proposals for

TABLE 3.5
Constitutional Amendments Acted On, 1967–1993

Article	Introduced in Legislature (Annual Mean)	Number Passed by Legislature	Number Passed by Voters	Percent Passed by Voters
1 Bill of Rights	18.0	2	2	100.00
2 Suffrage	9.0	0	0	NA
3 Legislature	15.0	5	2	40.00
4 Executive	7.4	0	0	NA
5 Officers and Civil Departments	13.6	1	1	100.00
6 Judiciary	28.2	16	9	56.25
7 State Finances	19.8	6	5	83.30
8 Local Finances	11.3	7	4	57.14
9 Local Governments	3.4	0	0	NA
10 Corporations	2.3	6	4	66.67
11 Education	3.6	0	0	NA
12 Defense	0.0	0	0	NA
13 Public Officers	4.7	4	4	100.00
14 Conservation	4.7	8	6	75.00
15 Canals	1.9	1	1	100.00
16 Taxation	6.1	1	1	100.00
17 Social Welfare	2.0	2	2	100.00
18 Housing	3.5	1	0	0
19 Amendments	3.6	1	0	0
20 When to Take Effect	6.0	0	0	NA
Total	164.4	61	41	67.21

constitutional change that appeared to allow more spending, borrowing, or taxation. This success rate for legislative proposals approximates the national average.

On average over this period, New York State passed 969 bills a year, which comprise 8 percent of those filed. The ratio of amendments passed to those introduced in the legislature (less than 1 in 100) indicates that, as intended, it is indeed more difficult to amend the state constitution in New York than to pass ordinary legislation.

There is a statistically significant relationship between the articles for which amendments are proposed in the legislature and those that are actually amended (Spearman's Rho = .48, significant at .05). Those most amended were articles on the judiciary, conservation, local finance, state finance, corporations, the legislature, and public officers. Few amendments over the quarter century since the last convention made fundamental changes in the structure of state government. The three passed in 1977 concerning the state judiciary are an exception in this regard. Had they passed at referendum, provisions establishing a fifth judicial department, altering the amending process, and changing the rules for erecting new counties would also have been of some structural significance.

CONCLUSION

There has been no shortage of constitutional change proposals introduced in the New York state legislature in recent years, including measures that would seriously restructure state government. Moreover, significant numbers of constitutional amendments have been passed by the legislature over the past quarter century, and many of these have been ratified at the polls. New York's legislative process for constitutional amendment has not, however, produced a substantial amount of structural change in state government during this period. Amendments passed by this route rarely deal with the distribution of power in state government, and those that do are not designed to limit or constrain the principal political institutions or actors.

A small number of legislators functioned in recent years as constitutional-change entrepreneurs, some because their institutional role demanded it, others seemingly out of personal commitment, and still others for apparently partisan reasons. Members in key leadership positions, however, rarely take a role in advancing constitutional change, and the threat of voters calling a constitutional convention in response to the automatic question does not appear to motivate preemptive action through the legislature in New York to make major reforms in the structure and operation of government, as does the constitutional initiative threat in other states.

Conventions must be actually held to affect the legislative change process, and then their impact comes, ironically, out of failure. Reforms that lost when New York voters rejected the new state constitution that was offered them in a single up or down vote in 1967 were passed by the legislature in subsequent years. The convention created a constitutional-reform agenda and a cohort of committed and connected partisans of change to advocate for it.

In sum, the record in New York State suggests that the legislative method for constitutional change is not an effective alternative for overcoming those aspects of the state constitution that are "bargains among self-interested politicians." This is true even when the legislature is under the threat of voters being able to bypass it to call a constitutional convention. At minimum this finding argues against rejecting the opportunity for a convention provided by the automatic question on the grounds that the legislative method for constitutional change is available. For fundamentally altering institutional relationships, this method is not a real alternative.

NOTES

1.   Alexander Hamilton, James Madison, and John Jay, Federalist No. 43, in *The Federalist Papers*, ed. Benjamin Fletcher Wright (Cambridge, Mass.: Harvard University Press, 1961), 315.

2.   Donald S. Lutz, this volume, chap. 2.

3.   League of Women Voters, "Michigan Doesn't Need Constitutional Convention," *Detroit Free Press*, 24 September 1994.

4.   Thomas Gais, "The New Dilemma of State Constitutional Change: Direct Democracy, Legislative Resistance and the Decline of Deliberative Procedures," *Temple Law Review* (forthcoming).

5.   Lutz, this volume, 27.

6.   Barbara Geddes, "Democratic Institutions as Bargains Among Self–Interested Politicians" (paper presented at the annual meeting of the American Political Science Association, San Francisco, Calif., September 1990), 1–29.

7.   Janice May, "State Constitutions and Constitutional Revision, 1992–93," in *Book of the States, 1994–95* (Lexington, Ky.: Council of State Governments, 1994), 2.

8.   Additionally, reflecting the federal character of the American national system, a method exists (though it has never been used) to bypass the national government entirely and amend the U.S. Constitution at the state level.

9.   Public Affairs Research Institute of New Jersey, news release, October 1994.

10.   Caroline Tolbert, "Direct Democracy and State Governance Policies" (paper presented at the annual meeting of the American Political Science Association, New York, September 1994), 1–32.

11.   David B. Magleby, *Direct Legislation Voting on Ballot Propositions in the United States* (Baltimore, Md.: John Hopkins University Press, 1984), 192.

12.   Gerald Benjamin and Michael Malbin, *Limiting Legislative Terms* (Washington, D.C.: CQ Press, 1994), 7.

13.   Massachusetts Constitution, art. 4; Alexander G. Gray, Jr., and Thomas R. Riley, "The Initiative and Referendum in Massachusetts," *New England Law Review* 26 (Fall 1991): 95–98.

Generally, the indirect initiative in the states is used for ordinary legislation, ensuring that the legislature will get a crack at a proposed change brought forward by petition before it goes into effect. Ohio places a measure before the legislature once it receives the signatures of 3 percent of the electors and requires action within four months. If the proposal is passed unchanged, it becomes law. If it is amended or nothing is passed, and petitions of an additional 3 percent of the electorate are filed, the original proposal goes to a popular vote. If a majority is in favor, the legislative action is superseded and the original proposal becomes law.

An alternative approach used in Michigan requires an initiative petition to be signed by 8 percent of the voters at the last gubernatorial election. The legislature is given forty days to act. If it fails to act a popular vote is held on the initiative proposal. If it enacts an alternative, both the initiative proposal and the legislative are to be presented to the public, with the one gaining the higher number of votes becoming law. There is no second petition process.

In Alaska, a law offered by initiative cannot be placed on the ballot until the legislature has met. If it passes the measure or one "substantially similar," the proposal does not go to the ballot.

14.   Robert Williams, "The Role of the Constitutional Commission," in *The New York State Constitution: A Briefing Book*, ed. Gerald Benjamin (Albany, N.Y.: Temporary State Commission on Constitutional Revision, 1994), 78–79.

15.   Lutz, this volume, 25.

16.   A detailed index to measure these differences has been developed by Donald S. Lutz. See ibid., 42–43, Table 2.1.

17.   Gerald Benjamin and Melissa Cusa, "Amending the New York State Constitution through the Legislature," in *New York State Constitution*, ed. Benjamin, 55–71.

18.   Lutz, this volume, 32–34, Table 2.1.

19.   Ibid., 40, Table 2.6.

20.   May, "State Constitutions."

21.   John W. Kingdon, *Agendas, Alternatives, and Public Policies* (Boston: Little, Brown, 1984).

22.   Ibid., 181.

23.   Gerald Benjamin and Robert Nakamura, eds., *The Modern New York State Legislature Redressing the Balance* (Albany, N.Y.: The Nelson A. Rockefeller Institute of Government, 1991).

24.   The number of amendments introduced in New York concerning the Bill of Rights (Article 1) is misleading, for almost half focus on removing the constitutional prohibition on gambling, inappropriately located in this portion of the document.

25.   See, for example, Burt Neuborne, "State Constitutions and the Evolution of Positive Rights," *Rutgers Law Journal* 20 (Summer 1989): 888; Christine Ladd, "Note: A Right to Shelter to the Homeless in New York State," *New York University Law*

School Review 61 (May 1986): 272; Dann Braveman, "Children, Poverty and State Constitutions," *Emory Law School* 38 (Spring 1989): 576–614; Bert Lockwood, R. Collins Owens, and Grace A. Severyn, "Litigating State Constitutional Rights to Happiness and Safety," *William and Mary Law Quarterly* 2 (1993): 1–28; Gerald Benjamin with Melissa Cusa, "Social Policy," in *New York State Constitution*, ed. Benjamin, 231–241.

26.   See Frederick Miller, "New York State's Judicial Article: A Work in Progress," in *Effective Government Now for a New Century*, ed. Temporary New York State Commission on Constitutional Revision (Albany, N.Y.: Commission and the Rockfeller Institute of Government, 1995), 83–98.

II

CASE STUDIES: CAMPAIGNS FOR CONSTITUTIONAL CHANGE

4

Creating a State Constitutional Right to Privacy: Unlikely Alliances, Uncertain Results

Rebecca Mae Salokar

In November of 1980, the citizens of Florida voted to amend their state constitution by including an explicit, free-standing right to privacy. It was not the first time that such an amendment had been placed on the ballot. In fact, only two years earlier, the same measure had been rejected by over 70 percent of the voters. For proponents of the amendment, the 1980 election marked the culmination of a three-year effort to restrict governmental intrusion into the private lives of individuals. Opponents, on the other hand, viewed its adoption as the beginning of numerous court battles over the legitimate power of state government to obtain information and to forbid "unacceptable" lifestyles and behavior. But, the real story behind the right-to-privacy amendment goes beyond the arguments over the policy's substance. What accounted for the initial failure of the constitutional amendment in 1978, and its subsequent adoption in 1980, is best understood as a function of substantive concerns combined with procedural tactics and the contextual political environment in which the amendment process took place. In short, this is a classic tale of politics.

Although a great deal of research has been dedicated to understanding the arguments and debates of the Founding Fathers of this nation for the purpose of interpreting the U.S. Constitution, state constitutional history has generally been ignored. This oversight is due, in large part, to the fact that the constitutional issues that most directly affect citizens, their individual rights, are matters lodged in the U.S. Bill of Rights and subject to interpretation by the U.S. Supreme Court rather than by state courts. While the Supreme Court welcomed litigation over civil rights and liberties and ruled in favor of the individual, there was little demand for state courts to address such issues. To obtain a favorable holding from the highest court in the nation simply precluded the need to litigate in each of the fifty states.

However, the ideological transformation of the U.S. Supreme Court under Chief Justices Warren Burger and William Rehnquist, and the refusal of the Reagan and Bush administrations to staunchly defend individual rights during the 1980s forced advocates for the disenfranchised to look elsewhere for protection. Interest groups like the American Civil Liberties Union and the Lambda Legal Defense and Education Fund began searching through the fifty state constitutions for language that might expand individual rights. Even Justice William Brennan recognized the possibilities: "Rediscovery by state supreme courts of the broader protections afforded their own citizens by their state constitutions . . . is probably the most important development in constitutional jurisprudence of our times."[1]

Since the 1980s, almost all states in the nation have witnessed litigation efforts to expand individual-rights protections through their own state constitutions, and privacy rights have been particularly salient issues. For example, in 1992 the Kentucky courts were asked to overrule the state's sodomy statute and to find a privacy right within the Kentucky Constitution.[2] In Hawaii, a case is working its way through judicial channels, challenging the state's traditional notions of marriage.[3] As scholarly interest naturally follows this trend in state litigation, public law researchers have found state-based studies more complicated. Rather than simply examining the decisions and litigation activity of one court system, we must now consider the constitutional developments in each of the fifty states and in the federal system.

This chapter is presented as a case study of the battle to include a right to privacy within the Constitution of the State of Florida. Although each state's history with the amendment process will differ due to procedural distinctions embedded in their particular constitutions, it is important to note that substance — what the amendment will or will not do— may not be the sole determinant of success or adoption. Rather, as my research shows, a sensitivity to procedural issues, interest group motivations, alliances and lobbying, and matters that are, quite frankly, outside the debate over the particular policy concern are key elements of a state's constitutional history.

I have organized this chapter into four sections. Florida's constitutional history, a history of frequent change, serves as an introduction to the saga of the constitutional right to privacy in Florida. What is evident from this history is that Floridians have not had a particular attachment to their constitutions; there has been an apparent willingness to amend, revise, and revisit the basic document as frequently as necessary. The state's constitutional history sets the stage for the initial battle to incorporate an individual right to privacy in the Florida Constitution. These first efforts, which took place in 1978, are the focus of the second section of this chapter in which I document the substance of the policy and analyze the factors that led to the amendment's electoral defeat. In the next section, I then describe the strategy that resulted in the successful adoption of the right to privacy in 1980 and the keys to that success. How the right to privacy has been used by both litigants and the courts of Florida is the focus of the fourth section. Finally, some general observations on the politics of constitution making serves as a conclusion.

FLORIDA'S CONSTITUTIONAL HISTORY

The state of Florida has had a long history of constitution-building and a great deal of experience in amending its basic laws. Since its admission to the United States in 1845, the state has adopted six different constitutions.[4] The original document was drafted in 1838 by constitutional convention and was approved by popular vote the following year. It was not until 1845, however, when Florida was granted statehood, that the 1838 constitution became the official constitution, and it was to serve the state for only a short period of time.

In January 1861 Florida joined South Carolina and Mississippi in seceding from the Union. As a result, the 1838 Florida Constitution was abandoned in favor of allegiance to the Confederacy and a new constitution was adopted. Following the Civil War, Florida adopted yet another constitution in order to regain admission to the Union. Its initial constitution following Reconstruction (1865) was rejected and a subsequent document was finally accepted in 1868. The 1868 Constitution was later revised in 1885, marking the end of the Reconstruction Era in Florida.

The 1885 Constitution served the state of Florida for over eighty years. Eventually, however, obsolete language, an antiquated executive and administrative organization, and civil rights successes at the national level (particularly with respect to reapportionment) mandated wholesale change of Florida's basic law. Additionally, by the mid-1960s, the 1885 Constitution had been amended over 150 times resulting in a lengthy document embedded with contradictions. Thus, a Constitution Revision Commission was organized in 1965 to draft a new constitution for the legislature's review. Following a few minor changes by the legislative bodies, the new constitution was approved by the voters in 1968.

In a novel development, the 1968 Constitution institutionalized Florida's tendency to revisit and revise its constitution on a regular basis by providing for a mandatory reexamination of the document ten years after its adoption and every two decades following the initial review. Under Article 11, Section 2, a Constitution Revision Commission made up of thirty-seven members is tasked to "examine the constitution of the state, hold public hearings, and . . . file with the secretary of state its proposal, if any, of a revision of this constitution or any part of it."[5] Recommendations of the commission are then subject to a popular vote at the next general election or under certain circumstances, at a special election. A simple majority vote in support of the revisions or amendments is required for adoption.

Article 11 also allows for three of the more traditional means of constitutional revision by legislative proposal, citizen initiative, or by constitutional convention.[6] By joint resolution with three-fifths of its membership's approval, the state legislature can propose either amendments or a wholesale revision of the state's constitution subject to the approval of the state's voters. Citizen initiatives, on the other hand, are restricted to single-subject amendments and require evidence of public support through signed petitions prior to being placed on the ballot.[7] A state constitutional convention may also be called by citizen petition following the approval of such a convention by a majority of the voters.

Given its constitutional history and the mechanisms embedded in the 1968 Constitution, one might justifiably argue that the citizens of Florida truly believe that their constitution should be a working document and that they are at least willing to entertain changes to the basic law. John J. Bertalan's recent research on Florida's amendment process reveals that between 1969 and 1992, some ninety-two amendments were put before the state's voters. Of these, sixty-five were adopted (70.65 percent).[8] In short, like other southern states, the people of Florida seem to view their constitution as a working document subject to frequent revision. This differs significantly from the national citizenry's attachment to the U.S. Constitution.[9]

THE FIRST BATTLE FOR PRIVACY

The first Florida Constitution Revision Commission (CRC) mandated by the 1968 Constitution assembled in 1977 to begin the task of examining the state constitution for possible revisions.[10] Talbot (Sandy) D'Alemberte, a lawyer and former legislator from Dade County who had worked on previous constitutional amendments, was named to chair the CRC by Democratic Governor Reubin Askew. D'Alemberte was a member of the Florida Bar's Board of Governors and was widely recognized for his scholarly research on the state's constitution. Not surprisingly, the majority of the thirty-seven–member commission were lawyers. But the body also represented a diverse range of interests. Included, for example, were university professors, activists from the League of Women Voters and teacher's unions, insurance and business executives, former legislators, and an accountant.[11]

The suggestion that a right to privacy be considered for inclusion in the state constitution was made by Commissioner and Chief Justice Ben Overton (who named himself to the commission) at the first organizational meeting of the CRC on July 6, 1977. Citing the advances in technology and the resulting intrusions on personal privacy in addition to the widespread concern over privacy matters in both the state and federal legislative and judicial arenas, Overton argued that the commission should take up the issue. In the public hearing phase of the commission's work that took place in August and September 1977, the Florida chairperson for Common Cause, Gerald P. Cope, Jr., also testified on behalf of the development of a free-standing right to privacy.[12]

Following a series of ten public hearings in which it heard from over 600 witnesses, the CRC set about its work by establishing nine substantive committees in early October. Chair D'Alemberte, who favored including privacy in the Florida Constitution, established a separate committee to deal specifically with privacy and related issues. The Ethics, Privacy, and Elections Committee was asked to review Article 6 (suffrage and elections), Article 3, section 18 (conflict of interest), Article 2, section 8 (ethics in government) and Article 1, section 4 (freedom of speech and press) and section 12 (searches and seizures). It was in this committee that the first and fullest substantive discussion of a right to privacy took place.

Agreement within the committee was quickly obtained on the principle of a constitutional right to privacy, but the nature of that right was the subject of much discussion, debate, and compromise.[13] The key issues revolved around whether to protect the individual from private as well as public intrusions, the standard of review that a privacy claim should receive from the courts and whether that standard ought to be made explicit in the language of the amendment, and finally, the specific language that should be used in defining "privacy." Additional concerns addressed the impact that such a right to privacy would have on existing statutes and constitutional measures like criminal searches, Florida's Government in the Sunshine mandate, required financial disclosure laws, and the ability of the state to govern in the arena of social behavior.

Gerald Cope's testimony and writings were instrumental to the discussions that took place in October and November. As a courtesy to the committee, Cope provided examples of free-standing privacy amendments that had been adopted in several states. Although several state constitutions address the notion of privacy with respect to search and seizure provisions, in 1972, three states (Alaska, California, and Montana) had adopted specific language that set privacy rights apart from unwarranted searches. Cope personally preferred the language of the Montana Constitution in that a clear standard of review, "a compelling state interest," was made explicit. But the committee members argued that setting such a standard would result in a weakened right of privacy rather than a vigorous one.[14]

The proposal adopted by the committee in late November and sent to the full commission reflected a number of compromises. It included both a "self-executing right" to privacy for individuals with respect to governmental intrusions and directive that the legislature take action to protect individuals from interference in their personal lives by private actors.[15] Despite the diligent work of the committee and its efforts to compromise, further revisions were made by the full CRC and its Committee on Style and Drafting. What resulted was the deletion of the latter protection against private intrusions and the inclusion of a qualification to eliminate possible conflicts with financial disclosure laws, searches and seizures, and other constitutional matters affecting privacy. The provision eventually adopted by the full commission provided for what appeared to be a very straightforward, vigorous right to privacy:

Section 23. Right of Privacy. — Every natural person has the right to be let alone and free from governmental intrusion into his private life except as otherwise provided herein.

In addition to its work on privacy, the CRC had over 800 constitutional issues and reforms that were raised during the public hearing stage of its work. Culled from this laundry list, over 200 matters were placed on the CRC's agenda and subsequently received the attention of the commission through its committees. After months of work, the end result was a litany of major and minor proposed revisions to 103 sections of the Florida Constitution that would be placed before the voters in the November 1978 general election.

Unlike the procedures that resulted in the adoption of the 1968 Constitution, the CRC was under no obligation to formally submit their proposed revisions to the legislature for approval or amendment. Furthermore, although key members of the state legislature served on the CRC, their participation did not ensure the vocal and visible support of the legislative body as a whole. In fact, two legislative efforts, one in 1977 and one in 1978, to force the CRC to subject its proposals to legislative review failed.[16] The message that was sent from the state house should have been clear: Legislators would not be guaranteed advocates of the commission's proposals.

The final major decision by the CRC in late April 1978 involved the matter of how to present the wide-ranging revisions to the citizens of the state. The 1968 Constitution had been packaged as three separate ballot measures and the division proved to be a successful strategy. Discussions among the commissioners focused largely on how to best guarantee that the bulk of their proposals, some of which simply dealt with eliminating archaic language, would be approved by the voters. The strategy that emerged involved bundling the proposed changes to seventy-three sections of the constitution into an "omnibus proposal" that would be voted up or down as a whole. The more controversial revisions were crafted into an additional seven ballot measures. Finally, the order in which the revisions would appear on the ballot was considered to be important. Thinking that the voters may reject one or several of the more controversial measures, the CRC decided that the omnibus proposal should be listed first to prevent it from being tainted by possible "no" votes on other measures.

The right to privacy found its way into the omnibus proposal, which was offered to the voters as "Revision 1 Basic Document." Rather than attempt to identify all the major changes included in the revision, the ballot language was crafted to be all-encompassing.

Proposing a revision of the Florida Constitution, generally described as the Basic Document, embracing the subject matter of Articles I (Declaration of Rights), II (General Provisions), III (Legislature), IV (Executive), V (Judiciary), VI (Suffrage and Elections), VIII (Local Government), X

(Miscellaneous), XI (Amendments) and XII (Schedule), except for other revisions separately submitted for a vote on this ballot.[17]

Included in the omnibus package were provisions that touched on criminal matters,[18] open government,[19] judicial hearings[20] and grand jury procedures,[21] term limits for cabinet members, the creation of a state department of health, and the elimination of liability limits on state and local government. But, the ballot measure never mentioned the word "privacy" or the specific elements of these key changes.

What the CRC considered to be the more controversial reforms were to be presented to the voters as seven other separate ballot issues that included a "little ERA," the establishment of single-member districts, a nonlegislative reapportionment commission, the replacement of the elected cabinet by gubernatorial appointments and the removal of the Department of Education from the cabinet, the establishment of an appointed Public Service Commission, tax reforms, and modifications to the judicial selection process.

With the submission of the ballot measures to the secretary of state on May 9, 1978, the work of the CRC was formally completed. There was no provision in the 1968 Constitution for funding the publication of the CRC's work, publicizing the proposed measures, or educating the public on the meaning of the proposals beyond the constitutional requirement that a notice of election and the language of the proposals be published in "one newspaper of general circulation in each county in which a newspaper is published" in the tenth and sixth weeks preceding the election.[22] When the CRC tried to obtain legislative funding to produce its report to the citizens of Florida, the bill was vetoed by the governor as too costly ($750,000.00).[23] Ultimately, a 22-page pamphlet was funded at a cost of $7,309.00, and approximately 125,000 copies were distributed to the public with a cover letter from Chairperson D'Alemberte encouraging duplication and dissemination of the document.

Turnout for the November general election was expected to be high across the state. In addition to the CRC's proposals, Florida was witnessing a heated race for the governorship between Bob Graham and Jack Eckerd as well as the biannual congressional elections and legislative races. What the CRC could not anticipate or control, however, was the development of yet another ballot measure affecting the state's constitution. Using the initiative process, casino gambling advocates had managed to garner enough signatures to place a proposed constitutional amendment on the November ballot that would legalize gambling in the

South Florida area. As a result, Reubin Askew, the lame duck governor, focused his attention on defeating casino gambling and did little to support or draw attention to the CRC's work. In retrospect, the casino gambling measure both detracted from what could have been a healthy, wide-ranging public debate over the CRC proposals and, more important, consumed the energy and resources of the political leadership that should have supported the CRC's work. With the all-out campaign against casino gambling, the message that was being delivered to the voters was simply, "Vote no."

The nature of the omnibus proposal guaranteed that the alliances that formed to lobby for or against the revision would be unique. What public debate there was made for interesting political bedfellows. Conservatives concerned with limiting government's intrusion into private business affairs, medical practitioners who wanted to further preserve their privileged communications with patients, and gay organizations who saw the privacy provision as legitimizing personal lifestyle decisions unofficially joined ranks with defense attorneys supporting the reforms to transactional immunity, pretrial release and grand jury procedures, and "good government" advocates who lobbied for changes in the judicial selection procedures, open government and terms limits for the cabinet.

The support of gay rights organizations was particularly troubling to the executive director of the CRC, Steven Uhlfelder, who was also an aide to Governor Askew. In an interview with the *Miami Herald*, Uhlfelder indicated that he had discussed the privacy amendment with a member of Gay Rights Amendments Never Die and had strongly suggested that the amendment would not protect gay and lesbian lifestyles. "For them to make an issue of this and create a furor — it's ridiculous," Uhlfelder told the press. Even the two key advocates of the privacy provision, Chief Justice Overton and Chair D'Alemberte, reportedly agreed that amendment would not, "because of its intent and wording," protect homosexual behavior.[24]

Opponents to the privacy provision included the attorney general and numerous state prosecutors who feared that Revision 1 would restrict the state's power to conduct searches, and moral conservatives who warned of legalized homosexuality and drug use. Perhaps most surprising, the state's Democratic party, whose members dominated the CRC and the elective branches of government, announced its opposition to five of the ballot measures, including the omnibus proposal. Major newspapers in the state like the *Miami Herald* failed to endorse Revision 1, the omnibus proposal, arguing that "the bad in Revision 1 outweighs the good." Even the Florida Bar Association's Constitution Committee was split 5-5 on the omnibus proposal and would not make a recommendation to its membership.

To exacerbate issues even further, Anita Bryant funded a late campaign against Revision 2, the proposal to include gender nondiscrimination in Florida's basic rights clause. Bryant, who had waged a successful referendum campaign against a gay rights ordinance in Dade County in the mid-1970s, once again raised the specter of homophobia by taking out advertisements in the mass media markets suggesting that Revision 2 — not the privacy provision — would legalize homosexual behavior and marriages.[25] Bryant's attacks on Revision 2 undoubtedly had some spillover effect on the one amendment that was being visibly supported by gay rights organizations.

The results of the November 7 election proved to be a major disappointment for the members of the CRC. Not one of their eight revision measures managed to gain the support of the voters. The omnibus proposal, which strategists had thought would be the least controversial, failed by a wide margin (71 percent to 29 percent).[26] The casino gambling initiative was also rejected by 72 percent of the voters. Although 2.4 million voters had cast a ballot in the gubernatorial race, the number of votes registered on each of the eight constitutional revision measures was significantly lower. Only 2,071,928 votes were registered on the omnibus proposal. Even the little ERA, Revision 2, which had been highly publicized and was, by far, the most understandable measure of the eight, only attracted 2.2 million voters (58 percent to 42 percent).

The after-election analyses suggested that several factors led to the demise of the constitution revisions, as a whole. First, the decision to separate the revisions into eight ballot measures caused confusion for the voters and diluted whatever leadership support may have been garnered. Second, the campaign against casino gambling likely spilled over into voters' decisions on the CRC's proposals. In short, voters went into the voting booth with a propensity to vote against any constitutional changes. Since the Florida Constitution had been fully revised only ten years earlier, one reporter further suggested that the public may not have seen any pressing need to incorporate such wholesale changes as those promoted by the CRC.[27] Even Chesterfield Smith, the chairperson of the 1968 CRC, suggested, "There was no call for reform, no anger at the rascals who are doing things to us . . . the people in general were satisfied with our form of government in Florida."[28]

Despite nearly a year and a half of work and extraordinary efforts to tap the public's interest in its constitution, Florida's first experiment with an innovative revision commission appeared to be fruitless. However,

Governor-elect Bob Graham suggested otherwise at a press conference following the election. Rather than abandoning the commission's work, he indicated that several of the proposals would likely be introduced to the legislature for adoption consideration in future legislative sessions. His prediction held true; less than two years later, Florida once again considered a constitutional right to privacy.

ROUND TWO AND A REVIVAL OF PRIVACY

On January 17, 1980, the Florida Supreme Court handed down a decision that provided the spark for a second effort to establish a constitutionally based right to privacy within the Florida Constitution. In *Shevin v. Harless, Schaffer, Reid and Associates, Inc.*,[29] the court rejected a lower court's finding that the due process clause of the Florida Constitution (Article 1, section 9) provided a constitutional right to disclosural privacy. The case pitted Florida's Public Records Law[30] against an individual's interests to keep certain personal information private. Seeking to obtain the records of a private consulting firm's search for a managing director of a public utility, a newspaper reporter invoked the Public Records Law, requiring the state attorney general to file for a writ of mandamus against Harless, Schaffer, Reid and Associates. The consulting firm and a number of the applicants argued that both the U.S. and Florida Constitutions protected individuals from government intrusion through a right to disclosural privacy. The Florida Supreme Court disagreed. With respect to the state constitutional arguments, it concluded that "there is no support in the language of any provision of the Florida Constitution or in the judicial decisions of this state to sustain the district court's finding of a state constitutional right of disclosural privacy."[31]

The timing of the court's decision was important; the Florida legislature was just about to open its regular session and legislators were busy seeking out proposals for new legislation. In the previous year, the legislature had approved two constitutional amendments that were to appear on the March 1980 ballot, and several of the issues proposed by the 1978 CRC were still ripe for legislative action.

On January 18, 1980, Representatives Jon Mills, Curt Kiser, Lee Moffitt, and Bill Sadowski prefiled a joint resolution that would create Article 1, section 23 of the Florida Constitution, the right to privacy.[32]

Every natural person has the right to be let alone and free from unwarranted governmental intrusion into his private life.[33]

It was a bipartisan venture with Kiser, the Republican minority leader, joining forces with the three Democrats. Their initial proposal, HJR 387, was nearly identical to the language proposed by the CRC with two significant exceptions. First, the word "unwarranted" was included to clarify the types of governmental intrusions that would be protected, and second, the authors had abandoned any reference to potential conflicts with other aspects of the Florida Constitution, an issue that the CRC had been so careful to address.

HJR 387 was referred to the Committee on Governmental Operations and its subcommittee on executive reorganization held hearings in early March. Not surprising, the committee drew on the expertise of Patricia Dore, a legal scholar who had served on the staff of the CRC and who remained a strong advocate of a state right to privacy even after its 1978 defeat. The written records of the legislative committee's work reveal that issues similar to the substantive debates of the Ethics, Privacy, and Election Committee of the CRC were addressed, producing several drafts of a committee substitute for HJR 387. The original committee substitute for HJR 387 reinstated the provisional language ("except as otherwise provided herein") to accommodate potential conflicts with the ethics provisions of the constitution, which mandated financial disclosure by public officials (Article 2, section 8). The second draft, submitted following hearings at which Dore testified, eliminated the word "unwarranted" in referring to the type of governmental intrusion, and resulted in an amendment that was identical to the CRC's ballot measure.

Section 23. Right of privacy. — Every natural person has the right to be let alone and free from governmental intrusion into his private life except as otherwise provided herein.

In late March, Senator Jack D. Gordon requested a copy of the house committee's work and on April 24 joined with Senator Dempsey Barron in introducing SJR 935, a privacy amendment proposal containing the house's language. The bill was referred to the Rules and Calendar Committee, as required by senate procedures, for consideration. But, the house's work was still unfinished.

The final and most dramatic change to the language of the amendment seemingly resulted from the careful consideration of the *Shevin* decision. At issue in *Shevin* was a conflict between an alleged privacy right and a Florida statute (the Public Records Law), not a constitutional provision. Adopting the language of the CRC's privacy right would have meant that any future conflict between privacy and the Public Records Law would result in the statute's unconstitutionality. Not only would the Public Records Law be at risk, Florida's Government in the Sunshine Law, a statute that ensured public access to a wide range of governmental meetings, might also fall victim to the right of privacy.[34] This had not been a problem for the CRC in 1978, since the Omnibus Proposal called for the elevation of both of these laws to constitutional status (as Article 1, sections 24 and 25). Since that proposal had been rejected by the voters, however, access to public meetings and public records remained embedded in statutory law.

To prevent the possible demise of these two statutes, the house committee's final revision of the joint resolution added a second sentence to ensure that no court would reject either the mandate of open meetings or access to public records in favor of an individual's right to privacy: "This section shall not be construed to limit the public's right of access to public records and meetings as provided by law." This explicit language would also curtail some of the opposition that the privacy amendment had received during the 1978 election.

The house committee reported out its version of the bill on April 23, and the committee substitute to HJR 387 was passed by the Florida House of Representatives on May 6 by a vote of 98 to 4. The bipartisan support for the bill was paralleled by the bipartisan opposition; two Democrats and two Republicans voted "nay."[35] The engrossed bill was immediately certified to the senate, where it was referred to the Committee on Rules and Calendar. In the meantime, the senate committee amended its version to reflect the final house bill, and SJR 935 was favorably reported to the senate on May 6. When SJR 935 came to the senate floor on May 14, Senator Gordon offered a motion to withdraw CS/HJR 387 from the Rules Committee and substituted it for the senate's measure.

The debate on the senate floor is indicative of what little opposition there was to the bill. During the committee hearings, only one senator, Democrat Edgar M. Dunn, had expressed serious opposition to the measure, repeatedly warning that a right to privacy would open the door to consensual sex by homosexuals and would broaden women's rights to abortions. On the floor of the senate, Dunn offered yet another amendment to change the language from "free from governmental intrusion" to "free from any unreasonable governmental intrusion." His amendment failed and CS/HJR 387 was passed by the senate, 34 to 2. In addition to Dunn's negative vote, Senator Pat Frank, a fellow Democrat, also voted against the measure.

Several aspects of these legislative efforts to amend the Florida Constitution are worthy of some discussion. First, the sponsors of the bill were some of the most powerful members of the state legislature in 1980. Both Mills and Moffitt were key members of the Democratic party in the state and both were being groomed to become the speaker of the house. Kiser, the Republican sponsor and minority leader, was known as one of the most "effective and responsible legislators," even by members on the other side of the aisle.[36] Dempsey Barron, who served a stint as president of the senate and cosponsored the senate's legislation, is best known in Florida history as one of the state's most powerful conservative Democrats. He had also served on the 1978 CRC. More important, Barron was, for years, the leader of the dominant governing coalition in the state senate. Jack Gordon, on the other hand, was one of the most liberal Democrats in the senate and was one of the few of his ilk who could work well with Barron. The coalition that brought the privacy amendment to the floor of the state legislature could not have been stronger.

This broad-based coalition translated into widespread bipartisan support. Republicans and Florida's conservative Democrats, concerned especially with the implications of the *Shevin* decision, saw the privacy amendment as a tool to protect the business and financial records of individuals and as a way to limit government's ever-growing interference into personal matters. Liberal Democrats, on the other hand, were interested in individual freedom on a broad scale. Clearly, the U.S. Supreme Court's decisions in *Roe v. Wade*[37] (extending the privacy right to abortion decisions) and the *Griswold* constellation of cases[38] served as a vision of what a Florida right to privacy could protect in the future.

Finally, the privacy amendment battle two years earlier provided some critical lessons that eased the way, both legislatively and electorally, for the 1980 effort to amend the constitution. Legislative sponsors did not have to work through what might have been lengthy debates to draft the language of their amendment; the CRC's privacy amendment provided a ready model. Potential issues in 1980 had been addressed and virtually resolved during the CRC's extensive debates. Furthermore, legislative sponsors called on the expertise of those who had worked through these earlier debates, people like Professor Dore and Senator Barron, who provided ready rebuttals to any serious opposition. The supporters could also anticipate the arguments that would be raised by the electorate and had the overwhelming legislative support to point to in convincing voters of the policy's merit. But, most important, the privacy amendment now had a core of visible and "legitimate" advocates, a group of political leaders who were ready and willing to defend the ballot measure when it went before the citizenry in November.

The right to privacy amendment was not the only proposed change to the Florida Constitution to be considered by the voters in November. Ironically, a proposal to eliminate the CRC received first billing among five constitutional amendments on the 1980 ballot. The right to privacy appeared as Amendment 2 and was followed with another of the CRC's previous proposals. Amendment 3 was essentially a legislative house-keeping measure that had also been buried in the 1978 omnibus proposal; it would eliminate the first reading of proposed bills in the state legisla-ture in lieu of the publication of a bill's language in the legislative journals. Amendments 4 and 5 were finance measures that allowed municipalities to use state bonds (instead of higher priced private bonds) for water facilities and liberalized municipalities' use of gas tax funds for road repairs, respectively.

The joint resolution to include a right to privacy was filed with the secretary of state nearly six months before the November election. This gave advocates and opponents plenty of time to debate and discuss the issue. But, unlike the CRC's 1978 proposals, which had attracted a high degree of public attention, the debate over the 1980 privacy amendment was much more subdued. Governor Bob Graham and the prosecuting attorneys of the state continued to oppose the measure, arguing that it would hamstring criminal investigations, but little other opposition surfaced. In fact, several of the state's chambers of commerce joined in supporting the amendment. And while gay rights activists continued to support a right to privacy, their visibility was generally limited to their own publications and community. Significantly absent from the 1980 debates were Anita Bryant and her fundamentalist followers. Senator Ed Dunn was, perhaps, the only visible opponent that continued to lobby against the measure on moral grounds.

Once again, the state's largest newspaper, the *Miami Herald*, came out against the privacy amendment. In its editorial of October 29, 1980, the *Herald* used what might be considered deceptive tactics to persuade its readers to vote against the bill. Publishing only a portion of the amendment's language ("every natural person has the right to be let alone and free from governmental intrusion into his private life") and omitting the qualifying language that the legislature had so carefully included, the editorial board argued that the right would be unlimited, would provoke a flood of litigation, and would curtail the efforts of law enforcement personnel.[39] In 1978, the newspaper's criticism remained unanswered; this was not the case in 1980. Senator Jack Gordon, one of the bill's sponsors and a legislator from Miami Beach, quickly replied. In his editorial response, published the day before the election, Gordon pointed out the *Herald*'s glaring omission of the qualifying language and noted the experience of states that had a similar free-standing right to privacy. "Our study of their experience since 1972 is that neither the police nor other public agencies have been inhibited from carrying out their essential functions."[40] Gordon also highlighted the fact that the bill had received widespread bipartisan support in the legislature and argued that the amendment gave citizens an opportunity to get government "off our backs."[41]

On November 4, 1980, Floridians finally adopted a free-standing constitutional right to privacy. Amendment 2 was passed handily with 60 percent of the voters supporting its adoption. Only the amendment to eliminate the CRC failed (56 percent opposed). The proposal to eliminate first readings in the legislature enjoyed the strongest support (67 percent) among Florida voters while Amendment 5, allowing municipalities to use gas tax revenues for road repairs, passed by the slimmest margin (55 percent).[42]

Like the 1978 elections, significantly fewer voters chose to register their support or opposition on the constitutional amendments than on other measures. The key race on the ballot in 1980, the presidential contest between incumbent Jimmy Carter and Ronald Reagan, attracted over three and one-half million Florida voters to the polls.[43] Yet, only two and one-half million voters (70 percent) cast a ballot on Amendment 2 and even fewer voted on the other four constitutional amendments.[44] This is not surprising; in 1980, many voters probably went to the polls only for the presidential race and were less educated about the other ballot provisions. Research on turnout rates for judicial retention elections suggests similar patterns. Hall and Aspin's study of retention elections for major state trial judges found that "at least one-third of the voters passed up the opportunity to vote in retention elections."[45] This "roll-off" phenomenon probably holds true for constitutional ballot provisions that traditionally attract less media attention, are often viewed as less important to the voter, or are simply confusing to the inattentive citizen.

But, unlike retention elections, which provide "few cues to help voters in the voting booth,"[46] the 1980 ballot language on the right to privacy may have aided in its passage. When voters went to the polls on November 4, 1980, they did not see the language of the actual privacy amendment with all of its caveats. Rather, the ballot simply stated, "Proposing the creation of Section 23 of Article 1 of the State

Constitution establishing a constitutional right of privacy." For those who had not followed the debates over the right to privacy, the ballot language probably proved to be persuasive, in and of itself. Unfamiliar with the warnings of open homosexuality, increased abortions, legalized use of marijuana and limits on police investigations, the voter who considered Amendment 2 for the first time in the voting booth would be hard pressed to vote against it. Surely, the uninformed voter could have believed, based simply on the ballot language, that additional rights and protection for the individual citizen would prove to be a good thing. On the other hand, the more educated voters had probably studied the ballot in its entirety and had shaped their decisions prior to November 4. Unfortunately, survey research prior to the election and exit polling, which might have allowed confirmation of such a hypothesis, is not available on the constitutional ballot measures.

IMPACTS AND IMPLICATIONS

Shortly after the passage of the Florida right to privacy amendment, jubilant gay rights activists declared that they would initiate a campaign for a national constitutional privacy provision and would begin to file court cases in Florida to test the limits of the state's new right for gay issues. The first promise turned out to be a hollow one; such a campaign has yet to materialize. The second promise, however, came to fruition late in the 1980s. The delay in testing the limits of Florida's right of privacy amendment can probably be attributed to two facts. First, the best organized gay community in the state was still feeling the repercussions of a stinging defeat of a Dade County gay rights ordinance at the hands of Anita Bryant. That battle had cost the community dearly in terms of political capital and resulted in some members returning to their "closets." More important, however, in the early 1980s, the politics of AIDS demanded the gay community's attention, political energy, and dedication. The search for test cases on gay rights necessarily became a back-burner issue in Florida following the 1980 election.

It is no surprise, however, that the Florida courts were asked to interpret the scope of the privacy amendment on a range of other issues, issues that had merited the careful attention of the amendment's sponsors during both the 1978 and 1980 campaigns. In a series of cases decided between 1981 and 1985, Florida courts entertained challenges that pitted the statutory right of access to public records against an individual's right to disclosural privacy.[47] Repeatedly, the courts interpreted the privacy amendment exactly as its drafters had intended; the right to privacy did not curtail the public's right to know. It was not until 1985 that the Florida Supreme Court had to consider the right of privacy on its own merits.

In its first decision to explicate a standard of judicial review and consider a textual interpretation of the constitutional provision, the Florida Supreme Court adopted the "compelling state interest standard." Under this standard of review, the state is tasked with the burden of proving that an intrusion on an individual's privacy was both justified and accomplished by the least intrusive methods.[48] *Winfield v. Div. of Pari-Mutuel Wagering* was the first case to reach the supreme court in which the state had sought to obtain records that were traditionally considered private, an individual's financial and banking records. The court's decision in *Winfield* recognized that the drafters of the Florida right to privacy intended "to make the privacy right as strong as possible. . . . It can only be concluded that the right is much broader in scope than that of the Federal Constitution."[49] At the same time, however, the court accepted the state's arguments that its investigation into the pari-mutuel industry served a compelling purpose and had been accomplished by the least intrusive means. In a subsequent case, *Rasmussen v. South Florida Blood Service*, the court swung the pendulum back to the individual; civil discovery rules could not be used to force disclosure of the identities of blood donors who might have transmitted the HIV virus.[50]

During the mid-1980s, cases began reaching the courts' dockets that addressed a different type of privacy, namely, the freedom of an individual to make personal decisions. Although the Florida Supreme Court had entertained such a case even before the privacy amendment had been adopted,[51] Article 1, section 23, seems to have broadened the court's acknowledgement of decisional autonomy. Several right-to-die and right-to-refuse-treatment cases have been resolved in favor of the individual, regardless of their competence at the time of the decision.[52] But, perhaps, the most well-known privacy decision in Florida constitutional history was handed down in late 1989. It was a decision that Senator Ed Dunn had anticipated.

As the U.S. Supreme Court began modifying its interpretation of the right to privacy with respect to abortion during the latter half of the 1980s, several state legislatures moved to heighten restrictions on abortion availability in their own states. Florida's legislature joined that trend and in the summer of 1988, passed a parental consent statute. In a challenge to the law, the Florida Supreme Court ruled in *In re T.W.* that minors, as natural persons, enjoyed the protection of the constitutional right of privacy in their decision to obtain an abortion, and further, the state had no justifiable compelling interest in curtailing that right. The parental consent statute was declared unconstitutional.

This 1989 decision received widespread media coverage and, perhaps single-handedly, revived the interests of gay rights groups. In the years since that ruling, gay activists have sought to overturn the state's ban against homosexual adoptions, administrative agency decisions to prohibit lesbians and gay men from qualifying as foster parents, and have challenged discriminatory actions in the workplace and housing availability. Although none of these cases has reached the docket of the state's highest court, several trial court decisions have resulted in favorable outcomes for gay advocates and Florida's constitutional right to privacy has been instrumental in those rulings.[53]

The judicial interpretation of Florida's right to privacy is still at an early stage. Although there has been a moderate degree of litigation since its adoption, the fullest contours of this individual freedom remain to be defined. Despite the ominous warnings of opponents to the right to privacy, no torrent of cases has flooded the courtrooms of the state. In the few decisions that have been handed down on the issue, the courts have balanced the needs of government against the fundamental rights of the individual; the right has not been interpreted, as opponents sug-gested, as one that "outlaws all governmental intrusion into the private lives of the people, including those that might otherwise be justified by compellingly legitimate public purposes."[54] As the drafters intended, Florida courts have acknowledged the robustness of the right to privacy as a fundamental freedom. In the *Winfield* decision, for example, the supreme court acknowledged that the words "unwarranted" and "unreasonable" were rejected both by the drafters and by the voters of the state, and the justices interpreted this to mean that privacy deserved the most vigorous protection.[55] Yet, the court's decisions continue to protect the state's overriding affinity for the public's "right to know" by upholding the citizens' access to public records and open governmental meetings even in the shadow of the constitutional right to privacy. What seems clear from the decisions handed down to date is that the language or text of the Florida constitutional right to privacy has served as an accurate reflection of the intentions of its drafters.

PROCESS, CONTEXT, AND JUDICIAL INTERPRETATION

The saga of Florida's right to privacy, as a preliminary exploration of state constitutional politics, sheds some light on our thinking more generally about public law in the states and the politics of change. How is change accomplished procedurally? What are the strategies that contribute to the success or failure of a constitutional revision or amendment? Finally, is the substantive nature of constitutional change really important and, if so, to whom?

The first message from the Florida experience is most vivid. Process matters. The decisions made by the CRC to incorporate the right to privacy into the omnibus proposal sealed its demise in 1978 for several reasons. First, opposition to the other measures included in Revision 1 naturally spilled over to the privacy clause. While ensuring an odd coalition of supporters, the tactic also guaranteed an equally diverse core of opponents. All this changed in 1980, when a bipartisan, broad-based coalition supported a single policy change untainted by peripheral issues.

Second, that the ballot language of the 1978 omnibus proposal failed to include a specific reference to the right of privacy meant that only informed voters could make a substantive decision on the measure in the voting booth. Those citizens who had not studied (or understood) the CRC's pamphlet or who had been excluded from the public discourse over the revisions were probably unaware of the privacy right included in Revision 1. In 1980, the ballot language provided a cue to the uninformed voter, a cue that most likely proved persuasive.

The fact that the CRC was not constitutionally bound to submit its proposed revisions to the state legislature is yet a third factor that illuminates the importance of process. The 1968 Constitution, which devised the CRC method of revision, allowed the commission to skirt legislative approval even in the face of expressed concerns, and resulted in the exclusion (and perhaps alienation) of potential political support. The 1980 privacy amendment, however, was solely the product of legislative action, thereby guaranteeing that visible political support would be forthcoming at the general election.

A second lesson from the case study concerns a sensitivity to the context in which constitutional change takes place, particularly those events or activities that are beyond the control of the drafters of constitutional reform. When the CRC began its work in 1977, it could not have anticipated the fact that a casino gambling measure would also appear on the November 1978 ballot. Although the degree to which this issue tainted voters' opinions on the CRC's proposals is unknown, the fact that the citizens received a very loud message to reject one ballot proposal likely spilled over to the CRC's eight constitutional ballot measures. Additionally, the appearance of Anita Bryant in opposition to the "little ERA" probably reminded voters of her earlier campaign against gay rights in Dade County, a campaign that received widespread attention. Bryant's appearance, combined with the fact that gay rights activists took a very public stance in favor of the right to privacy in 1978, further impaired the passage of Revision 1.

The 1980 ballot did not provoke such visible opposition. In fact, the general message received by voters was to vote "yes" on most of the constitutional ballot measures. Municipal leaders worked diligently in support of the two amendments that would benefit local governments' financial operations. Legislative leaders who had supported the right to privacy were also lobbying for Amendment 3, a provision to expedite the legislative process. Only the first constitutional ballot measure, the proposal to eliminate the CRC, was vigorously opposed by the media, by those who had drafted the 1968 Constitution and others who had served on the first commission in 1978 and by "good government" advocates who wanted to preserve Florida's innovative tool for revisiting its basic law.

Given the importance of process and context, one must seriously question the degree to which the amendment's substance, a right to privacy, really played a role in its defeat in 1978 and its subsequent passage in 1980. The language of the amendment proposed in 1978 was identical to that presented to the voters in 1980. Did the voters change their minds about privacy rights in the short span of two years or was their initial rejection of Revision 1 predicated on other tangential factors? I suggest that the latter explanation is more fitting. Voters rejected the 1978 omnibus proposal, a series of constitutional changes that happened to include a right to privacy. Even if the right to privacy had been extracted and presented to the voters as a separate ballot measure in 1978, the visibility of gay rights groups, the vocalizations of Bryant, and the presence of the casino gambling measure would have probably led to a similar result.

This research also presents a difficulty for those who would rely on original intent doctrine as a means for judicial interpretation of state constitutional law. Just whose "intent" does one seek in the context of state constitutional reform? Voters are clearly participants in the reform process. As the history of Florida's privacy right suggests, however, electoral outcomes might not reflect the citizens' support or rejection of a constitutional measure. Rather, electoral outcomes might simply be the result of a complex web of contextual variables that may or may not be related to the substance of the constitutional amendment. One would be hard-pressed to argue, for example, that the people of Florida completely reversed their stance on an individual right to privacy between 1978 and 1980.

We can also look to the drafters of the constitutional language for guidance in interpretative exercises. As the Florida case suggests, however, simply reviewing the legislative history of 1980 may not tell the whole story. Clearly, the major discussions over a right to privacy took place during the CRC's work two years earlier. That was the arena in which the language of the amendment was debated, crafted, and revised. In reality, the legislature entered the discussions at midstream, well after the key issues had been debated and the language matters resolved. Thus, the legislative history in this case is not nearly as instructive as the reports of the CRC.

In sum, what my analysis suggests is that studies of constitutional change, particularly in state political systems, must be sensitive to the complexities of the process and the vagaries of the broader political environment; it is not enough to simply evaluate the merits and demerits of the policy under consideration. This is not to say that substance should be ignored. Rather, its consideration must be couched in a contextual analysis of factors that may not be germane to policy under study.

Models for such an approach are numerous. Public policy researchers have traditionally explored the nontextual bases for legislative and administrative decisions. Increasingly, public law scholars consider contextual factors, variables like interest group activity and judicial selection processes, in explaining judicial decisionmaking. As the focus shifts to state constitutional law, researchers must be willing to emulate and adapt those tools that have been proven successful to other areas of inquiry and bring these techniques to bear on this relatively undeveloped inquiry into state constitutional politics. This case study is but one small effort to move in that direction.

NOTES

1. William J. Brennan, Jr., "Special Section," *National Law Journal*, 29 September 1986, S-1, citing a speech given on August 8, 1986. See also Brennan, "State Constitutions and the Protection of Individual Rights," *Harvard Law Review* 90 (January 1977): 489–504.

2. *Kentucky v. Wasson*, 842 S.W.2d 487 (Ky. 1992). Although the constitution of Kentucky does not include an explicit right to privacy, the state supreme court found the sodomy statute to be unconstitutional under state law using equal protection analysis and finding an implicit right to privacy.

3. *Baehr et al. v. Lewin*, 852 P.2d 44 (Haw. 1993).

4.   For an extensive account of Florida's constitutional history, see Michael V. Gannon, "A History of Florida to 1900," in *Florida's Politics and Government*, 2d ed., ed. Manning Dauer (Gainesville: University of Florida Press, 1984), 22–30; and Manning Dauer, "Florida's Constitution," in *Florida's Politics and Government*, ed. Dauer, 93–96. See also Talbot D'Alemberte, *The Florida State Constitution: A Reference Guide* (Westport, Conn.: Greenwood Press, 1991), 32–34, an analysis of the current constitution and the right to privacy.

5.   Florida Constitution, art. 11, sec. 2c. Under sec. 2a, the membership of the Constitutional Revision Commission includes the attorney general and appointments made by the governor (fifteen members), the speaker of the house (nine), the president of the senate (nine), and chief justice in consultation with the other justices (three). The governor designates one of the members to be the chairperson.

6.   An additional means of constitutional revision was adopted by Florida voters in 1988. The Taxation and Reform Commission operates very much like the Constitutional Revision Commission. It meets every ten years to review fiscal matters and propose constitutional reforms. Two of its three proposals were approved by the voters in 1992, following its first meeting.

7.   Petitions must be "signed by a number of electors in each of one half of the congressional districts of the state, and of the state as a whole, equal to eight percent of the votes cast in each of such districts respectively and in the state as a whole in the last preceding election in which presidential electors were chosen" (Florida Constitution, art. 11, sec. 3).

8.   John J. Bertalan, "Revising the Florida Constitution" (paper presented at the annual meeting of the Florida Political Science Association, Winter Park, Fla., April 1993).

9.   For a discussion of the distinctions between state and national constitutions, see G. Alan Tarr, "Constitutional Theory and State Constitutional Interpretation," *Rutgers Law Journal* 22 (Summer 1991): 841–861; and G. Alan Tarr, "Understanding State Constitutions," *Temple Law Review* 65 (1992): 1169–1195.

10.   There was some initial confusion over the exact timing as to when the first Constitution Revision Commission should be assembled. The matter was settled at the request of the governor by the Florida Supreme Court (*In re Advisory Opinion of the Governor Request of November 16, 1976 [Constitution Revision Commission]*, 343 So. 2d 17 [Fla. 1977]).

11.   Steven J. Uhlfelder, "The Machinery of Revision," *Florida State University Law Review* 6 (Summer 1978): 575–588.

12.   Cope also published a law review article urging the CRC to consider a free-standing privacy provision (Note, "Toward a Right of Privacy as a Matter of State Constitutional Law," *Florida State University Law Review* 5 [1977]: 631–745), and later provided a rigorous analysis of the language adopted by the CRC and the need for the provision (Gerald P. Cope, Jr., "To Be Let Alone: Florida's Proposed Right of Privacy," *Florida State University Law Review* 6 [Summer 1978]: 671–773).

13.   For an excellent history of the committee's work, see Cope, "To Be Let Alone," 723–728; and Patricia A. Dore, "Of Rights Lost and Gained," *Florida State University Law Review* 6 (Summer 1978): 609–670.

14.   Cope, "To Be Let Alone," 725.

15.   Ibid., 727–728. The privacy rights were offered as a new section to Article 1 of the Florida Constitution. Section 23, as proposed, read, "Every individual has the

right to be let alone and free from governmental intrusion into his private life," and "the legislature shall protect by law the private lives of the people from intrusion by other persons."

16.   Uhlfelder, "The Machinery of Revision," 576 (citing Florida House Joint Resolution 1998 [1977]; *Florida House of Representatives Journal* 719 [Reg. Sess. 1977]; Florida House Joint Resolution 1522 [1978]; and *Florida House of Representatives Journal* 560–561 [Reg. Sess. 1978]).

17.   Florida Constitution Revision Commission, "Proposed Revision of the Florida Constitution" (Tallahassee: State of Florida, 1978), 2.

18.   Transactional immunity, which existed as a statute, would have been elevated to constitutional status. Additionally, state judges would be required to consider alternatives to money bonds for pretrial release candidates.

19.   Florida's Government in the Sunshine and public records laws, which existed as statutes, would have been elevated to constitutional status. A key element of the revision, however, permitted officials to close hearings and records "when it is essential to accomplish overriding governmental purposes or to protect privacy interests."

20.   Revision 1 would open judicial hearings unless the Florida Supreme Court or state legislature moved to close them. Additionally, the meetings of the judicial nominating commissions would be public.

21.   Revision 1 would permit witnesses before the grand jury to be accompanied by an attorney.

22.   Florida Constitution, art. 11, sec. 5(a). In fact, this lack of funding extended to compensation for the members of the commission who were only provided travel and per diem expenses for their attendance at the sixty-plus meetings and hearings (Uhlfelder, "The Machinery of Revision," 587).

23.   L. Harold Levinson, "Interpreting State Constitutions by Resort to the Record," *Florida State University Law Review* 6 (Summer 1978): 573, note 17, citing June 23, 1978, letter from R. Askew to B. Smathers, secretary of state (veto message).

24.   "Constitution . . . Gays for 1," *Miami Herald*, 1 November 1978, A5.

25.   The National Organization for Women (NOW) quickly called for a boycott of the commercials by every television and radio station and Common Cause issued a statement calling the Bryant claim "patently absurd" ("Constitution . . . Just ridiculous," *Miami Herald*, 2 November 1978, A25). But, despite these efforts, Bryant attracted even more attention by claiming that she was being censored.

26.   Only the revision to eliminate the elected cabinet fared worse, garnering support from only one-fourth of the voters.

27.   John Van Gieson, "Confusion Killed Constitutional Revisions," *Miami Herald*, 9 November 1978, A25.

28.   Ibid.

29.   379 So. 2d 633 (Fla. 1980).

30.   *Florida Statutes*, chap. 119 (1975).

31.   379 So. 2d 633, 639 (Fla. 1980).

32.   The bill was formally introduced and referred to the Committee on Governmental Operations on April 8, 1980 (Legislative Information Division, *History of Legislation, 1980 Regular Session, Special Sessions C, D, and E* [Tallahassee, Florida: Joint Legislative Management Committee], 96).

33.   Florida House Joint Resolution 387 (1980).

34. *Florida Statutes*, sec. 286.011 (1977).

35. Republicans Fred Burrall and Fred Tygart joined Democrats Ralph Haben and Jack Hagler in opposing the resolution. Control of the house at the time of the vote was in the hands of the Democrats, 88 to 32.

36. Telephone interview with former Senator Jack Gordon, 30 September 1993.

37. 410 U.S. 113 (1973).

38. *Griswold v. Connecticut*, 381 U.S. 479 (1965); *Eisenstadt v. Baird*, 405 U.S. 438 (1972); and *Carey v. Population Services International*, 431 U.S. 678 (1977).

39. Editorial, "Risk of the Unknown Too High in New Proposal on Privacy," *Miami Herald*, 29 October 1980, A6.

40. Jack D. Gordon, "Florida's Constitutional Amendments," *Miami Herald*, 3 November 1980, A7.

41. Ibid.

42. I suspect that the use of the word "tax" in Amendment 5 caused some confusion and fear among Florida voters who have a strong propensity to resist new taxes. This amendment's sole purpose was to allow municipalities to use gas tax revenues for road repairs. Previously, these funds were restricted to new road construction. The amendment did not levy any new taxes.

43. The total votes cast in the presidential race in Florida were 3,679,657.

44. Total votes cast (from highest to lowest) on 1980 constitutional amendments: Amendment 2 — 2,581,869; Amendment 1 — 2,464,447; Amendment 5 — 2,451,368; Amendment 4 — 2,431,850; and Amendment 3 — 2,382,915.

45. William K. Hall and Larry T. Aspin, "What Twenty Years of Judicial Retention Elections Have Told Us," *Judicature* 70 (April–May 1987): 347.

46. Ibid.

47. See, for example, *Mills v. Doyle*, 407 So. 2d 348 (4th Fla. Dist. Ct. App. 1981); *Florida Board of Bar Examiners re: Applicant*, 443 So. 2d 71 (Fla. 1983); and *Forsberg v. Housing Authority of City of Miami Beach*, 455 So. 2d 373 (Fla. 1984).

48. *Winfield v. Div. of Pari-Mutuel Wagering*, 477 So. 2d 544, 547 (Fla. 1985).

49. Ibid., 548.

50. 500 So. 2d 533 (Fla. 1987).

51. *Satz v. Perlmutter*, 379 So. 2d 359 (Fla. 1980).

52. See, especially, *JFK Memorial Hospital v. Bludworth*, 452 So. 2d 921 (Fla. 1984); *Public Health Trust v. Wons*, 541 So. 2d 96 (Fla. 1987); and *In re Guardianship of Estelle M. Browning*, 568 So. 2d 4 (Fla. 1990).

53. *Seebol v. Farie*, No. 90–923–CA–18 (Fla. 16th Cir. Ct. 1991); *Cox and Jackman v. Dry*, No. 91–3491–CA–01 (Fla. 12th Cir. Ct. 1993); *Amer v. Children's Home Society*, No. 92–14370 (Fla. 17th Cir. Ct., filed 1992); *Matthews v. HRS*, No. 92–07141–P (Fla. 13th Cir. Ct., filed 1992).

54. Joe Little, "Florida's Constitutional Amendment," *Miami Herald*, 3 November 1980, A7.

55. *Winfield v. Div. of Pari-Mutuel Wagering*, 477 So. 2d 544, 548.

5

The Politics of Term Limitations

John David Rausch, Jr.

The drive to enact legislative term limitations has emerged as the political phenomenon of the 1990's. Since 1990, voters in 16 states have approved citizen initiatives limiting the tenure of their elected representatives in state legislatures and, in most states, their congressional delegations. The term-limit phenomenon has spread across the country at a dizzying speed. Term-limit campaigns have emerged in many states simultaneously. To what extent is the term-limit movement a national movement with state components? Has the nature of the movement changed during its brief history? Does the term-limit movement's reliance on direct democratic processes signal a movement away from making public policy through the normal legislative process? Who are the primary actors in the term-limit movement? In finding answers to these questions, we will better understand those groups that have sought out direct democratic devices to pursue their objectives.

As part of this effort, this chapter examines the drive for term limitations from its emergence in 1989 and 1990 to its maturation in 1993 and 1994. The politics of term limits in selected states are examined in an effort to address the issue of whether or not the phenomenon is a national movement with state components. Further, the term-limit phenomenon is identified as one effort of the people to bypass and constrain their elected representative bodies. This chapter argues that the term-limit phenomenon is an elite-driven movement directed by self-appointed political entrepreneurs whose primary goal is to limit government. While it will be noted that some term-limit advocates are working to make legislatures more responsive and responsible, the bulk of the evidence points to actors who desire less government.

DEFINING AN ELITE-DRIVEN MOVEMENT

Most observers of the term-limit phenomenon label it a "movement." Unfortunately, the term-limit movement fits uncomfortably within the sociological definition of "mass or social movements."[1] Social-movement theory suggests that people organize spontaneously to solve a problem, a leader emerges from within the group, and some conflict (violent or nonviolent) occurs with status quo interests. The present analysis presents evidence that the term-limit phenomenon is not spontaneous and that the elite leadership, reasonably defined, emerges before the birth of the movement. For this reason, the term-limit phenomenon is an "elite-driven movement." The analysis that follows argues that while term limits enjoy much support from the electorate, the issue would never reach the ballot without the actions of a small number of well-placed individuals.

A BRIEF HISTORY OF TERM LIMITATION
IN THE UNITED STATES

Limiting the number of terms an elected official may serve is far from a new idea.[2] Members of the Continental Congress were limited to serving three years out of every six. The early constitutions of several states required rotation in office. However, at the insistence of the Federalists, term limitation was not included in the new federal constitution. Today, many executives serve with limited terms, including the president. It was not until 1990 that the first legislative term limitations were enacted.

In 1990 voters in Oklahoma and California approved initiatives to limit the tenure of their state legislators, and Colorado voters approved a measure limiting their congressional delegation.[3] The failure of a term-limit initiative in Washington State in 1991 did not slow the drive for term limits. In fact, it may have assisted the term-limit movement in developing a more national focus and it allowed term-limit advocates feedback on their proposals. In November 1992 term limits, now primarily targeted at Congress, were approved by the voters of fourteen states, including California, Florida, Michigan, Ohio, and Washington. Term-limit advocates targeted the nine remaining states, which had not yet approved congressional term limits, with the citizen initiative. In 1994 active campaigns to get the issue on the ballot were occurring in at least five of the nine states. Table 5.1 lists the states that have acted on term-limit initiatives. Voters in Alaska, Colorado, Idaho, Maine, Massachusetts, Nebraska, Nevada, North Dakota, Oklahoma, and Utah considered term-limit initiatives in 1994.[4] Information about these initiatives is contained in Table 5.1.

Congressional term limitations have been discussed in state legislatures, but no legislation has been enacted. During the spring of 1993, New Jersey almost became the first state to enact congressional term limits via the legislative process. A bill passed the house and the governor was willing to sign any term-limit measure, but the legislation died in the senate after a staff report questioned the constitutionality of state-imposed term limits on federal officeholders. Term-limit legislation also made progress in the New Hampshire legislature in 1993. The first session of the 103d Congress saw a large number of term-limit proposals introduced, but none was debated and brought to a vote. While the concept of term limitation has been wildly successful in states with the initiative process, noninitiative states have seen little term-limit activity. One should not conclude that the term-limit movement has not penetrated noninitiative states. In many noninitiative states, there are groups working to change state constitutions to allow for a direct popular vote on issues like term limits.[5] The first success of these groups is the state of Mississippi, where voters added the right of initiative to the constitution in 1992.

The development of the term-limit movement can be divided into phases. In Table 5.1, one begins to see these phases emerge temporally. The first phase includes the 1990 efforts in Oklahoma, Colorado, and to some extent, California. Each was the result of forces indigenous to the state and the campaigns involved little activity from forces outside the state. The unsuccessful Washington State effort in 1991, as well as the rarely discussed failure in Nevada in 1992,[6] are uncomfortably placed in a transition phase. In this phase, the influence of agents from outside the state began to grow, and the influence of outsiders was an issue in the campaigns.

The third phase involves almost all efforts in 1992. In the third-phase states, we find outside groups working hard to see that term-limit initiative campaigns are successful. In several of these states, term-limit

TABLE 5.1
State-by-State Initiative Activity on Legislative Term Limitations, 1990–1994[*]

State	Identifier	Proposal Type[a]	Federal Limits	State Limits	Ballot Access[b]	Yes (percent)
1990						
Oklahoma[c]	State Question 632	CA	None	12 years (lifetime ban)	No	67
California	Proposition 131[d]	CA	None	House: 12 years Senate: 12 years (consecutive)	No	48
	Proposition 140[e]	CA	None	House: 6 years Senate: 8 years (lifetime ban)	No	52
Colorado	Amendment 5	CA	12 years (consecutive)	8 years (consecutive)	No	71
1991						
Washington	Initiative 553	S	House: 6 years Senate: 12 years Combined: 12 years (consecutive)	House: 6 years[f] Senate: 8 years Combined: 10 years (consecutive)	No	46
1992						
Arizona	Proposition 107	CA	House: 6 years Senate: 12 years (consecutive)	House: 8 years Senate: 8 years (consecutive)	g	74

State	Identifier	Proposal Type[a]	Federal Limits	State Limits	Ballot Access[b]	Yes (percent)
Arkansas	Proposed Constitutional Amendment #4	CA	House: 6 years Senate: 12 years (lifetime ban)	House: 6 years Senate: 12 years (lifetime ban)	g	60
California	Proposition 164	CA	House: 6 years Senate: 12 years (consecutive)	None	Yes	63
Florida	Amendment 9	CA	House: 8 years Senate: 8 years (consecutive)	House: 8 years Senate: 8 years (consecutive)	Yes	77
Michigan	Proposal B	CA	House: 6 years Senate: 12 years (consecutive)	House: 6 years Senate: 8 years (lifetime ban)	No	59
Missouri	Constitutional Amendment #12	CA	None	House: 8 years Senate: 8 years (lifetime ban)	No	75
	Constitutional Amendment #13	CA	House: 8 years Senate: 12 years (lifetime ban)	None	No	74
Montana	Constitutional Initiative 64	CA	House: 6 years Senate 12 years (consecutive)	House: 6 years Senate: 8 years (consecutive)	Yes	67

Nebraska[g]	Measure #407	CA	House: 8 years Senate: 12 years (consecutive)	Senate: 2 terms (consecutive)	h	68
Nevada	j	CA	House: 6 years Senate: 12 years (consecutive)	None	Yes	NA
North Dakota	Initiated Measure #5	S	House: 12 years Senate: 12 years Combined: 12 years (lifetime ban)	None	Yes	55
Ohio	Issue 2	CA	House: 8 years Senate: 12 years (consecutive)	None	No	66
Ohio	Issue 3	CA	None	House: 8 years Senate: 8 years (consecutive)	No	68
Oregon	Measure #3	CA	House: 6 years Senate: 12 years (lifetime ban)	House: 6 years Senate: 8 years (lifetime ban)	Yes	69
South Dakota	Constitutional Amendment A	CA	House: 12 years Senate: 12 years (consecutive)	House: 8 years Senate: 8 years (consecutive)	No	63
Washington	Initiative 573	S	House: 6 years Senate: 12 years (consecutive)	House: 6 years Senate: 8 years Combined: 14 years (consecutive)	Yes	52

State	Identifier	Proposal Type[a]	Federal Limits	State Limits	Ballot Access[b]	Yes (percent)
1993						
Maine	Initiative Petition 1993, chap. 1	CA (indirect)	None	House: 8 years Senate: 8 years (consecutive)	No	67
1994						
Alaska	Measure #4	CA	House: 6 years Senate: 12 years (consecutive)	None	Yes	63
Colorado	Amendment 17	CA	House: 6 years Senate: 12 years (consecutive)	None[j]	Yes	51
Idaho	Proposition 2	CA	House: 6 years Senate: 12 years (consecutive)	House: 6 years Senate: 12 years (consecutive)	Yes	59
Illinois	k	CA	None	House: 8 years Senate: 8 years (consecutive)	Yes	NA
Maine	Question #1	CA (indirect)	House: 6 years Senate: 12 years (consecutive)	None	Yes	63
Massachusetts	Question #4	CA (indirect)	House: 8 years Senate: 12 years (consecutive)	House: 8 years Senate: 8 years (consecutive)	Yes	52

Nebraska	Measure #408	CA	House: 6 years Senate: 12 years (consecutive)	Senate: 12 years	Yes	68
North Dakota	1	CA	House: 6 years Senate: 12 years (consecutive)	None	Yes	NA
Oklahoma	State Question 662	CA	House: 6 years Senate: 12 years (consecutive)	None	Yes	67
Utah	Initiative A	CA	House: 8 years Senate: 12 years (consecutive)	House: 8 years Senate: 8 years	Yes	35^m

Notes: The information presented in this table is summarized; full text of the measures should be consulted for full detail.

[a]CA = constitutional amendment; S = statute.

[b]Ballot access regulation would allow an incumbent to run for reelection, but his or her name could not appear on the ballot; the incumbent would be allowed to run a write-in campaign.

[c]Oklahoma voted on state legislative term limits on September 18, 1990.

[d]Proposition 131 was proposed by gubernatorial candidate and state attorney general John Van de Camp. Cosponsored by California Common Cause, it included a number of other campaign reforms including a provision for the public financing of state legislative campaigns.

[e]Proposition 140 was spearheaded by former state senator and Los Angeles County Supervisor Peter Schabarum. It also included a number of other provisions such as ending the legislative pension system and cutting legislative staff. The pension provision was later found unconstitutional by the state supreme court. The court found the remainder of the proposal within constitutional bounds. See *Legislature v. Eu*, 816 P.2d 1309 (Cal. 1991), *cert. denied*, 112 S. Ct. 1292 (1992).

[f]Initiative 553 included a retroactivity clause that would have counted past service against the limit. Therefore, any incumbent who had served twelve or more years would have been required to leave office after one additional term.

[g]Nebraska's term-limit initiative was invalidated by the state supreme court in May 1994 due to a lack of valid signatures. See *Duggan v. Beermann*, 245 Neb. 907 (1994 Neb. LEXIS 112).

[h]Yes for federal offices; no for state offices.

[i]Measure was declared unconstitutional and ordered removed from the ballot by the Nevada Supreme Court in *Stumpf v. Lau*, 839 P.2d 120 (Nev. 1992).

[j]Colorado voters approved state legislative term limits in 1990. The 1994 initiative brought the state's congressional limits in line with other states.

[k]The term-limit initiative in Illinois was barred from the ballot by the state supreme court after the Chicago Bar Association filed a protest of the initiative's constitutionality under the state constitution. According to the Illinois Constitution, initiatives may not "alter the structure" of government.

[l]The term-limit initiative was barred from the ballot by a decision by the state attorney general that many signatures had been collected improperly.

[m]The Utah Legislature passed and the governor signed term-limit legislation in the spring of 1994.

Source: Sula P. Richardson, *Term Limits for Federal and State Legislators: Background and Recent State Activity*, Report 93-122 GOV (Washington, D.C.: Library of Congress, Congressional Research Service, 1993), tables 2, 3; interviews with officials in the offices of secretary of state for those states acting on term limits after 1993.

leaders emerge from within the state, but they are found unsuitable by the national organizations and are replaced by more suitable leaders at the first opportunity. Term-limit operatives at the national level see that additional resources are sent to states where campaigns are in "trouble."

By the time the remaining initiative states become involved in congressional term-limit campaigns, the movement has reached a "franchising" stage. In this stage, national term-limit advocates (now operating as one large group) select persons to serve as term-limit leaders in each of the states, provide the leaders with the resources necessary to write and qualify the initiatives, and offer campaign strategy after the proposal has been certified for the ballot. This final stage is least understood, primarily because it is ongoing.

SELECTING STATES FOR ANALYSIS

Performing a careful examination of each term-limit campaign would require more space than is available in a chapter-length analysis. Therefore, a few cases have been selected for detailed examination. Data from other states will be utilized to substantiate a point where necessary. For the purposes of understanding how the term-limit movement has nationalized, this chapter examines the process and politics leading to the adoption of term limits in four states: Oklahoma, Washington, Michigan, and Florida.

The cases were selected purposely in order to achieve a look at the term-limit movement at its different phases. Oklahoma was the first state to experience a statewide initiative campaign on term limits and even though only state legislators were limited, the campaign offers important insights. Washington's experience is important because two efforts were necessary before term limits were approved by voters. It also was the only state where a term-limit initiative failed to be approved and I consider it the first state with a significant amount of outside assistance. Michigan also illustrates the role of outside assistance on a statewide campaign. But in Michigan, the outside assistance proved beneficial, almost necessary. Florida, which was the most indigenous of all of the fourteen campaigns in 1992, provides the observer with a glimpse at some of the differences between the national groups that have emerged as powerful actors in the term-limit movement.

It may seem difficult to generalize from these disparate states. However, this analysis concludes that as the term-limit movement has nationalized and matured, the state-level campaign matters much less than what is taking place on the national level. Therefore, state differences are not as important.

FOUR (OR FIVE) SAMPLES OF TERM-LIMIT CAMPAIGNS

Oklahoma: "Governor . . . we want to beat them."[7]

On September 18, 1990, voters in the state of Oklahoma decided that the tenure of their elected state representatives and senators needed to be limited. In Oklahoma, term limits can be attributed to the efforts of one individual, a businessperson who appointed himself the term-limit leader of the state. An examination of this first campaign shows the relative lack of influence the mass electorate has in the process of enacting term limits while it also depicts a state campaign in its most pure state. A comparison of Oklahoma's campaign with the 1990 term-limit effort in Colorado would find more similarities than differences.

When Oklahoma voters approved State Question 632 (SQ 632) in 1990, term limitation appeared to be a novel idea. Legislative term limits were enacted through the use of the citizen initiative, not the legislative process. There had been many proposals to limit the terms of legislators (specifically the terms of members of congress) but none reached fruition.[8] By approving SQ 632, Oklahoma voters were indicating that they believed the legislature had become too powerful, unresponsive, and downright silly. Examples of the legislature's power and silliness include "stopping the clock in the capitol just before constitutionally mandated adjournment and later arguing — successfully — in court that because the legislature had never adjourned it remained in the same 'legislative day,' if not the same calendar day."[9] Oklahomans also endured a legislative pay raise enacted by an independent compensation board and watched a speaker be overthrown. By 1990 voters were understandably upset with their legislature.

Tulsa businessperson Lloyd Noble had "often thought . . . that we [Oklahomans] could limit our state legislators via the initiative-petition process."[10] In 1989, when a blue-ribbon commission appointed by the governor to recommend changes in the state constitution failed to consider term limits, Noble decided to take a deeper look into the concept. He commissioned Cole Hargrave Snodgrass & Associates, a political consulting firm in Oklahoma City, to conduct a poll of Oklahomans. The survey's goal was to determine the level of popular support for term limits. With more than 70 percent of the Oklahomans surveyed supporting the concept of term limits, Noble saw a winning idea and decided to launch an initiative effort.[11]

In the fall of 1989, Noble filed a proposal with the Oklahoma secretary of state to limit the length of service of Oklahoma legislators to twelve years. The proposal also stipulated that these twelve years could be served in either chamber or both. For example, a member of the state house could serve four years in that body and seek election to the state senate where he or she would be able to serve only eight more years.[12]

The proposal had been carefully drafted by "a former legislator, a current legislator — both attorneys — and a personal friend who was also the personal attorney for the late Senator Bartlett."[13] The lawyers took several factors into account in drafting the measure. First, it had to conform to the "single-subject rule." The results of the initial survey also were taken into account; although there was support for term limits of eight or even six years, more respondents favored at least twelve years. The proposal "could not include federal offices because it might anger popular politicians" like U.S. Senator David Boren, who was serving his third term, and U.S. Senator Don Nickles, who was going to announce his intent to run for a third term.[14]

With the proposal drafted, Noble's next step was to begin circulating petitions. Circulators, paid with funds raised by Noble's newly organized Oklahomans for Legislative Reform, gathered the second highest number of signatures on an initiative petition in the prescribed ninety-day period. The signatures were certified by the secretary of state and the certification was validated by the state supreme court.

After the signatures on the petitions were validated, Noble persuaded Republican Governor Henry Bellmon, a supporter of term limits, to place the question on the primary run-off ballot in September 1990. Both men wanted to avoid the general election clutter and distractions, but of greater importance was the desire to have Oklahoma be the first state to enact term limits. Noble recalls telling Governor Bellmon, "Governor, [term limits in] Colorado and California are going to be on the ballot in November [1990]. We want to beat them."[15] This may seem pure boosterism on the part of the two men, however, in Oklahoma, there is a "tendency . . . for contentious policy questions to get settled at the ballot box on primary or runoff ballots." This effectively spares candidates from taking positions on controversial state questions in their campaigns.[16]

Oklahoma became the first state to enact term limits in September 1990 when voters approved the measure by a margin of almost 2 to 1.[17] Most of the credit for the initiative's success can be credited to Noble and to a disgruntled electorate upset over the heavy-handed way their legislature flaunted constitutional directives.

Noble, whose family is known throughout the state for their philanthropic efforts, is a Republican who once ran unsuccessfully for a seat in the state house. The pro–term-limit effort was spearheaded by an organization, Oklahomans for Legislative Reform, bankrolled primarily by Noble and other members of his family. The total budget for the campaign including advertising was $220,000.[18] According to campaign reports filed with the state, most of the money was raised in-state. Noble went into debt financing the measure, debt he had not expected given the overwhelming popular support for the measure.[19]

Noble's organization was bipartisan as most of the Republican minority in the state legislature and a number of key Democrats, including former governor Raymond Gary, enthusiastically supported the idea.[20] Simultaneously, Democratic gubernatorial candidate David Walters, while not specifically endorsing Noble's proposal, implied support and ran his own successful campaign against "professional politicians."[21] During his campaign, Walters ran a commercial attacking professional politicians. Because of Walters' advertising efforts, Noble spent less than he might have.

Noble encountered little enthusiasm for his proposal from one segment of the Oklahoma population. Many corporate leaders gave lip service to his initiative but failed to provide any substantial resources. While many chief executive officers liked the idea, their government affairs staffs cautioned against active support or financial contributions. The government affairs "people" did not want "to offend the legislature."[22]

Noble did find an enthusiastic supporter in media tycoon Edward L. Gaylord. Among other holdings, Gaylord owns the Oklahoma Publishing Company (OPUBCO), the parent company of the state's largest newspaper, the *Daily Oklahoman*. Gaylord, a billionaire, has been labeled "the richest and arguably the most powerful person in the state."[23] The government affairs staff at OPUBCO did not have to worry about angering the legislature because the body is frequently the subject of front-page editorials in the paper. OPUBCO and Gaylord gave large financial contributions to Noble's efforts and the *Daily Oklahoman* displayed its support editorially.

Public opinion data present a measure of mass support for term limitations. "The concept [of term limits] was never weaker in public opinion polls than the two-to-one margin it garnered on [election day]."[24] Survey data support that contention. A survey of Oklahoma residents taken in advance of the election found similarly strong support coupled with limited variation across demographic categories.

Almost no opposition emerged to challenge the initiative, although one group, The Committee to Protect the Rights of Oklahoma Voters in Elections, emerged less than a week before the election. Its leadership included a former chair of the state Democratic party and the party's former executive director. The organization could muster little effective opposition. Some minimal opposition to the initiative came from current members of the state legislature. Former speaker of the U.S. House of Representatives Carl Albert was the most visible politician who opposed the initiative, but Albert's efforts may have been "too little, too late."[25] Noble was lucky little opposition emerged considering his inability to raise large sums of money in support of his effort.

With the initiative successfully approved by Oklahoma voters, Lloyd Noble had made his mark. Less than a year later, he directed the Oklahomans for State Question 640, a group that raised money and campaigned for the passage of a proposal commonly called the "no taxation without a vote of the people" initiative. State Question 640 was successful.

Several insights emerge with a close examination of the history of term limits in Oklahoma. First, almost every part of the process involved Oklahomans. Noble is an Oklahoman who previously had campaigned unsuccessfully for the state house. To conduct the survey that resulted in his decision to campaign for term limits, he chose an Oklahoma City political consulting firm. He relied on two Oklahoma lawyers, State Senator Gary Gardenhire of Norman and attorney Wilson Wallace of Ardmore, to write the initiative.[26] Almost all the money spent in the campaign was raised from Oklahoma sources with little assistance from outside and no help from national term-limit groups. The second factor is that Noble wanted the initiative to succeed and attract attention from across the country. His initial survey showed that limits of eight or even six years could pass, but twelve-year limits were shown to be more easily approved. Noble "very much wanted it [the limit] to be retroactive," but was talked out of that strategy with good reason.[27] The initiative was simple and clear with no loopholes other than the grandfather clause, and it met the legal requirement of dealing only with one subject. Noble wanted Oklahoma to be first and it was.

Washington: "Second time a charm"[28]

The effort in Washington State in 1991 is part of the transitional phase of the term-limit movement's development. As in Oklahoma, the key actor in Washington was self-appointed. Unlike Lloyd Noble, she is a "liberal" activist. Other factors that differentiate term-limit activity in Washington from the efforts that preceded it include an increase in the influence of large contributors from outside the state, the role of a national term-limit organization, and the writing of the term-limit proposal without any input from Washington voters. The 1991 campaign was unsuccessful, although postmortems do not agree why it failed.[29] While the first campaign can be considered part of a transition, the second campaign in 1992 clearly shares characteristics with the other states in the second phase.

Sherry Bockwinkel, a liberal and Democratic activist, began the movement to place a term-limit proposal on the Washington ballot by drafting the proposal, allegedly, in her Tacoma living room.[30] Bockwinkel organized the group LIMIT (Legislative Initiative Mandating Incumbent Terms) to spread the idea of term limits around the state. The core group in LIMIT consisted of several members of Mike Collier's campaign staff. Collier was a liberal Democrat defeated in a primary attempt to unseat U.S. Representative Norm Dicks, the more conservative Democratic incumbent. Bockwinkel emerged from Collier's unsuccessful campaign frustrated at the lack of attention paid to a challenger in a primary election. As an example of the lack of attention given to challengers, the League of Women Voters refused to invite Collier to debate Representative Dicks.[31]

LIMIT's activities were nominally directed by a steering committee. The committee included Bockwinkel, who soon became LIMIT's executive director; Gene Morain, "a retired businessman who provided seed money [and] served as treasurer"; and Professor Robert Struble, noted for his research and advocacy of rotation for legislators. There were never more than thirty members of the committee. The steering committee had no real power as it met at the request of Bockwinkel. It was often engaged in conflict over the wording of the proposal, particularly during the discussion of retroactivity. No members of LIMIT's steering committee were ever elected by Washington voters or even by the larger "membership" of LIMIT.[32]

Interests outside Washington made an appearance early in the process. In December 1990 Bockwinkel and Morain attended a conference sponsored by two national term-limit groups, Citizens for Congressional

Reform (CCR) and Americans to Limit Congressional Terms (ALCT), held in San Jose, California. At the conference, the Washingtonians learned about term-limit activities from activists in other states.[33]

In January 1991 LIMIT released the wording of its initiative and began collecting signatures. It was at this point when the perception of the term-limit campaign began to change. In contrast to the states that had previously enacted term limits, Bockwinkel initially encountered some difficulty in collecting the signatures needed to get the initiative on the ballot. The problems have been attributed to both a lack of organization and a lack of funding. In the early days of the effort, Bockwinkel was the only paid staffer; all petition circulators were volunteers. These volunteers, although committed to the cause, were mainly residents of the Tacoma vicinity and most of their efforts were focused in that area. LIMIT was unable to attract either state or national attention.[34]

In March a delegation of national term-limit activists visited Bockwinkel. The group included Cleta Mitchell, representing ALCT; LaDonna Lee, a founder of ALCT; and Shari Williams, executive director of Americans Back in Charge and a successful term-limit activist in Colorado. By April CCR began making monetary contributions. CCR was a subsidiary of Washington, D.C.–based Citizens for a Sound Economy, whose board members "range from conservative Republicans to libertarians." CCR eventually contributed large sums of money to the term-limit effort in Washington. Records reveal that CCR contributed $176,970.89 to LIMIT from April 1991 through July 8, 1991.[35] CCR also hired National Voter Outreach, an initiative consulting firm from California, to collect signatures.

An election campaign often is decided more by perception than reality.[36] This was certainly the case for the Initiative 553 (I-553) campaign. Initiative 553 was the number given the LIMIT proposal by the Washington secretary of state. With the assistance of CCR and National Voter Outreach, enough signatures were collected to get the initiative on the November 1991 ballot. The campaign, unlike those in other states, was marked by a number of perception problems. There was a strained relationship between Bockwinkel's LIMIT and the CCR. Operatives paid by CCR thought Bockwinkel was very liberal and very opinionated. She was accustomed to working with volunteers and not familiar with raising and spending large sums of money. CCR's workers operated out of a plush suite of offices in Seattle while most of LIMIT's business was conducted from a small office in Tacoma or Bockwinkel's living room. Bockwinkel was not even informed about the sources of

CCR's funds.[37] In the end, CCR ran a separate campaign loosely coordinated with LIMIT's activities.

Even with the retroactivity clause, opponents had a difficult time getting organized. The proposal's retroactivity clause simply stated that time already served in office would be considered in applying term limits. Incumbents who had already served the maximum time allowed would be forced to retire after one additional term. Even though this would have forced most of the congressional delegation out of office by 1994, the delegation did not want to participate in attacking what appeared to be a popular movement within Washington. In October the Tacoma *Morning News Tribune* ran an investigative story on the sources of funding for the term-limit campaign.[38] This was the beginning of the worst perception problems for LIMIT.

The information that the term-limit campaign was being funded largely by outsiders allowed term-limit opponents to reframe the debate and mobilize the state's congressional delegation. Term limit opponents ran advertising that suggested to voters that their state would lose clout in Washington if the delegation, notably Speaker Thomas Foley, was required to retire early. The ads developed questions about California's desire for Washington water supplies (former California governor Jerry Brown spent several days in Washington speaking in support of congressional term limits). Did the wealthy industrialists who contributed to the term-limit effort want to despoil Washington's coastline with oil platforms and the threat of oil spills? (Two of the contributors were the Koch Brothers of Kansas, owners of a conglomerate that controls a pipeline company among other interests.) Initiative 553 failed to be approved by a vote of 54 percent to 46 percent.

Exit polls showed that the clout issue worked in weakening support for term limits. A poll commissioned by the national Democratic Congressional Campaign Committee and the statewide term-limit opposition after the election found that over 20 percent feared that Washington would lose clout in Congress if term limits were approved. Nearly as many felt that it was wrong for Washington to unilaterally limit congressional terms.[39] No research has been conducted on whether Washington voters would have supported state legislative term limits if separated from congressional term limits.

Even though they were defeated, LIMIT and other activists refused to stay down for long. For term-limit activists, particularly at the national level, the 1991 defeat in Washington was a valuable learning experience. Term-limit proponents were able to analyze the techniques used by opponents and turn the opposition's strategy on them in 1992. One important lesson was "not to have a term limit election by itself." The strategy was updated to include the rule that a term-limit vote should always be held during a general election thereby forcing incumbent legislators to run on the issue. Sherry Bockwinkel was given more control over the campaign in 1992. Bockwinkel has become a vaunted symbol of the term-limit movement "with her Birkenstocks and long frizzy hair."[40] Bockwinkel's strength as a symbol derives from the fact that she is not the typical term-limit leader. Most are white males with conservative political agendas.

Without belaboring the point, the 1992 campaign in Washington was much different from the 1991 campaign. Bockwinkel had more control. The perception that outsiders were going to take over Washington's resources was found to be an empty argument. The 1992 initiative (I-573) incorporated many changes, which exit polls showed had concerned voters in 1991. The retroactivity clause was removed. A section was included specifying that Washington's congressional term limits would not take effect until ten other states passed similar measures, thus weakening opponents' arguments on the clout issue.

LIMIT was successful in 1992 due in part to the distractions caused by presidential and congressional elections. Contributors who might have given to groups opposing term limits had to prioritize their contributions. Incumbents had to campaign for themselves, often against opponents outspoken on term limits. In fact, Speaker Foley had a strong challenger in 1992. Heather Foley had to direct the campaign, an effort reportedly conducted from the Speaker's rooms in Washington, D.C. Raising less money, but with more contributions coming from in-state, LIMIT was able to campaign successfully for approval of I-573. On November 3, 1992, Washington joined thirteen other states in passing a term-limit initiative by a vote of 52 percent to 46 percent, the narrowest margin of any state. The story of term limits in Washington is not over. In February 1994 a federal judge in Seattle ruled that the congressional term limits specified in the initiative were unconstitutional. As Speaker Foley is one of the plaintiffs on the lawsuit, it is expected that this decision will be appealed to the U.S. Supreme Court.[41] Bockwinkel and LIMIT have moved on to other initiatives including the CLEAN initiative, which is an ethics package; the "three-strikes-you're-out" mandatory sentencing initiative; and other efforts at cutting government waste. LIMIT also filed a lawsuit aimed at overturning state legislation prohibiting paid petition circulators.

Florida: "I had money and some time."

Unlike other campaigns in the large second phase of the term-limit movement, Florida's campaign was the most indigenous. Like others in this phase, the term-limit activist had assistance from outside the state, primarily from the Colorado-based group Americans Back in Charge. Phil Handy, a Winter Park financier and financial advisor to former Republican governor Bob Martinez, founded and chaired Citizens for Limited Political Terms. The campaign was called "Eight Is Enough" because the initiative prohibits incumbents from the ballot after serving eight years in office. Handy believes his campaign was the best organized term-limit effort in the nation, an interesting mix of volunteer effort combined with large amounts of his own money.[42] For this reason, the Florida term-limit campaign provides a useful case for study.

Prior to 1990, Phil Handy was known for his financial operations and his work for statewide Republican candidates. In 1989 Handy "and some Australian partners . . . borrowed about $360 million to finance $400 million worth of acquisitions." By late 1990 he had sold his interest in each of the acquisitions for a nice, but undisclosed, profit.[43] After dismissing a run for political office himself, he decided to give term limits a try. He had "gotten wind" of the term-limit campaigns in Oklahoma, Colorado, and California and he had some extra money and time. He also was a business associate of Terry Considine, Colorado'a term-limit proponent and chair of Americans Back in Charge.[44] On what seems a lark, Handy set about organizing a campaign to put a term-limit initiative on the Florida ballot.

Initiatives are not an industry in Florida. In fact, before 1992 only six initiatives had appeared on the Florida ballot and only three had been approved.[45] A term-limit campaign in Florida had to be "well organized, well orchestrated and be a state-wide campaign, which in Florida means at least seven major media markets."[46] It would be an effort that would take "more time than [he] expected" and, as indicated by campaign finance records, $130,950 donated by forgiving a loan to Citizens for Limited Political Terms.[47]

Handy began his term-limit effort without polling public opinion. Instead, he gauged public opinion by standing "in front of post offices and Wal-Marts . . . and ask[ing] people to sign a petition."[48] The campaign was kicked off at an April 1991 press conference where Handy stated that "if eight years is long enough for Ronald Reagan to be president . . . and for Reubin Askew to be governor . . . then it's long enough for members of the [Florida] Legislature, the [Florida] Cabinet and the U.S. Congress," all officials to be affected by his initiative.[49]

In November 1991 Handy's efforts met their first obstacle. Term-limit opponents, including U.S. Representative Larry Smith (D.-Broward County) and the National Conference of State Legislatures, sued in the Florida Supreme Court to stop the initiative. Congressional term limitation enacted by the state is illegal, the opponents argued, because it adds qualifications to service not identified in the constitution. The initiative also violated state procedural regulations since it involved more than one subject — term limits on the state legislature, members of Congress, and executive officials. Representative Smith was able to enlist the aid of the chief counsel of the U.S. House, Steven Ross, in preparing an amicus brief. This led to an outcry by Republicans in the U.S. House, who saw taxpayer funds being used to oppose term limits.[50] The Florida Supreme Court ruled that the initiative met all requirements for a ballot question and deferred judgment on the constitutionality of state-enacted term limits until after the initiative was decided by the voters.

Throughout the campaign, Handy dealt primarily with one national term-limit group, Americans Back in Charge of Denver, Colorado. He refused to deal with Citizens for Congressional Reform because "CCR made their financial involvement subject to a six-year term limit for the U.S. House of Representatives."[51] Although Citizens for Limited Political Terms accepted money from U.S. Term Limits, Handy refused to alter his initiative. He felt he could work with Americans Back in Charge who functioned primarily as a political consultant "looking in from time to time to see how things were going."[52]

After fifteen months of circulating petitions, Eight Is Enough submitted 529,268 signatures to the secretary of state's office in July 1992. This was the largest number of signatures collected for an initiative in Florida with about half being collected by volunteers. Handy was unable to have the initiative appear on the ballot as Amendment 8. Instead he had to encourage voters to "vote yes on Amendment 9."[53]

Even though he ran a model campaign, Handy's efforts were not unopposed. A group calling itself Restore Our American Rights (ROAR) was organized by state labor leaders, former lawmakers, and lobbyists to develop an educational campaign to counteract the popularity of Eight Is Enough. During its brief existence, ROAR was unable to raise more than $10,000 and eventually gave up the fight in mid-September.[54] Local political observers and wits could not ignore the fact that ROAR consisted of little more than five former or present lobbyists, leading the group to be referred to as FLIT, Five Lobbyists in Tallahassee.

The Eight Is Enough proposal won approval by a margin of 77 percent to 23 percent. The landslide occurred even as a number of long-term state legislative and congressional incumbents were reelected. On the day after the election, term-limit opponents filed a lawsuit in federal court in Tallahassee. Although the lawyer who filed the suit predicted lawsuits in all fourteen states where term limits were approved, legal questions were raised in only five.[55] As of February 1994 no action on the suit was scheduled. Phil Handy moved on to serve as the manager of Jeb Bush's gubernatorial campaign. Handy was proud of his campaign because it received only 20 percent of its funding from outside Florida and even though he eventually had to hire a campaign manager to handle the day-to-day activities, Handy did not pass any control of the campaign to a group from beyond the state's borders.

Michigan: A Local or a National Effort?

The campaign in Michigan exemplifies many of the key features of the second phase of the term-limit movement. The bifurcated leadership of the campaign changed after signatures were collected and the initiative was placed on the ballot. There was a substantial opposition that had to be neutralized by experienced political professionals (not professional politicians). The degree of outside assistance was also higher than in the other states examined in this chapter. However, the outside assistance was not as easy to discern as it was in Washington in 1991.

The term-limit process began in Michigan in the spring of 1991 when Dick Jacobs, former Libertarian Party candidate for governor and U.S. Senator and a Republican primary candidate for the state Senate in 1990, created a group to place two initiatives on the ballot. One was a measure to change the state tax system and the other was a term-limit initiative. Jacobs acknowledged that the signature collection effort was slow. In the first month, only 200 volunteers had been collecting statewide.[56]

Early in the campaign, there were apparently two efforts at collecting signatures. Tim Purdy, identified as a member of the Campaign to Limit Politicians' Terms, indicated in a published report that his group was also collecting signatures but that it was not working in a coordinated effort with Jacobs.[57] Purdy was working in Michigan at the request of Ron St. John, the first executive director of Citizens for Congressional Reform. Purdy and St. John had worked on initiatives together in Arizona. It was Purdy's job to organize the volunteers to collect signatures while Jacobs was to handle paperwork and legal details.[58] This is the first instance of a bifurcated campaign process and it may have caused problems. By the summer of 1992, term-limit campaigns in several states "were in trouble." Michigan was one of those states.[59]

The term-limit initiative proposed by Jacobs included the limits commonly recognized as standard. Members of the U.S. House would be allowed to serve three two-year terms and Senators could serve two six-year terms. The initiative also included term limits for members of the state legislature and executive officials. The proposal bears a strong resemblance to the initiatives acted on in other states in 1992. In fact, Jacobs took the sample language presented to him by Shari Williams of Americans Back in Charge and Eric O'Keefe, a political consultant from Wisconsin and board member of U.S. Term Limits, photocopied it, and filed it with the Michigan secretary of state. The initiative was filed almost too early for campaigners to build an organization.[60]

Opposition to term limits emerged behind the leadership of lobbyist and congressional spouse Debbie Dingell. With the assistance of the chairman of the Upjohn Corporation, Dingell was able to build "a coalition of business and union groups." The strong opposition, although it appeared to many to be self-serving, caused anxiety among term-limit proponents. A *Detroit Free Press* poll taken only one week before the election showed term limits with 72 percent support. On election day, after a week of campaign ads, term limits received only 59 percent of the vote.[61] The strong opposition caused term-limit proponents at the national level to deem the campaign "in trouble" and lend more professional assistance.

Because of the vigorous anti–term-limit effort, proponents were forced to spend much money in the last stages of the campaign. U.S. Term Limits donated $314,000 to the campaign in the two weeks before the election. Michigan Citizens Against Term Limits, the opposition coalition that comprised Michigan Common Cause, the League of Women Voters and other groups, received more than $160,000 in the final weeks of the campaign.[62]

Unlike earlier term-limit efforts, it is difficult to identify one person responsible for the proposal's success. A term-limit initiative was originally the idea of Dick Jacobs, a Holland, Michigan, businessperson and unsuccessful candidate for public office. While Jacobs was working to gain support for his idea, Tim Purdy organized volunteers to collect signatures as an activist with the Campaign to Limit Politicians' Terms. By the end of the campaign, Steve Mitchell, a professional political consultant, was handling the "day-to-day" details for the effort and Dick Headlee of Taxpayers United was taking credit for the term-limit idea.[63] Several different political forces were at work to create this shuffling of positions. The first is that the pro–term-limit forces did not expect strong opposition. When opposition did emerge, activists at the national level decided that professional campaigners were needed. The second force was the amount of money flowing into the campaign from national term-limit groups. Changing local leadership should be expected as those who finance the efforts must "ensure that the support is going toward actual [term-limit] efforts and that the local people are serious."[64] Term limits may have been a local idea, but the campaign needed outside assistance to be successful.

CONCLUSION

The term-limit phenomenon has continued to spread despite questions of the constitutionality of state-imposed congressional term limits. The discussion presented above provides a narrative analysis of the development of a term-limit movement and the ability of that movement to use state-level constitutional change through the initiative process to further goals drawn on a national level. This section draws generalizations about the term-limit movement, raises issues relating to the question of accountability in term-limit campaigns, and links the term-limit movement with a number of other "citizen" efforts to change their government.

The Term-Limit Movement

It is obvious that the term-limit movement in 1994 does not resemble the movement in 1990. However, rather than maturing into a loose organization of state efforts to limit legislative terms, the movement has developed a strong national organization that "franchises" term-limit campaigns to the states. Early in the 1991 effort in Washington State, national groups moved into the state and tried to usurp power from the local organization already there. This technique was a failure. For the 1992 campaigns, national groups assisted term-limit efforts at the state level by sharing information across states. In problem states like Michigan, national activists were not afraid to suggest professional political consultants who would run the campaign after the local "movement people" worked to get the issue on the ballot. In many cases, the consultants were paid directly by one of the national groups. There were cases of individuals starting initiative efforts and being unable to get organized efficiently. These efforts were either assimilated into state groups assisted by the national organizations or ignored completely. Early indications of the 1994 campaigns suggest that national groups are involved much more deeply in efforts to change state constitutions to limit congressional terms.

The congressional term-limit campaign in Oklahoma began in November 1993. By spring 1993 Lloyd Noble had decided he did not want to be involved in an effort on congressional terms because of the constitutional question.[65] During the summer of 1993 term-limit activists at the national level discussed possible candidates for term-limit leader in Oklahoma and finally selected Walt Hill, a former state representative and official in the Department of Agriculture during the Bush administration. At any point during the summer of 1993 a person could have emerged to begin a campaign for limiting congressional terms in Oklahoma, but one conservative activist in the state reported that they were forced to wait for money to come in from Washington (where U.S. Term Limits is headquartered).

U.S. Term Limits, now the leading national group in the movement, provides money for legal assistance in drafting initiatives to meet local requirements and to handle any legal challenges, assistance in dealing with the press, and sponsors occasional strategy sessions where state leaders meet to discuss their campaigns.[66] In return for this assistance, U.S. Term Limits requires that the initiative include provisions limiting U.S. House members to six years in office and Senators to twelve years. The untrained eye may see a trend developing in the nation for six- and twelve-year term limit. This is a strategy, not a trend.

The Nature of the Term-Limit Leader

The narrative presented above describes an idea developed and sold by a small number of individuals. Term-limit activists are self-appointed and, in almost all cases, do not consult with the electorate in preparing proposals. These activists are largely unaccountable. Previous research has recognized the problem of accountability in the initiative process.[67] In the initiative process, the voter only approves the initiative, first at the qualification stage and later in the voting booth, if the initiative qualifies for the ballot. The voter has no input into the content of the initiative and the initiative cannot be altered by voters who view the concept as sound but dislike the proposal. In the case of term-limit initiatives, only voters in California in 1990 were provided the opportunity to choose between different permutations of term limits. However, each proposal (Propositions 131 and 140) contained other legislative reforms that may have influenced vote decisions. In other states, alternative term-limit measures were often circulating at once, but national groups selected only one to support with their resources. Usually, that initiative proposed six-year term limits for U.S. House members and twelve-year term limits for Senators.

Term-limit activists are not accountable to the general voting public. However, their actions are accountable to one group of people, those who give the money. The persons spearheading early term-limit efforts only needed to concern themselves with satisfying contributors and groups within their states. As the term-limit movement has developed into a more national effort, state-level activists are becoming more accountable to the national groups. Here again, the national groups are only accountable to their contributors. Primarily this means only those persons who are able to contribute large sums of money. We have seen that Sherry Bockwinkel's term-limit message was not being heard until outside contributors started pouring money into the effort. Money has been a significant theme among term-limit activists interviewed for this research. Most agree that "money is always needed to spread the word about a good idea."[68]

While the question of the accountability in the initiative process has always been a concern, only in the case of term limits does it pose a significant problem. Advocates of term limits propose to alter the connections between the electorate and their elected representatives. Nothing of this magnitude has ever been attempted through the initiative process. In thinking about term-limit activists and their goals, one would immediately come to the conclusion that these activists seek revenge on legislators for some past transgression. Term-limit activists also might be seeking a method of gaining name recognition for future political endeavors.

In each of the cases presented in this chapter and in other cases under examination in other research, evidence to support both conclusions can be found. Lloyd Noble of Oklahoma sought a seat in the state legislature prior to conducting his successful term-limit campaign. Sherry Bockwinkel in Washington worked on the campaign staff of a challenger virtually ignored in the rush of interest groups to support the congressional incumbent. In Michigan, Dick Jacobs was a perennial Libertarian and Republican candidate for public office. However, there is evidence that he viewed term limits as one way of limiting the size and taxing power of government. Other actors in Michigan had political pasts and aspirations. These include Dick Headlee, who had once been a candidate for governor, and Glenn Steil, who in 1993 campaigned for a vacant congressional seat in a special election. Phil Handy, Florida's term-limit leader, seems to violate the "revenge or aspiration." Other persons not examined in this chapter include Terry Considine of Colorado, the

Republican candidate for the U.S. Senate in 1992, and Pete Schabarum of California, a former Los Angeles county supervisor and former state senator who several people have suggested "got back" at the state senate.[69]

Term-limit activists fall into one of two camps, identified by the goals of the activists and their past political activities. The largest group comprises those who desire a smaller government and fewer taxes. Persons interested in "better government" constitute the other faction. This chapter has examined campaigns run by activists from both groups. The campaign in Washington State in 1991 is a good example of the problems caused by the interaction of the two camps. Sherry Bockwinkel, the symbolic "good government" term-limit activist, found it difficult to work with the more conservative, and often libertarian, "small government" forces. Each of the other leaders, in Oklahoma, Florida, and Michigan, fall in the small government faction. U.S. Term Limits, the leading national group, clearly is dominated by contributors who favor limited government and are willing to pay for it. The ability to raise significant sums of money is one key feature of the small government group. Since it is easier to attract contributors with "deep pockets" to a "make government smaller" campaign, the good government group must resort to mobilizing larger numbers of volunteers. As the initiative process becomes more professionalized, mobilizing volunteers will become increasingly difficult as everyone will want to be paid. The potential for conflict between the two factions is present and the term-limit movement may have to endure internal friction in the future.[70]

The Nature of Constitutional Change

The term-limitation phenomenon has important implications for the future of legislative bodies and the connections between constituents and legislators. The term-limit movement also portends the future of state constitutional change. Citizens are seeing the initiative process as the only method to "retake their government." The characters on the cover of the National Referendum Movement's brochure ask, "Since We the People are sovereign, why can't we vote on significant issues that affect our lives?" Various groups have emerged to help "We the People" get the ability to vote on important issues.

Groups proposing term limits and other legislative reforms are following the Progressives' preferred method for constitutional change, state-by-state reform via the citizen initiative. This method, referred to as the "Wisconsin idea," has been copied by Americans Back in Charge, headed by former Colorado state senator Terry Considine. Renaming it the "Colorado idea,"[71] the goal of this method is to force Congress to consider a constitutional amendment by enacting congressional term limits on a majority of members of Congress. The Colorado idea, altered slightly, has been adopted by groups who desire a national referendum, school choice, and even a balanced-budget amendment. One of the projects of Americans Back in Charge is to pass initiatives in the states calling on Congress to propose a constitutional balanced-budget amendment.

This chapter presented an analysis of term-limit campaigns in several states. While term limits offer a challenge to legislatures and legislators, the movement developing to enact term limits also represents the future of state constitutional change by initiative. Apparently, the people do not believe legislatures can solve the difficult problems, and therefore, the only solutions will come through the initiative process. However, this analysis has given some indication of the lack of accountability of the persons who lead initiative campaigns. The average voter only partici-pates in the final decision regarding legislation, while at least in theory, the citizen can offer suggestions throughout the normal legislative process. As the initiative process becomes more professionalized and initiatives become more expensive to qualify, the threat exists of an elite takeover of the process. We are already seeing this elite-dominated takeover of the term-limit phenomenon.

NOTES

1. Doug McAdam, John D. McCarthy, and Mayer N. Zald, "Social Movements," in *Handbook of Sociology*, ed. Neil J. Smelser (Beverly Hills, Calif.: Sage, 1988), 695–737.

2. Mark P. Petracca, "Rotation in Office: The History of an Idea," in *Limiting Legislative Terms*, ed. Gerald Benjamin and Michael J. Malbin (Washington, D.C.: CQ Press, 1992), 19–51.

3. Gary W. Copeland and John David Rausch, Jr., "Term Limits in Oklahoma, Colorado, and California in 1990," in *Legislative Term Limits: Public Choice Perspectives*, ed. Bernard Grofman (Boston: Kluwer-Nijhoff, in press).

4. Susan B. Glasser, "Term Limits Measures Win (Except in Utah)," *Roll Call (Washington, D.C.)*, 10 November 1994, 3.

5. See "The Bottom Up," 1 January 1994. "The Bottom Up" is the newsletter of the National Referendum Movement.

6. Ed Vogel, "Term Limits Advocates Won't Fight Ruling," *Las Vegas Review Journal*, 26 September 1992, 1.

7.   Gary W. Copeland and John David Rausch, Jr., "Sendin' 'Em Home Early: Oklahoma and Legislative Term Limitations," *Oklahoma Politics* 2 (Fall 1993): 33–50.
8.   Sula P. Richardson, *Congressional Terms of Office and Tenure: Historical Background and Contemporary Issues*, Report 91–880 GOV (Washington, D.C.: Library of Congress, Congressional Research Service, 1991).
9.   Gary W. Copeland, "Term Limitations and Political Careers in Oklahoma: In, Out, Up, or Down," in *Limiting Legislative Terms*, ed. Benjamin and Malbin, 140.
10.   Lloyd Noble, "Lessons from State Campaigns," in *Term Limits: Sweeping the States?*, Heritage Lecture 397, ed. David M. Mason (Washington, D.C.: Heritage Foundation, 1992), 24.
11.   Ibid.
12.   Copeland and Rausch, "Sendin' 'Em Home Early," 35.
13.   Noble, "Lessons from State Campaigns," 24.
14.   Personal interview with Tom Cole, president of Cole Hargrave Snodgrass & Associates, 6 May 1993.
15.   Noble, "Lessons from State Campaigns," 26.
16.   Patrick B. McGuigan, "Better Sooner Than Later: How the Oklahoma Term Limitation Came to Pass" (paper presented at the annual meeting of the Western Political Science Association, Seattle, Wash., 3 March 1991).
17.   John Greiner, "Voters Pass Measure Limiting State Lawmakers' Terms," *Daily Oklahoman*, 19 September 1990, 1, 2.
18.   Noble, "Lessons from State Campaigns," 32.
19.   Personal interview with Cleta Deatherage Mitchell, director of the Term Limits Legal Institute, 6 May 1993.
20.   Copeland and Rausch, "Sendin' 'Em Home Early," 36.
21.   Steve Lackmeyer, "Walters Backs Limiting Terms in Legislature," *Daily Oklahoman*, 28 May 1990, 8.
22.   Rob Martindale, "Noble Beats Establishment to Win Term Limits," *Tulsa World*, 21 October 1990, A1, A4.
23.   David R. Morgan, Robert E. England, and George C. Humphreys, *Oklahoma Politics and Policies: Governing the Sooner State* (Lincoln: University of Nebraska Press, 1991), 4–6.
24.   McGuigan, "Better Sooner Than Later," 7.
25.   Copeland, "Term Limitations," 142.
26.   McGuigan, "Better Sooner Than Later," 11.
27.   Noble, "Lessons from State Campaigns," 24.
28.   Robert Struble, Jr., "Second Time a Charm: Term Limits in Washington State" (paper presented at the annual meeting of the Western Political Science Association, Pasadena, Calif., March 1993).
29.   Ibid.; David J. Olson, "Term Limits Fail in Washington: The 1991 Battleground," in *Limiting Legislative Terms*, ed. Benjamin and Malbin, 65–96.
30.   Timothy Egan, "Campaign on Term Limits Breeds Unusual Alliances," *New York Times*, 31 October 1991, A1, A14.
31.   Olson, "Term Limits Fail," 70–71.
32.   Struble, "Second Time a Charm," 9–10.
33.   Olson, "Term Limits Fail," 71.
34.   Ibid., 73.
35.   Ibid.

36.   Struble, "Second Time a Charm," 7.

37.   Personal interview with Richard Arnold, CEO of National Voter Outreach, 30 April 1993; Scott Maier, "Outside Money Muddles Who's Boss," *Seattle Post-Intelligencer*, 31 August 1992, A6.

38.   Patti Epler and Les Blumenthal, "Push for Limits: Is It the People or the Powerful?" *The Morning News Tribune* (Tacoma, Wash.), 13 October 1991, A1, A8.

39.   Olson, "Term Limits Fail," 83–85.

40.   Maier, "Outside Money," A6; personal interview with LaDonna Lee, president of Eddie Mahe Company and a founder of Americans to Limit Congressional Terms, 6 May 1993.

41.   Joel Connelly, "Term Limit Law Struck Down," *Seattle Post-Intelligencer*, 11 February 1994, A1, A7.

42.   Personal interview with Phil Handy, chair of Citizens for Limited Political Terms, 5 April 1993.

43.   James R. Hagy, "Handy's Newest: Term Limitations," *Florida Trends*, March 1991, 61.

44.   Handy interview.

45.   Tom Fielder, "The Term Limitation Movement is Headed toward Florida," *Miami Herald*, 23 December 1990, C6.

46.   Phil Handy, "What Next? Initiatives and Other Efforts," in *Term Limits*, ed. Mason, 41.

47.   Amy E. Young, "The Money behind the Movement," *Common Cause*, Summer 1993, 38.

48.   Handy, "What Next?" 41.

49.   "Limits on Terms Urged," *St. Petersburg Times*, 16 April 1991, B4.

50.   Howard Troxler, "Rascals Never Go without a Fight," *St. Petersburg Times*, 6 November 1991, B1; "House Lawyer Opposing Term Limits," *St. Petersburg Times*, 7 November 1991, A2; "Can the State Constitutionally Impose Term Limits on Members of Congress?: A Legal Debate," in *Limiting Legislative Terms*, ed. Benjamin and Malbin, 251–261.

51.   Stuart Rothenberg, "Transplanting Term Limits: Political Mobilization and Grass-Roots Politics," in *Limiting Legislative Terms*, ed. Benjamin and Malbin, 105.

52.   Handy interview.

53.   Elizabeth Willson, "Group Says It Will Get Term Limits on November Ballot," *St. Petersburg Times*, 15 July 1992, A1.

54.   Term-Limit Opponents Give Up," *St. Petersburg Times*, 16 September 1992, B4.

55.   Elizabeth Willson, "Term Limits Quickly Land in Court," *St. Petersburg Times*, 5 November 1992, 1B; "State-By-State Legal Update," *The Legal Limit*, November 1993, 3–4.

56.   Jon Brandt, "Jacobs Forms Varied Alliance in Bid to Limit Taxes, Terms of Politicians," *Grand Rapids Press*, 16 June 1991, F4.

57.   Ibid.

58.   Personal interview with Tim Purdy, director of Pennsylvanians for Term Limits ("Titles in term limits don't always mean anything"), 28 June 1993.

59.   Interview with Mitchell.

60.   Interview with Purdy.

61.   Michael Rust, "Voters Put a Cap on Lawmakers' Terms," *Insight*, 30 November 1992, 11, 32.

62.   Dawson Bell, "Last-Minute Cash Showered on Term Limits Battle," *Detroit Free Press*, 2 November 1992, 3.

63.   Rust, "Voters," 32.

64.   Personal interview with Edward H. Crane, president of the Cato Institute, 10 June 1993.

65.   Rob Martindale, "Term-Limit Campaigner May Lose Post," *Tulsa World*, 7 May 1993, A9. The Associated Press wrote the story a little differently: "A national group seeking to limit terms for members of Congress has deposed a Tulsa oilman who led the drive for term limits for state legislators." "Oklahoma Term-Limits Leader to Resign Post," *Associated Press*, 7 May 1993.

66.   "St. Louis: Gateway for Term Limit Movement; National Leaders Gather to Discuss 1994 Strategy; News Conference on Saturday, Dec. 4," *PRNewswire*, 3 December 1993.

67.   David B. Magleby, *Direct Legislation: Voting on Ballot Propositions in the United States* (Baltimore, Md.: Johns Hopkins University Press, 1984), 184–186.

68.   Personal interview with Robert Murphy, former Oklahoma Libertarian activist, 17 December 1993.

69.   Tom Waldman, "Proposition 140 — Pete Schabarum's Parting Shot," *California Journal*, 1 December 1991, 553–555.

70.   James M. Perry, "Advocate Groups for Congressional Term Limits, though United in Cause, Clash over Strategy," *Wall Street Journal*, 25 August 1993, 10.

71.   Ronald D. Elving, "Congress Braces for Fallout from State Measures," *Congressional Quarterly Weekly Report*, 29 September 1990, 3144.

6

Crime as a Boogeyman: Why Californians Changed Their Constitution to Include a "Victims' Bill of Rights" (and What It Really Did)

Candace McCoy

What happens when state courts disagree with federal courts over constitutional standards? Relying on "independent state grounds,"[1] many state supreme courts have said that a state's constitution is the primary law governing rights of its citizenry. As long as the state affords more rights to a criminally accused person than does the U.S. Constitution via Supreme Court case law, there is no violation of federal law. Of course the states cannot fall short of the federal standard so as to provide *less* protection to a defendant than would federal law, for if they do the higher standards of the federal Constitution will apply and thus bring state law into line with federal. But the states can provide *more* rights. Thus the federalist interplay between national and state standards occurs in the arena of judicial rulings and resulting precedent.

Many state supreme courts have used this states' rights approach to render U.S. Supreme Court case law on the Fourth and Fifth Amendments essentially inapplicable to the acts of local police.[2] They have done so because they think the U.S. Supreme Court has not diligently and appropriately protected the constitutional rights of the criminally accused, preferring instead slavishly to accept police arguments about the difficulties of operating under constitutional constraints.

Paradoxically, giving citizens more rights than the U.S. Constitution requires is often unpopular. The voting public in whose name these rights are developed and invoked is in no mood to hear about how carefully the courts protect the rights of criminals. Given the chance, citizens inflamed over the crime issue will readily abandon civil liberties and direct their anger and fear against anyone who is foolhardy enough to support unpopular law. The genesis and implementation of California's Proposition 8, a "Victims' Bill of Rights" passed on the referendum ballot in 1982, is an apt example of moral entrepreneurship that did indeed give citizens that chance. The results were predictable, but the story of how Proposition 8 was conceived and passed was scarcely foreordained. If anything, it perfectly illustrates the political objectivity of the popular initiative and referendum, a device that is a ready tool for either the right or the left and that enables interest groups or self-interested politicians of any persuasion to circumvent judicial or legislative standards that would otherwise not be vulnerable.

INVENTING THE BOOGEYMAN

There actually was a time in living memory when crime was not regarded as a tremendous social problem. Until the late 1960s, people who were asked in open-ended questions to list the social issues of most concern to them rarely placed crime high on the list.[3] The past three decades, however, produced a spiral of unease, fearmongering, and a consequent continual rise in fear of crime — all in the context of crime trends over three decades that have actually held mostly steady except in a few specific and frightening categories.[4] Nowhere is this dynamic more apparent than in California, a state whose politics are often regarded as a bellwether for the direction of the nation's social discourse. Since the 1960s, California politics about the crime issue have endured heated debate, personal image-making and attack, recall of sitting judges, an initiative proposed and guided through the electoral process by dedicated law-and-order ideologues, and an actual impact of that initiative described as misleading at best and antithetical to public accountability at worst.

The conditions that gave rise to the California crime phenomenon and its subsequent effect on local and constitutional politics are common throughout the nation. Although people living today in nonghetto neighborhoods do not experience significantly more street crime per capita than did their 1960s counterparts, they are considerably more fearful and militant about it. Why is that? The causes, of course, are surely varied, and we cannot prove with certainty that any particular factor is more important than another — or even, if one factor were most important, how much more so it is. Nevertheless, several phenomena seem intuitively related to heightened fear of crime. For example, the media are increasingly sophisticated in their technological reach, and they continue to rely on sensational crime news because it sells well. In addition, a new type of popular television show, the simulation or "docu-drama," blurs the distinction between fact and fiction in concentrating on crime and medical emergency reenactments. The main purpose of such shows is to draw the viewer into a vicarious experience of the crime or medical emergency, which in turn could have the unintended consequence of encouraging many viewers to feel personally victimized and thus fearful.[5] Another factor leading to heightened fear of crime may be that crime itself has changed for the worse — not in rising crime rates in the great bulk of criminal categories, but in specific subcategories of crimes upon which the public mood fixates.[6]

Media sensationalism and the changing nature of some crimes are surely important factors explaining the rise in fear over the past three decades,[7] but equally important is that street crime has been "socially constructed." As Stuart Scheingold states:

The punitive overtones of volitional criminology resonate intensely and insistently with contemporary culture in the United States. But these punitive predispositions are socially constructed and are not uniformly distributed within the society. The politics of criminal process is thus conducted within a fluid cultural context, which, since it is socially constructed, is responsive to political initiatives. The state is, in other words, both constrained by the prevailing culture and a powerful instrument for shaping it. . . . The state has strong incentives for encouraging a . . . punitive interpretation of crime and anomie.[8]

By "socially constructed," Scheingold means that the crime issue would not be so monumentally salient to the general population were it not for powerful political actors who have shaped and even created public fear of crime. To be sure, the presence of particular social variables provides fertile soil into which these actors can plant the seeds of fear and punitiveness. Even if actual incidence of crime per capita is roughly the same, something changed over the last three decades: anomie. *That* social variable increased. In the classic Durkheimian sense of the term, people began to feel disconnected — for reasons probably having very little to do with crime. And when more people feel disconnected, they begin to believe that social norms themselves are irrelevant.

"Anomie stems from impunity — the realization that violations of society's most fundamental rules will go unpunished."9 If the increasingly anomic public could be reassured that norm violations *would* be punished, the person who offers that reassurance would be a hero. Enter the politician and a socially constructed boogeyman.

A primary example to which many commentators refer is George Bush's callous manipulation of the image of Willie Horton in his 1988 presidential contest against Michael Dukakis. Horton had been imprisoned for committing a first-degree assault. He was granted a weekend release, and while thus free he committed a horrible rape and murder. Dukakis was governor of Massachusetts at the time, and he supported the short-time release program through which Horton had been granted a weekend pass. Bush's advertisements showed a picture of Horton, black and menacing, and recounted the crime while placing blame on Dukakis. A vote for Michael Dukakis, the subtext of the advertisement could read, was a vote for a candidate who was soft on crime and not willing to control blacks. Many analysts credit the ad for boosting Bush's momentum in the final days of the race, which he won handily.

In essence, Bush created a boogeyman and then convinced the voters he could protect them from it. The image of crime (interspersed with racial images, a separate and seamy presentation) is thus created, massaged, and manipulated for personal political gain. But perhaps this analysis is more than slightly paranoid: Conspiratorial politicians actually invent the crime issue out of whole cloth, get people to believe them, thus frighten people so much that the voters look for a savior, so the voters then elect the politicians who started the whole thing to begin with? To the contrary — everyone knows, the popular explanation says, that the cycle begins not with politicians but instead with victims of crime themselves. Frightened and angry, they demand that something be done, and politicians respond with hard-line legislation that has little effect on soft-headed judges and revolving-door justice, thus allowing crime to continue unchecked, and beginning anew the cycle of victimization and political responsiveness.10 But data do not support this commonsense understanding, nor do the histories of various statewide campaigns to reform criminal law and procedure by changing state constitutions, such as California's. Instead, observing local anticrime campaigns supports the version of crime as socially constructed for personal political gain, whether it be political office or vindication of a particular ideology.

Consider the example of California's Proposition 8, the Victims' Bill of Rights that used the referendum device to force state constitutional case law back from "independent state grounds" so as to adhere to the bare-bones federal standards. Throughout the 1970s, anticrime politicians had persistently tried to get their ideas translated into legislation, but the state legislature rebuffed them. The state's supreme court, controlled by "liberal legalists,"[11] also resisted the arguments of these hard-line anticrime crusaders, who included local assistant prosecutors and elected state representatives. These struggles occurred at a time when Californians were certainly deeply concerned about social unrest but in which there was no deep-seated or consistent alarm about street crime — an observation that undermines the commonsense assertion that angry citizens are the initial impetus for passing anticrime legislation. Although there are many examples of such citizen activism in relation to particular crimes,[12] broad-based crime-related legislation is usually initiated by politicians who may or may not sincerely believe that statutory reform will significantly affect the crime rate.

Proposition 8 is an example of anticrime legislation and constitutional amendments conceived, drafted, promoted, and implemented by a dedicated group of moral entrepreneurs — politicians who probably sincerely believed that giving constitutional rights to criminals makes crime worse. They also were tireless self-promoters who used the crime issue to convince the voters to elect them. They include Ed Meese, a local assistant district attorney who eventually became attorney general of the United States under Ronald Reagan, and George Nicholson, another assistant district attorney who longed to be governor of California but eventually had to settle for a superior court judgeship in Los Angeles. They were frustrated after trying to convince the state legislature to pass legislation overturning case law from the state supreme court or to pass statutes on their law-and-order "wish list." But these failed efforts seemed to fuel their determination. Soon they turned to the only political forum left open to achieve their goals: the wide-open initiative and referendum process, with its roots firmly planted in populist history and its modern manifestations closely tracking shifting public opinion on a variety of hot topics.

Although the drafters and promoters of Proposition 8 were anticrime activists, their primary intent was that the initiative should drastically change the state's court procedures in criminal cases. (Nevertheless, the connection between tough court procedures and low crime rates, while apparently a matter of faith for law-and-order activists, is unproven.) The state constitutional changes passed in this referendum would wipe out any state case law that gave more protections to criminal defendants than the federal Constitution did, and it changed several other local court procedures, too. To achieve these goals, its promoters had to convince the voters to pass the proposition, and to do so they had to package and sell the legislation. To the boogeyman of crime was added another powerful symbol: his victim.

THE GENESIS OF PROPOSITION 8 — NOT A VICTIM IN SIGHT

Poll data from California in the 1960s depict a public fairly unconcerned about crime.[13] As Gusfield and Edelman would say, citizens were quiescent on the issue.[14] By the 1980s, however, voters approved by an overwhelming majority a ballot initiative designed to curtail constitutional rights of criminal defendants, which the group of law-and-order politicians had portrayed as a powerful means of decreasing crime. Considering that the initiative, Proposition 8 on the June 1982 primary ballot, was titled "A Victims' Bill of Rights," a voter would readily surmise that the interest group that had drafted and promoted the initiative was a victims' advocacy organization. Not so.

The people who drafted, proposed, and promoted the Victims' Bill of Rights were not crime victims. They were the group of right-wing politicians, described above, whose views had been regularly ignored in the liberal politics of California throughout the 1960s and 1970s. They truly believed that crime was the primary social issue of the era and that permissive courts actually encouraged criminal activity by not imposing harsh punishment on factually guilty arrestees. To them, the Fourth, Fifth, Sixth, and Fourteenth Amendments to the Constitution were primarily procedural hurdles to be swiftly jumped on the quick race to conviction and punishment.[15]

In debates over the proposition, they did not state whether any of them personally had actually been a victim of crime, but they surely considered themselves to be victims of the liberal politics of the state supreme court. As a prosecutor handling serious felony cases, for instance, Proposition 8's drafter George Nicholson had lost repeatedly in court and negotiations because of the state supreme court case law.

There is little question that the California Supreme Court under Chief Justice Rose Bird was a classic example of a judicially activist bench and that its activism was from the left. Liberals and conservatives alike regarded the court as result oriented and insensitive to traditional judicial roles, even going so far as to regularly disregard *stare decisis*. Many prosecutors at the time took pains to explain their opposition to the Bird court not as disagreement with its antiprosecution pronouncements, but as disgust with its arbitrary and mindlessly antigovernment decision-making.[16] Given the leftist tilt of the activist Bird court — which is not to say that rightist judges cannot be equally activist[17] — it is hardly surprising that right-wing opposition coalesced early and remained constant until Bird eventually was recalled on the popular ballot and was stripped of her seat on the bench.[18] The first election in which conservatives had tried to unseat Bird was in 1978. (She held onto her judgeship, largely because of support from feminists who thought she had been targeted because she was the first female supreme court chief justice in California's history, not because of the substance of her judicial opinions.)

The same people who eventually proposed and promoted Proposition 8 in 1982 had worked hard to unseat Bird in 1978, so it is safe to say that one of the conditions leading to this anticrime legislation and constitutional amendments in California was the presence of a well-organized group of right-wing legal professionals capable of mounting a statewide attack on case law with which they vehemently disagreed. Another condition leading to passage of Proposition 8 was the conflating of due-process values and liberal ideology in the public mind. The anticrime activists encouraged this analysis.

But a concern for due process, generally defined as "fundamental fairness" in court procedures, is theoretically a value to be cherished by citizens and legal professionals of all political stripes. Ideally, due process is politically neutral, affording identical opportunity for any party to come into court and present a case through well-established procedural stages with well-understood structural expectations. But when a politically activist court from either side of the ideological fence begins to build elaborate rules of procedure and require "ever more exacting"[19] standards of proof, the suspicion grows that the judges are simply using procedural standards to make it harder for disfavored parties to prevail. Of course, such an ideological choice is part of the U.S. Constitution itself, in which the Founders by writing the Fourth, Fifth, and Sixth Amendments consciously chose to favor defendants over the government so as to prevent prosecutors from railroading the innocent. The question is whether a court will expand these procedural protections and also whether the judges are doing so because they dislike the government rather than because they think the procedures essential to "a well-ordered scheme of liberty."[20]

The ex-prosecutors who proposed and advocated Proposition 8 said that the California Supreme Court under Rose Bird had expanded state constitutional case law not from a concern for "fundamental fairness" but from a rabid antigovernment bias. Quite probably, the justices on that court were *both* due-process advocates *and* antigovernment thinkers — a connection that is not necessarily made in the minds of the many judges who are simultaneously pro–due process and pro-prosecution. For these jurists, the issue of how *much* process is due tends to be resolved quickly in favor of precluding extensive procedural challenges, as long as the usual "fundamentally fair" procedures have been followed.

Whatever the objective truth about the thinking processes of the Bird court justices, the point is that the proponents of Proposition 8 were capable of convincing voters that liberal justices used due process to free criminals, presumably from a "soft-headed" misunderstanding of the enormity of the crime problem.

While the purpose of Proposition 8 was to overturn case law on criminal procedure from the state supreme court, the legislation also included many provisions about pretrial processes and sentencing that had been proposed and defeated in the state legislature.[21] These included a limitation on plea bargaining, harsh treatment of habitual offenders, the right of each victim to speak at the sentencing of the offender, and a presumption of restitution for victims in each sentencing. The latter two are the only provisions of Proposition 8 that can objectively be said to relate to "victims' rights," which was the title of the referendum as voters read it in the voting booth. The other provisions concerned victims' rights only under an interpretation that equates victims' rights with court procedures limiting due process.

That interpretation is not based on the actual behavior of most victims. It is difficult to know exactly what victims really want in serious felony cases, other than that almost all agree they want an apology from the offender and restitution for loss of property, wages, and psychological well-being. Beyond that, in regard to court participation, offender sentencing, or legislative reform, what a particular victim wants is a very personal decision that varies tremendously among individual people.[22] But the conservatives who drafted Proposition 8 simply assumed that victims want harsh punishment of their victimizers, with as few constitutional protections in court proceedings as possible.

Other than the requirements of allocution at sentencing and presumption of restitution, Proposition 8 contained no provisions for direct victim influence in criminal prosecutions. Instead, it was simply assumed that victims wanted a harsh criminal justice system and that by providing it, Proposition 8 was a victims' Bill of Rights. The name "Victims' Bill of Rights" was as much a political slogan intended to invoke the image of the innocent victim in order to justify limiting due process for offenders as it was an indication of concern for flesh-and-blood victims of crime.

PROVISIONS OF PROPOSITION 8 AND THEIR IMPACT

First and foremost, Proposition 8 was a list of actions required at various stages of criminal prosecutions. It added new provisions to the state's penal code, and even more important to the fundamental structure of California law, it added new sections to the state's constitution. So its provisions as passed by the voters had different legal characteristics. Some were legislation (usually, only the state legislature writes laws that add to the penal code) and others were constitutional amendments.

To observers who think of constitutional change in terms of the federal model, this may seem strange. The only way to change the U.S. Constitution is through amendment, a difficult process requiring an act of Congress and ratification by a majority of state legislatures. (Of course, case law from the U.S. Supreme Court in effect also changes the Constitution as the Court slowly interprets the document over time, a process that is the same among the states' courts and their constitutions.) But in California and some other states, the fundamental state constitution may be amended or enlarged by laws passed directly by the people.

The device by which this is accomplished in California is the state's "proposition," known to political scientists as the initiative and referendum. When approved by voters on a special ballot, initiatives pass new laws, while referenda block laws already passed by the legislature but with which the voters disagree. The purpose of propositions originally was to enable citizens who were angry at a state legislature controlled by special interests[23] to take matters into their own hands. This exercise in direct democracy is not uncommon; twenty-six states provide for some sort of initiative ballot. California's is especially powerful because it permits a majority of voters to amend the state constitution, the fundamental law of the jurisdiction.

Appellate cases interpreting California's Constitution, which themselves have the status of constitutional law, can also be amended through a ballot "proposition." (Insofar as a proposition adds new law to the constitution, it operates as an initiative; when it changes old law, including appellate case law, it operates as a referendum.) In this way, the group of law-and-order politicians who so despised the decisions of the state supreme court were able to overturn most of that court's criminal procedure pronouncements. The supreme court over which Rose Bird presided was a classic example of a body that gave more rights to the criminally accused than the U.S. Constitution, as interpreted by the federal Supreme Court, required. By rendering inactive the Bird court case law, Proposition 8 represented the winning trump card in a nasty game of give-and-take between conservative, hardline ideologues and their equally ideological counterparts on the left.

What were these particular provisions? Examples of new constitutional standards that Proposition 8 set into law and that directly overturned cases from the state supreme court are: (1) a scaled-back exclusionary rule; (2) a requirement that prior felony convictions be proven before the jury in open court; (3) a requirement that "public safety," not whether the defendant would be likely to show up in court for trial, must be the basis of bail decisions; (4) permission to make unlimited use of prior criminal convictions for purposes of impeaching the credibility of the defendant at trial[24]; and (5) abolition of the "diminished capacity" defense.[25]

These provisions seem puzzling in their technical detail. Most people accustomed to the federal Constitution would be surprised to see such specific standards, since the federal constitutional provisions governing criminal procedure are the very general policy statements of the Fourth, Fifth, Sixth, Eighth, and Fourteenth Amendments. Specifics such as a remedy for Fourth or Fifth Amendment violations (the exclusionary rule) or rules for impeaching witness credibility are left to case interpretation, not made part of the text of the document. If Congress wanted to abolish the exclusionary rule outright, for instance, it could not.[26] To change the Supreme Court case law that promulgated and upheld the exclusionary rule, Congress can bite around its edges by carving out huge exceptions to it, or Congress can approve a constitutional amendment abolishing the rule. Such an amendment would have to be ratified by the states, of course. These actions are very difficult to accomplish.

But the California Constitution can be much more easily amended, because initiatives approved directly by voters and thus bypassing the legislature have the force of constitutional law. The result is a cluttered document covering minutiae on a variety of subjects, but at least, arguably, it is the result of a directly expressed popular will. In the case of Proposition 8, the legal effect was to amend the state constitution and thus eliminate "independent state grounds" for the majority of criminal procedure standards enunciated by the unpopular state supreme court.[27]

The political effect was not so clear cut. George Nicholson, the drafter and promoter of the proposition, was a candidate in the Republican primary election for governor on the same ballot as Proposition 8. Clearly, he had hoped that his close identification with an anticrime law would help his election chances. It did not; he was defeated, although the proposition was approved. Somewhat surprising, it did not pass overwhelmingly. Only 56.4 percent of the state's voters approved it, while 43.6 percent did not. Perhaps this indicated some opposition to using the plight of victims as an opportunity to limit the scope of the constitutional rights of defendants, but more likely it reflected voter loyalty to the editorial opinions of the *Los Angeles Times*. The *Times* had come out against the measure as a "quick fix" likely to hurt the justice system but make no difference on crime.

The practical effect of the proposition is what matters most, of course. Whether it prevented crime is completely unprovable one way or another because of the oldest methodological glitch in criminology: You cannot measure deterrence, because by definition if it works nothing happens, and if nothing happens there is nothing to measure. In addition, even if we could prove that crime has declined — crime in California did decline somewhat in the period immediately after passage of Proposition 8, for instance, though it soon crept back up to previous levels — we cannot ascribe causation. Crime goes down or up depending on a wide variety of factors, and legislation may or may not be one of them.

Certainly, however, we can assess the impact of Proposition 8 on court functioning. Most of Proposition 8's provisions were aimed at reform of criminal procedures, with the underlying assumption that crime would decrease if courts got tougher. Although criminologists cannot assess whether crime decreased, they *can* measure whether sentencing became more severe after the measure passed and, if so, whether the change was probably attributable to the new law. They can also observe and assess the impact of such provisions as victim restitution and allocution at sentencing. More difficult is to evaluate the effect of the law on criminal prosecution — pretrial processes such as bail and plea bargaining, trial rules related to witness impeachment, and so on. These are more difficult to evaluate only because to do so requires an insider's understanding of how the procedures worked before the law was passed as well as after.

Very briefly, here is an overview of what Proposition 8 actually did. Note at the outset, however, it is very difficult to assess the effects of those provisions that actually changed the state's constitution, because they were very broad and thus almost impossible to evaluate empirically. For instance, Proposition 8 added the "right to safe schools" to the state constitution. It carved back the exclusionary rule so as to fit the federal standard. It required restitution for crime victims. All these were made provisions of the state constitution. School safety is extremely difficult to measure, as is — perhaps surprisingly — the effect of the exclusionary rule.[28] As for restitution, all indications are that courts had been regularly requiring restitution be paid even before Proposition 8 amended the state constitution, so the effect of the new constitutional provision was simply to continue business as usual.

Proposition 8 also amended the state's penal code; in essence, these provisions wrote new statutory law. Sentences for serious felons were required to be harsher, victims were to be given the right to speak at sentencing, plea bargaining was to be limited, and other court reforms regarding evidentiary standards of proof were required.

Sentencing severity is studied in two ways. First is the probation/prison dichotomy: whether a convicted offender received a county jail sentence coupled with probation or whether the offender received a state prison term, which would be a harsher sentence. The second way to measure sentencing severity is the average length of prison terms of that group of offenders who did go to prison. Results of analysis using the probation/prison measure, over time in a time-series analysis of sentences imposed, indicates that "the Victims' Bill of Rights did not cause more people to be sentenced to prison. Rather, "the post–Proposition 8 increase in imprisonment . . . was only the continuation of a trend begun earlier" and also the statistical result of sending mentally disturbed sex offenders to prisons instead of asylums.[29] But perhaps the length of sentence of those offenders who did indeed go to prison became longer? State and local statistics do not bear out this prediction. "Proposition 8 did not push aggregate sentence lengths upward. Offenders sentenced to prison did not, on the average, receive longer prison terms."[30] However, of that very small group of offenders who were sentenced as habitual criminals — which assumes a conviction and proof of prior record, which the prosecutor in his or her discretion may choose to include at sentencing or not — in all probability prison sentences did indeed become harsher.[31]

Victim allocution at sentencing was another Proposition 8 requirement. All victims had the right to attend the sentencing, submit facts to the court about the crime and its effect on the victim, and speak in court about the preferred sentence. An impact study found that only a minority of victims actually exercised the right and showed up in court for the sentencing, but those who did were satisfied with court procedures.[32] There is no way to assess whether victim allocution at sentencing influenced judges one way or another in determining the final sentence.

Proposition 8 also added to California's penal code a "limitation on plea bargaining."[33] Its effect was neither to increase sentencing severity nor decrease the volume of plea bargaining. But it *did* change the way plea bargaining was conducted, and in doing so it simply sped up the process so that serious felons would plead guilty very quickly, often within a few days of arraignment.[34] This is exactly what its drafters had intended. Experienced prosecutors, they wanted to dispose of serious cases quickly and with the minimum of evidentiary or legal challenge. The result of Proposition 8's "limitation" on plea bargaining was that a significant percentage of cases that formerly had been subjected to preliminary hearings instead ended in guilty pleas within a few days of arrest.

Preliminary hearings, which usually take about an hour, are pretrial proceedings in which victims may testify or see other evidence against the defendant produced in open court. If there is enough evidence to establish probable cause to hold the defendant, the case would be sent on to the trial court. Prior to Proposition 8, most defendants would plead guilty after the preliminary hearing but before the trial. The effect of Proposition 8 was to convince them to plead guilty even before the preliminary hearing, thus avoiding a technical plea bargaining "ban" that Proposition 8 had placed on the trial court.

While this outcome of the new law was surely what its drafters had intended, it is exactly antithetical to the usual understanding of the meaning of "victims' rights." In a preliminary hearing, a victim can testify, or at least confront the defendant by providing proof of guilt to be used in court. The victim and the public can see in open court the evidence that will be used to prove guilt beyond a reasonable doubt, or they will see evidence that may look shaky and thus might not reach that standard of proof necessary for conviction. By pushing plea bargaining to a pretrial stage even before the preliminary hearing, Proposition 8 served its drafters' intent of limiting due process, but it can scarcely be said that the impact of the law was to help victims. Perhaps equally important, one of the few chances for public accountability of the guilty plea process — that is, the one time when evidence is aired in public and not in private negotiations between the prosecutor and defender — was closed.

CONCLUSIONS: CONDITIONS ASSOCIATED
WITH CONSTITUTIONAL LAWMAKING
THROUGH THE INITIATIVE BALLOT

California's experience with constitutional amendment through the initiative and referendum ballot is not unique, but the story of Proposition 8 in 1982 is a particularly stark case study of this electoral device in action. It clearly isolates several factors present in the political life of the state in the late 1970s and throughout the 1980s that, taken together, constitute observable conditions from which any political entity would expect constitutional change to emerge. There are three major factors: (1) an ideological war over an important question of public policy (in this case, crime and due process), (2) sociological conditions under which manipulation of public opinion was possible, and (3) the availability of the initiative and referendum device to pass constitutional amendments.

The issues in the ideological war over crime and punishment in California throughout the 1970s and 1980s are not difficult to imagine, because proponents of each position baldly stated their preferences and the reasons for them. The battle began because of judicial activism. The state supreme court, disregarding the traditional role of judicial restraint and adherence to precedent, chose invariably to oppose the government's position in a number of policy arenas. While the court's stance could be labeled "proconsumer" in tort cases or "antibusiness" in labor cases, in criminal procedure it would most correctly be labeled "antigovernment," and it painstakingly interpreted defendants' procedural protections so as to hold prosecutors to exacting standards of proof. Opponents of the court's decisions, though, explained these stances in public so as to successfully paint the court as "procrime."

Applying the Newtonian principle to politics, for every action there is an equal and opposite reaction. The actions of the state supreme court were met with vehement opposition from the right. A group of politicians and former district attorneys organized and began to work hard to change the supreme court case law. They doggedly and vehemently denounced the decisions as prodefendant and therefore, logically, as procrime. They also knew how difficult it was to be a prosecutor applying this case law, and they set out to make procedure more favorable to prosecution.

To do this, they skillfully manipulated public opinion as ammunition in the ideological war. Voters who were not initially alarmed about court standards were nevertheless experiencing a growing sense of anomie.

There was sincere concern over a real social problem, crime and disorder, that prompted voters to feel uneasy and alienated. Proponents of Proposition 8 skillfully encouraged them to express their frustration about perceived normlessness by focusing on a figure that represented the phenomenon: the criminal. This intensified citizens' fear of crime, although their risk of victimization had not objectively increased much. Socially constructed crime waves were blamed on a boogeyman — the criminal; a socially constructed sympathetic figure in whose name legislation would be passed gave its name to the proposition — the victim.

None of this legislation amending the state constitution and statutes could have been passed had California not permitted initiative and referendum on the popular ballot. In this case study, the device was used skillfully by right-wing ideologues who served both their own self-interests as prosecutors and what they perceived as the public good. But any group of entrepreneurs, whether from the right or the left, could use proposition process and politics to achieve their goals if they are thwarted in traditional lawmaking arenas. That is the real lesson about constitutional amendment that this case study teaches. Whether this political structure is wise depends on how much power individual citizens should have to change the state's constitution and statutes. In this case, as with most ballot initiatives involving fundamental legal change, a special interest group, not a public-minded citizenry, was the primary catalyst for making complex constitutional change.

NOTES

1. "Independent state grounds" can be defined as the situation whereby "citizens have greater rights in some respects under the constitution of their state than under the federal Constitution"; where "state constitutions are independent sources of civil rights and liberties" (Joseph R. Grodin, *In Pursuit of Justice: Reflections of a State Supreme Court Justice*, with a foreword by Justice William J. Brennan, Jr. [Berkeley: University of California Press, 1989], 122 and 124). Grodin's discussion of independent state grounds in that book is placed in the context of the California cases from the supreme court headed by Chief Justice Rose Bird, discussed in the text.

In general, see Brennan, "The Bill of Rights and the States: The Revival of State Constitutions as Guardians of Individual Rights," *New York University Law Review* 61 (October 1986): 535–553.

2. See Barry Latzer, "California's Constitutional Counterrevolution," chap. 7, this volume.

3. Stuart Scheingold, *The Politics of Law and Order: Street Crime and Public Policy* (New York: Longman, 1984), 43–46.

4. Samuel Walker, *Sense and Nonsense about Crime*, 2d ed. (Pacific Grove, Calif.: Brooks/Cole, 1989). Note also that while occurrence per capita of street crimes such as rape, armed robberies, or burglaries has not increased much over the past two decades, firearms use among younger and younger children has. Further, it only takes a few sensational and catastrophic crimes of terrorism on domestic soil, such as the World Trade Center and Oklahoma City bombings, to sow a feeling of helpless vulnerability in a population not otherwise statistically more subject to criminal victimization.

5. For a haunting account of how these shows are produced and how they distort their depiction of crime and police work, see Debra Seagal, "Tales from the Cutting-Room Floor: The Reality of 'Reality-Based' Television," *Harper's*, November 1993, 50.

6. For example, widely reported cases of car-jackings in which car owners were fatally injured, or drive-by gang shootings, or assaults and homicides committed by increasingly younger teenagers, all are big news stories that titillate and fascinate and eventually come to be regarded as examples of common crimes widespread in every neighborhood in every city. In fact, these crimes are mostly concentrated in poor or gang-infested neighborhoods, except for the one major change of the past decade that indeed is distributed across class boundaries: greatly increased gun use. Assaults that used to be committed with knives, from which victims would recover, are now committed with deadly instruments. Teenagers both in school and on the street no longer play status games with the switchblades of the 1950s; they do so with guns. The crimes have not changed but the means of committing them have become more deadly.

7. Most careful commentators agree that the connection between media depictions of crime and violence and general fearfulness is probably quite real, but nevertheless it is difficult to measure. In fact, it is a methodological nightmare. Although we can prove that "the frequency of actual victimization and the relative proportions of violent and property crime do not match people's concerns, the media are more suspect. When we chart its impact, media coverage of crime may be an important source of 'vicarious victimization.' On the other hand, there are a number of reasons to believe that the attitudinal and behavioral impact of media messages about crime may not be that significant. The media are sources of impressions about crime which are remote from actual events. Being at best secondhand accounts of crime, stories of specific incidents which are channeled to the citizenry in this way may be stripped of most of their emotional content. . . . Finally, we may not be able to discern much of an effect of the media because it [the effect] does not vary much. There is little variation from place to place in terms of media coverage. In one way or another, the bulk of the population is exposed to these messages. When almost everyone receives virtually the same message, studies of individual differences in media consumption and fear cannot reveal its consequences" (Wesley Skogan and Michael Maxfield, *Coping with Crime: Individual and Neighborhood Reactions*, vol. 124, Sage Library of Social Research [Beverly Hills, Calif.: Sage, 1981], 143–144).

8. Stuart Scheingold, *The Politics of Street Crime* (Philadelphia, Pa.: Temple University Press, 1991), 22.

9. Ibid., 17, paraphrasing Ralf Dahrendorf, *Law and Order* (London: Stevens, 1985).

10. James Q. Wilson is the leading presenter of the notion that crime legislation is an example of responsiveness to public outcry by elected representatives (Wilson,

Thinking about Crime, rev. ed. [New York: Basic Books, 1983]).

11.   The phrase is George Will's, from an editorial he wrote in the *Washington Post* denouncing the Rose Bird court. He says that liberal legalists "fear above all else 'arbitrary' government and would prevent it by purifying procedures — process, process, and more process, in the form of hearings, lawyers, and ever more refined evidentiary rules and more exacting burdens of proof" (Will, "Judicial Kerosene," *Washington Post*, 12 February 1986, 10).

12.   The best national example is efforts by the group Mothers Against Drunk Driving, which was a spontaneous outpouring of activism by people whose families were victims of drunk drivers and who believed the law was too lenient in punishing them. See also local examples of spontaneous grass-roots activism where heinous crime sparks intense grieving, concern, and lobbying for legislation to address the problem. An example is Megan's Law, the New Jersey statute passed in 1994, requiring notification of a community when a sex offender is paroled and will live there. Megan Kanka, a young girl from Hamilton, New Jersey, had been raped and murdered by a recently paroled sex offender. After the law went into effect, the first notification to a community provoked a frightening reaction. Neighbors set upon the person they thought was the parolee and beat him. It was the wrong person.

13.   Candace McCoy, *Politics and Plea Bargaining: Victims' Rights in California* (Philadelphia, Pa.: University of Pennsylvania Press, 1994), 12–13.

14.   Murray Edelman, *The Symbolic Uses of Politics* (Chicago: University of Chicago Press, 1964); and Joseph R. Gusfield, *The Symbolic Crusade: Status Politics and the American Temperance Movement* (Urbana: University of Illinois Press, 1963).

15.   This language is borrowed from Herbert L. Packer's seminal work, *The Limits of the Criminal Sanction* (Palo Alto, Calif.: Stanford University Press, 1968), in which he delineates the value systems of "crime control advocates" and "due process advocates" regarding the nature of constitutional rights.

16.   In any discussion of California courts written in 1995, it is hard to avoid reference to the O. J. Simpson case. The fair-minded judge in that case, Lance Ito, was a Los Angeles prosecutor at the time the Bird court controlled California criminal procedure. Outside the strictures of the trial courtroom, he exercised his right to free speech as many Californians do: on his license plate. It read: "7 BOZOS" (Jeffrey Toobin, "Ito and the Truth School," *The New Yorker*, 27 March 1995, 46).

17.   The most frequently cited contemporary example are the opinions of U.S. Supreme Court Justice Antonin Scalia. Unlike the California Supreme Court under Bird, however, the U.S. Supreme Court has no voting bloc of justices to almost always give a majority vote to the activists' preferences.

18.   See Preble Stolz, *Judging Judges* (New York: Free Press, 1981); and newspaper accounts of the election in November 1986, which describe Bird losing her judgeship in the second recall election in which opponents had tried to take it from her.

19.   Will, "Judicial Kerosene," 10.

20.   Procedural due process (as distinguished from substantive due process, a concept that carries its own intellectual baggage) was defined in a series of U.S. Supreme Court cases that first considered whether the federal Bill of Rights applied to the states. In *Palko v. Connecticut*, 302 U.S. 319 (1937), Cardozo defined procedural safeguards necessary to effectuate due process to be "of the very essence of a scheme of ordered liberty." Harlan simply defined due process as "fundamental procedural

fairness" (*Duncan v. Louisiana*, 391 U.S. 145 [1968], sec. 2). See other cases cited in *Duncan* to follow the incorporation debate.

21. For a list of such provisions, see McCoy, "Politics and Plea Bargaining," 22–23.

22. See a collection of articles in Arthur J. Lurigio, Wesley G. Skogan, and Robert C. Davis, eds., *Victims of Crime: Problems, Policies, and Programs*, Sage Criminal Justice System Annuals, vol. 25 (Newbury Park, Calif.: Sage, 1990).

23. Thomas E. Cronin, *Direct Democracy: The Politics of Initiative, Referendum, and Recall* (Cambridge, Mass.: Harvard University Press, 1989).

24. McCoy, "Politics and Plea Bargaining," 29 and footnotes accompanying that text. These particular provisions became section 28 of the California Constitution.

25. This was accomplished by adding section 25(a) to the penal code. See Frederic Ron Krausz, "The Relevance of Innocence: Proposition 8 and the Diminished Capacity Defense," *California Law Review* 71 (July 1983): 1197–1215.

26. Not to say it has not tried. It has codified the good faith exception to the warrant requirement (first enunciated by the Supreme Court in *United States v. Leon*, 468 U.S. 897 [1984]) and is now attempting to push further by formulating a good faith defense to searches made without a warrant, too. See bills before the 1995 session of Congress. The Supreme Court so far has declined to rule on the good faith exception to warrantless searches.

27. For example, the state's supreme court upheld the Proposition 8 provision carving back the standards for search and seizure and the exclusionary rule so as to comport only with federal case law. *In re Lance W.*, 37 Cal. 3d 873 (1985); *modified*, 38 Cal. 3d 412. See also McCoy, "Politics and Plea Bargaining," 44–45 for a more detailed list of cases upholding various provisions of Proposition 8. For a detailed insider's view of the *Lance* case and several others that arose under Proposition 8, see Grodin, *In Pursuit of Justice*, 102–117.

Compare examples of interpretive conundrums that arise when the opposite political configuration obtains: The state case law provides a stronger exclusionary rule than the federal. What happens if state police make the arrest in a case that is then prosecuted in federal court? A strong argument can be made that the strict state rule should apply in federal court, since the exclusionary rule is intended to control police misconduct and the police involved in the case were state police. See Kenneth J. Melilli, "Exclusion of Evidence in Federal Prosecutions on the Basis of State Law," *Georgia Law Review* 22 (Spring 1988): 667–739.

28. Thomas Y. Davies, "A Hard Look at What We Know (and Still Need to Learn) about the 'Costs' of the Exclusionary Rule: The NIJ Study and Other Studies of 'Lost' Arrests," *American Bar Foundation Research Journal* 3 (1983): 611–690.

29. McCoy, "Politics and Plea Bargaining," 97.

30. Ibid., 101. Data and methods of analysis to determine the impact of Proposition 8 on sentencing severity are presented in detail there.

31. Proposition 8's sentencing enhancements for habitual criminals presaged contemporary "three-strikes-and-you're-out" laws. The immense discretion accorded prosecutors under Proposition 8 resulted in the use of enhancements for recidivism as bargaining chips in plea negotiation. If the defendant would plead guilty, the enhancement would be dropped. Thus only a small percentage of offenders who faced the harsher sentences because of prior records actually had them imposed. But of those who did receive the enhancements, sentences were considerably more severe.

32.   Virginia Neto, *Victim Allocution in Sentencing in California* (Washington, D.C.: National Institute of Justice, 1984). See also Dean G. Kilpatrick and Randy K. Otto, "Constitutionally Guaranteed Participation in Criminal Proceedings for Victims: Potential Effects on Psychological Functioning," *Wayne Law Review* 34 (Fall 1987): 7–28.

33.   California Penal Code, sec. 1192.7.

34.   For a complete description of how this happened, procedurally, see McCoy, "Politics and Plea Bargaining," 89–95 and 97–124 (impact on guilty plea and trial rates and timing of pleas) and 129–166 (impact on professional norms of court workers).

III

CASE STUDIES:
THE CONSEQUENCES OF
CONSTITUTIONAL CHANGE

7

California's Constitutional Counterrevolution

Barry Latzer

This is a study of a largely successful popular attempt to redirect a state supreme court. In the 1980s a mobilized California electorate, distressed over many of the decisions of the highest tribunal in the state, especially on issues of criminal justice, used the ballot box to oust three of its justices and amend the state constitution in order to compel more favorable rulings. The strategy worked very effectively — up to a point. The court changed from a liberal, procriminal defendant institution, to a moderate (conservative?) body much more sympathetic to a law enforcement perspective. When, however, conservative groups pushed even further in the 1990s, seeking to replicate their success with another, even more sweeping state constitutional amendment, they were effectively rebuffed by the now-moderate supreme court.

Notwithstanding this somewhat unexpected ending, this study shows that state constitutional politics is distinct from the politics of the federal Constitution in at least two striking ways. First, because of the relative ease of making personnel changes on state courts, state constitutional politics is more likely to involve direct public campaigns against state judges. Second, because it is far easier to amend state constitutions than it is to amend the U.S. Constitution, state constitutional politics invites more frequent attempts to alter the constitutional text. These tactics are much more likely to be effective in altering policies at the state level than at the federal.

Consider first the position of state judges. Shielded by the aura of the black robe, state judges, like their federal counterparts, usually face only unfocused and unspecific public demands. The means usually used to persuade them — legal argumentation — is esoteric and subtle, a method of persuasion available only to professionals specially trained to communicate with courts. The public prefers to perceive its judges as impartial guardians of a higher law, as neutrals above the political fray, not as politicians subject to such rough and tumble activities as lobbying and electioneering. Nevertheless, an aroused public opinion can quite effectively change the policy orientation of a state supreme court.

State supreme court judges, when compared with their federal counterparts, have a special vulnerability. Unlike the justices of the U.S. Supreme Court, state judges are usually voted into, and sometimes may be voted out of, office. Judges of the U.S. Supreme Court (they are not called "justices" in the Constitution) are, of course, appointed by the president of the United States, with the advice and consent of the U.S. Senate, and without any direct public input.[1] They serve for as long as they wish "during good behavior," are insulated from direct popular sanction, and are almost never disciplined.[2] By contrast, state high court judges are popularly elected to their positions in twenty-three states, are subject to retention election after initial appointment in sixteen states, and may be removed by the voters in six states.[3] To be sure, the public does not readily discipline state judges, but California proves that it can happen.

Moreover, the state bench's most sacred tomes — the state constitutions — are much more amenable to revision than the U. S. Constitution and considerably more subject to direct popular influence. The U.S. Constitution, which provides for little direct public input into a cumbersome amending process, has seen only thirty-three amendments proposed to the states in all of American history, twenty-six of which have been approved.[4] Whereas the U.S. Supreme Court can rely with some assurance on the difficulty of altering the U.S. Constitution as a bulwark against effective second-guessing, the work of the state courts is much more subject to challenge. Nearly all of the states provide for some popular input on proposed state constitutional amendments, usually requiring only a simple majority to approve proposals made by state legislatures or state constitutional conventions.[5] Seventeen states, including California, allow state constitutional amendment by initiative, that is, adoption of amendments by direct popular vote without the prior approval of the legislature or of a constitutional convention.[6] As a consequence of these liberal amending procedures, the states have been accused of "amendomania"; over 8,000 state constitutional amendments have been proposed, over 5,000 approved.[7]

Both of the above tactics — unseating the judges and amending the state constitution — were utilized in California and, until the overplaying of the conservative hand in 1990, were utilized most effectively. In three hot-button areas of court activity respecting criminal justice — capital punishment, search and seizure, and *Miranda* rights — the California judiciary was forced to back off from aggressively liberal positions and adopt a more conservative stance.

This study is in seven parts. The first part provides background on the California Constitution and the California Supreme Court. Part two examines selected death penalty decisions of the California Supreme Court, comparing U.S. Supreme Court rulings on the subject and analyzing the impact of the California cases upon the state constitution and on California judicial politics. Parts three and four provide the same type of analysis for search and seizure and for *Miranda* cases, respectively. The fifth part relates how conservative forces in California compelled a rollback of many of the court's liberal decisions. Part six describes the limitation of the public initiative process. The chapter closes with some observations on state constitutional law and the redirection of state courts.

BACKGROUND: THE CALIFORNIA CONSTITUTION AND THE CALIFORNIA SUPREME COURT

The California Constitution, like the constitutions of the other forty-nine states, contains a bill of rights the text of which roughly parallels the Bill of Rights in the federal Constitution. In the state constitutions, the rights provisions are usually found in the first article of the document, whereas the Bill of Rights is an appended set of amendments. The state provisions are usually textually similar to the federal, sometimes identical, occasionally quite different. There is no necessary correlation between text and interpretation, however. Identical state and federal provisions have been construed differently, and dissimilar provisions are often construed identically.

The California Constitution provides rights for criminal defendants that appear to be very much like the rights established by the Fourth, Fifth, Sixth, and Eighth Amendments of the U.S. Constitution. Table 7.1 enables ready comparison of the federal and state text.

TABLE 7.1
Selected Criminal Justice Provisions in the U.S. and California Constitutions

California Constitution	U.S. Constitution
Article 1, section 13 Search and Seizure The right of the people to be secure in their persons, houses, papers, and effects against unreasonable seizures and searches may not be violated; and a warrant may not issue except on probable cause, supported by oath or affirmation, particularly describing the place to be searched and the persons and things to be seized.	Amendment 4 Search and Seizure The right of the people to be secure in their persons, houses, papers, and effects, against unreasonable searches and seizures, shall not be violated, and no Warrants shall issue, but upon probable cause, supported by Oath or affirmation, and particularly describing the place to be searched, and the persons or things to be seized.
Article 1, section 15 Self-Incrimination Persons may not . . . be compelled in a criminal cause to be a witness against themselves.	Amendment 5 Self-Incrimination nor shall any person be . . . compelled in any Criminal Case to be a witness against himself
Article 1, section 15 Double Jeopardy Persons may not twice be put in jeopardy for the same offense.	Amendment 5 Double Jeopardy nor shall any person be subject for the same offence to be twice put in jeopardy of life or limb
Article 1, section 15 Speedy Public Trial* The defendant in a criminal cause has the right to a speedy public trial.	Amendment 6 Speedy Public Trial In all criminal prosecutions, the accused shall enjoy the right to a speedy and public trial
Article 1, section 15 Confrontation to be confronted with the witnesses against the defendant	Amendment 6 Confrontation to be confronted with the witnesses against him

152

Amendment 6 Compulsory Process
  to have compulsory process for obtaining Witnesses in his favor

Amendment 6 Counsel
  to have the Assistance of Counsel for his defence

Amendment 6 Jury Trial
  by an impartial jury of the State and district wherein the crime shall have been committed, which district shall have been previously ascertained by law

Article 3, section 2 Jury Trial
  The Trial of all Crimes, except in Cases of Impeachment, shall be by Jury; and such Trial shall be held in the State where the said Crimes shall have been committed. . . .

Amendment 8 Punishment
  nor excessive fines imposed, nor cruel and unusual punishments inflicted.

Article 1, section 15 Compulsory Process
  to compel attendance of witnesses in the defendant's behalf

Article 1, section 15 Counsel
  to have the assistance of counsel for the defendant's defense, [and] to be personally present with counsel

Article 1, section 16 Jury Trial
  Trial by jury is an inviolate right and shall be secured to all. . . . A jury may be waived in a criminal cause by the consent of both parties expressed in open court by the defendant and the defendant's counsel. . . . In criminal actions in which a felony is charged, the jury shall consist of 12 persons. In criminal actions in which a misdemeanor is charged, the jury shall consist of 12 persons or a lesser number agreed on by the parties in open court.

Article 1, section 17 Punishment
  Cruel or unusual punishment may not be inflicted or excessive fines imposed.

* Comparable rights are also provided by the California Constitution, art. 1, sec. 29: "In a criminal case, the people of the State of California have the right to due process of law and to a speedy and public trial."

On their face, with the exception of certain jury and counsel rights, and a separate state right to privacy, the California and federal criminal justice rights are textually equivalent. However, after about 1970, the interpretation of the California Constitution by the state supreme court began to diverge significantly from the interpretation given the federal fundamental charter. This divergence, sometimes referred to as the "new judicial federalism," is at the heart of the controversy underlying this chapter.

From the time California became the thirty-first state in 1850 until over a century later, the criminal justice rights in Article 1 of the state constitution received relatively little attention from the California high court.[8] This changed dramatically in the 1970s, not coincidentally, at a time when the U.S. Supreme Court underwent significant personnel and doctrinal change. The end of the Warren Court and the rise of the Burger Court appeared to foretoken a narrowing of the federal constitutional rights of criminal defendants.[9] When the Burger Court signaled that it would no longer be looking to expand defendants' rights and would rather create exceptions that favored the prosecution, some of the state courts discovered that they could preserve and expand these rights by interpreting *state* constitutional bills of rights provisions more broadly than comparable federal provisions.[10] Such state court cases are generally not subject to Supreme Court review, and therefore they could not be reversed by the Burger or Rehnquist justices.[11] These state constitutional decisions were frequently a source of dissension because of their implications for criminal justice policy. The expansion of defendant's rights rendered prosecution and conviction more difficult at the very time when crime in the United States was rising to new heights.[12]

For a fifteen-year period, from 1971 to 1986, the California Supreme Court was among the most controversial of American tribunals. It was in the forefront of the new judicial federalism. It was one of the first and most persistent state courts of last resort to reject U.S. Supreme Court interpretations in favor of enlarged state rights. Prior to the 1970s, the California Supreme Court had established a national reputation under Chief Justice Phil S. Gibson (1940–1964), and under the intellectual leadership of Associate Justice Roger J. Traynor (1940–1970).[13] But most of the court's reputation was built on its work in traditional areas of state law, such as tort law, not in constitutional law, federal or state.[14] In criminal law, for example, although Traynor authored an opinion endorsing the exclusionary rule for illegal searches and seizures six years before the U.S. Supreme Court mandated it nationally in *Mapp v. Ohio,* the decision was grounded on judicially created rules of evidence, subject to legislative revision, not constitutional law, which is virtually immune from legislative review.[15] Thus, the court was "activist," but not in a way that created anatagonism with the state legislature.

We will now analyze some of the controversial California Supreme Court decisions made during the period extending from the 1970s to the 1990s in three areas: the death penalty, search and seizure, and *Miranda.* For each category the focus will be on the use of the state constitution to broaden rights beyond those guaranteed under the U.S. Constitution and the ways in which these decisions engendered significant opposition to the state high court.

THE DEATH PENALTY IN CALIFORNIA

Insofar as criminal justice policy is concerned, perhaps no issue separates liberals and conservatives more than capital punishment. Under the Eighth Amendment ("nor cruel and unusual punishments inflicted"), as currently construed by the Supreme Court, executions are permitted for homicides committed with certain specified aggravating circumstances, such as murder for hire, or during the commission of another serious felony, or murder of an on-duty police or corrections officer.[16]

The Supreme Court did not reach its position until 1976 in *Gregg v. Georgia,* and then only over the passionate protest of liberal Warren Court holdovers, William J. Brennan, Jr., and Thurgood Marshall. Four years earlier, in *Furman v. Georgia,* Brennan and Marshall had been part of the Court majority that declared the death penalty violative of the Eighth Amendment, but they alone contended that the death penalty was inherently and irredeemably unconstitutional.[17]

In 1972, shortly before the *Furman* ruling, the California Supreme Court, in *People v. Anderson,* resolved the death penalty question on state constitutional grounds, expressly eschewing the federal Eighth Amendment issue.[18] In 1965, Robert Page Anderson shot and killed a San Diego pawn shop clerk and was captured at the scene after a shoot-out with police. A jury found Anderson guilty of murder and sentenced him to death, a sentence initially upheld on appeal to the state supreme court.[19] However, the defendant sought further review with habeas corpus petitions and two years later, in 1968, the sentence was set aside.[20] It was reimposed by a second jury following another sentencing trial, and once again Anderson appealed to the California Supreme Court. This set the stage for the court's controversial 1972 state constitutional ruling.

The vote was 6-1 in favor of reversal. Chief Justice Donald R. Wright, appointed by Governor Ronald Reagan in 1970, wrote the opinion of the court. Justice Marshall F. McComb, who wrote the opinion in the first Supreme Court ruling in *Anderson,* upholding the death penalty, was the lone dissenter. The majority opinion made quite clear that it was relying upon the state cruel or unusual punishments clause, not the federal, for its decision. This is significant not only because of its implications for the construction of the state constitution but also for the procedural posture of the case. If a state court rests its decision on state and not federal grounds, the U.S. Supreme Court generally cannot review the case.[21] Thus, Anderson's victory could not be judicially challenged by the prosecution since no higher court could take jurisdiction.

With respect to the state constitution, Chief Justice Wright emphasized that, unlike the federal Eighth Amendment, Article 1, section 6 (later renumbered section 17), prohibits cruel *or* unusual punishments. The difference, he contended, was significant, because the use of the disjunctive signifies that either characteristic alone — cruelty or unusualness — would render a punishment unconstitutional. The federal provision, written in the conjunctive, requires proof that the penalty is both cruel *and* unusual. As the opinion progressed it soon became clear that this argument was unnecessary: The court found that the death penalty was both cruel and unusual. The court also dismissed as "mere speculation and conjecture" the contention that other state constitutional provisions, such as the one granting the supreme court "appellate jurisdiction when judgment of death has been pronounced," implied that capital punishment did not violate the state constitution.

As for the penalty's cruelty, the court declared: "The cruelty of capital punishment lies not only in the execution itself and the pain incident thereto, but also in the dehumanizing effects of the lengthy imprisonment prior to execution."[22] Regarding unusualness, the court noted that the penalty was rarely imposed in California and even more rarely carried out. Statistics were marshaled to demonstrate that this was part of a worldwide trend toward abolition.

Thus, even before the Supreme Court's *Furman* decision (temporarily) abolishing capital punishment, and well before the ultimate repudiation in *Gregg* of the *Anderson* position — that the death penalty is inherently cruel and unusual — the California Supreme Court struck boldly, creating virtually unreviewable state constitutional law. Unreviewable perhaps, but not irreversible. *People v. Anderson* was like a fire bell in the night. It plunged the state into a "profoundly polarizing controversy," which according to a California law professor, "gravely damaged the public credibility of the court."[23] Death penalty proponents quickly mobilized public support for a new constitutional amendment adopted through the public referendum process, and before year's end, Article 1, section 27, was added to the fundamental state charter.[24]

This article flatly overturned the *Anderson* ruling and reinstated the death penalty statute that *Anderson* had declared unconstitutional. More broadly, section 27 sought to remove the state constitution as an obstacle to the imposition of the death penalty by declaring that the statute could not be deemed to contravene any state constitutional provision. This proved ineffective. Although the California Supreme Court acknowledged that section 27 reinstated the death penalty,[25] it also held in *People v. Bean* that the judiciary retained authority to prohibit the death penalty on state constitutional grounds so long as it did not rule that the death penalty is *inherently* cruel or unusual.[26]

Meanwhile, the death penalty controversy shifted gears. In 1976 the state supreme court held that portions of the reinstated death penalty statute abridged the *federal* Constitution.[27] This sent death penalty proponents back to the public once again, and in 1978 a new voter initiative, Proposition 7, established another capital punishment law.[28] However, death penalty appeals under this law faced a revamped group of state supreme court justices. In 1975 Edmund G. ("Gerry") Brown, a Democrat, became governor, replacing Republican Ronald Reagan. By the time his second term would end in 1982, Brown would get seven appointments to the court, including the controversial Chief Justice Rose E. Bird, Brown's former secretary of agriculture. During Bird's tenure, from early 1977 until her removal from the bench ten years later, the California Supreme Court reviewed sixty-four capital cases and upheld the penalty in only six.[29] Moreover, Chief Justice Bird reportedly voted to reverse the sentence or conviction in every capital case in which she participated.[30] Generally these reversals were not based on constitutional violations but rather were due to erroneous jury instructions by the trial judges. In 1985 death reversals reached their zenith, with twenty-two rejections and no approvals during that calendar year alone. The following year, the electorate removed Bird and two other Brown appointments, Associate Justices Joseph R. Grodin and Cruz Reynoso, when they were required to stand for retention.

The Republicans also resumed control of the governorship in 1983, with the election of former attorney general George Deukmejian. Deukmejian was able to replace most of the Brown justices and his successor, Pete Wilson, another Republican, finished the job.[31] Although death penalty reversals continued in a significant number of cases in the three-year period immediately following the Bird removal in 1986, death penalty *approvals* increased even more markedly. Table 7.2 provides the number of capital reversals and affirmances by year from 1977, when Rose Bird became chief justice, to the end of 1993.

TABLE 7.2
Death Penalty Reversals and Affirmances by Year,
California Supreme Court

Year	Reversals	Affirmances
1977	0	0
1978	0	0
1979	2	0
1980	5	1
1981	2	1
1982	6	1
1983	4	1
1984	11	1
1985	22	0
1986	6	1
1987	8	4
1988	12	39
1989	10	14
1990	2	22
1991	2	22
1992	1	24
1993	1	11

Since 1988, with Deukmejian-Wilson appointments in full control, there has been a palpable change in the court's attitude toward the death penalty. As the table shows, approvals have outpaced disapprovals 132 to 28. Doctrinally speaking, the state cruel or unusual punishments provision has been neutered; it now provides no more rights than its federal counterpart. As a 1991 California Supreme Court case laconically declared: "As a general interpretive principle, imposition of the death penalty under California law does not violate the state proscription against cruel or unusual punishment (Cal. Const. art. I, § 17) to the extent it comports with the federal Constitution."[32] Thus, after years of turmoil in the wake of *Anderson,* the battle over capital punishment in California ended in a clear victory for the conservatives.

SEARCH AND SEIZURE AND THE
CALIFORNIA CONSTITUTION

Search and seizure law has been one of the great sources of con-tentiousness in the United States for the last three decades. The root of the conflict is that the most effective method of enforcing Fourth Amendment restrictions upon law enforcement activities requires that evidence of a defendant's guilt be excluded from the adjudication process, with the result that prosecution is rendered more difficult. The primary purpose of excluding or suppressing evidence is to deter law enforcers from violating constitutional restrictions.[33] Because full compliance with search and seizure rules is difficult to achieve, however, reliable evidence of guilt not infrequently must be excluded in criminal prosecutions.[34] In a period of high crime rates there is, understandably, much opposition to legal rules that work to the advantage of suspected criminals.

The Burger and Rehnquist Supreme Courts sought to adjust in favor of the police many of the Fourth Amendment requirements that could be expected to lead to the frequent exclusion of evidence. At the same time, the California Supreme Court, interpreting the search and seizure provision of the California Constitution, was adopting more defendant-friendly positions likely to lead to increased suppression of evidence. Although the language of the state provision is nearly identical to the Fourth Amendment,[35] the California tribunal frequently rejected the Burger and Rehnquist interpretations, instead adopting constructions more favorable to the defendant and less favorable to the prosecution. The California Supreme Court took full advantage of its authority to develop state rights that are broader (more defendant protective) than federal rights.[36] After analyzing some notable examples of this new judicial federalism, we will discuss the impact of the 1982 state constitutional amendment which was intended to eliminate broader California exclusionary rules.

The first issue involves what is known as the "search incident to arrest." Although the Fourth Amendment appears to favor advance judicial approval (warrants) for searches by police, there are certain recurring situations in which a warrant would be wholly impractical. Such a situation includes the period immediately after an arrest. The Warren Court upheld warrantless searches of the arrested person and the area in his immediate control on the grounds that arresting officers need to prevent the suspect from using a concealed weapon against them, or from destroying or hiding some piece of evidence of criminality.[37] In

United States v. Robinson, the Burger Court held that even for a minor arrest, such as driving with a revoked license, where there is no reason to expect to find any weapon or evidence, a full search incident to arrest is justified.[38] In support of its ruling, the *Robinson* majority pointed out the dangers in accompanying any suspect to the police station, and the advantages in having a uniform rule covering all arrests. But for those inclined to mistrust the police, *Robinson* seemed like an invitation to search individuals on the pretext that some minor offense occurred, but with the real aim of finding evidence of a more serious crime — a perversion of the search-incident rationale.[39]

In 1975, in *People v. Norman,* the California Supreme Court rejected the *Robinson* rule in an interpretation of the state search and seizure provision.[40] As did *Robinson,* the *Norman* case also began with a traffic infraction. Defendant was driving at 4:00 A.M. without headlights, and after being stopped by the police, he cursed the officers and drove off, running a red light and a stop sign. Ultimately he got out of his van with a black object in his hand. Ordered by the police to drop it, Norman threw it under the van. The police recovered and opened the object: a plastic tobacco pouch containing marijuana, cigarette papers, and seconal. Norman was arrested and prosecuted for drug violations, and he sought to exclude the contents of the pouch.

Under the *Robinson* rule, the search of the pouch would undoubtedly have been upheld as an incident to arrest for the offense of evading arrest. Under *Robinson,* following an arrest for any crime, even the relatively minor one of driving off to evade a traffic ticket, a search of the items within the arrested person's immediate control is legitimate. The California Supreme Court, however, ignored *Robinson,* and relying instead on the state constitution, suppressed the drugs. The court required that before searching the pouch, the police must have probable cause to believe that it contained evidence of crime, contraband, or weapons. Since there was no basis prior to the search for concluding that any of these things was in the pouch, the search was held to have violated Article 1, section 13, the search and seizure provision of the state constitution. Consequently, the drug charges against Norman had to be dropped.[41]

Of course, the implications of this decision far exceeded defendant Norman. In every arrest in California the authority of the police to search would henceforth depend on the nature of the crime and the circumstances surrounding the arrest.[42] If police exceed their authority, even inadvertently, evidence of crime could be suppressed, and a criminal might go free or obtain a more favorable plea bargain. This is less likely to happen under the simpler and more straightforward federal rule, where the fact of arrest in and of itself justifies a search. In short, the California Supreme Court sacrificed the simplicity of the *Robinson* rule and created a greater risk of exclusion of evidence, with all of its deleterious consequences for criminal prosecution, in an effort to impose greater restrictions upon the police.

The second issue in which California's highest court refused to adopt federal search and seizure law involved the searches of automobiles. As is the case with searches incident to arrest, the Supreme Court has long permitted certain warrantless searches of motor vehicles.[43] Under the so-called automobile exception, police may search a motor vehicle without a search warrant if they have "probable cause" to believe that it contains evidence of a crime. The justification for excusing a warrant is that the vehicle's mobility makes advance court approval of the search impractical (assuming that seizing the vehicle and holding it until the warrant issues is also an unjustified intrusion) and that there is a diminished expectation of privacy in automobiles.[44] Not until 1982, however, did the Supreme Court finally resolve the question of the spatial scope of such searches, that is, how much of the vehicle and the objects recovered from the vehicle may be searched. In *United States v. Ross,* the Burger Court held that automobile exception searches could extend to any part of the vehicle in which it was reasonable to expect to find the sought-after items, including the trunk, glove compartment, and any other concealed areas in which the evidence could be hidden.[45] This also justifies opening any closed containers found in the vehicle, such as briefcases, pocketbooks, luggage, knapsacks, and the like, if they are likely repositories for the evidence being sought.

Once again, relying on the state search and seizure provision, the California Supreme Court established rules considerably more restrictive of law enforcement officers. The state court rejected two planks of the federal rule. First, it said that probable cause to search a car does not necessarily justify a search of its concealed areas.[46] The *Wimberly* case illustrates. Wimberly was driving erratically at 2:30 A.M. when police stopped him. The officers saw a jacket, marijuana seeds, and a pipe on the floor of the vehicle, and they smelled the odor of burned marijuana. A search of the jacket uncovered a plastic bag of marijuana. The police then searched the trunk where they found a suitcase, which they opened with the defendant's keys. There they found a sizable cache of marijuana. The state high court suppressed the marijuana recovered from the trunk, while admitting the evidence found in the passenger compartment. It held that the state constitution protects privacy in the trunk. Unless the police have probable cause to believe that there is evidence in a concealed area of a vehicle (the same rule would apply to the glove compartment), they cannot search in the area without a warrant. By contrast, the United States Supreme Court's *Ross* decision would have permitted a search of any portion of a vehicle in which the evidence could be found, without any additional justification for searching concealed areas.

The California Supreme Court also rejected a second tenet of the *Ross* rule: that so-called closed containers may be opened and searched without additional probable cause over and above the justification needed to search the automobile. *People v. Ruggles* is the key case.[47] Police, suspecting that Ruggles was responsible for a series of motel clerk robberies, set up surveillance at a time when he was expected to commit another holdup. They watched as he removed a brown briefcase from the trunk of a car, entered his apartment building, and returned some ten minutes later with the briefcase. Ruggles then placed the briefcase back in the trunk and drove off. Police followed and stopped him. On the back seat of the car they saw narcotics paraphernalia; from the trunk they recovered two tote bags, halloween masks, and the brown briefcase. Police opened the briefcase and found, among other items, two guns, ammunition, handcuffs (the hotel clerks had been handcuffed by the robbers), and a bandanna.

The California Supreme Court suppressed the items found in the briefcase. The court reasoned that police had probable cause to search the vehicle, including the trunk, for weapons and other holdup evidence, but this did not justify a search of closed containers recovered from the vehicle. Under the state constitution, such containers could not be searched without a warrant.[48]

Thus, in two major areas of search and seizure law, searches incident to arrest and automobile exception searches, the California Supreme Court, relying on Article 1, section 13, of the state constitution, provided broader rights than defendants have under the Fourth Amendment as interpreted by the Burger and Rehnquist Supreme Courts. Liberals may have cheered the use of the state constitution to preserve rights against what they commonly perceived to be Supreme Court cutbacks, but conservatives viewed such rulings as favoring criminals and handcuffing law enforcement. Ultimately, the conservatives succeeded in rolling back these decisions, but before we tell how it is first necessary to consider the development of the *Miranda* rule under the California Constitution.

THE *MIRANDA* RULE IN CALIFORNIA

The Warren Court's 1966 decision in *Miranda v. Arizona* was a lightning rod for conservative critics of the judiciary.[49] *Miranda* compelled law enforcement agents nationwide to warn those taken into custody, prior to questioning them, that they have a right to remain silent, a right to an attorney, and a right to cut off the questioning. As early as 1971, in *Harris v. New York,* the Burger Court established an exception to the rule.[50] Normally, if police fail to meet *Miranda* requirements, if, for example, they do not read all of the famed warnings about the right to counsel and silence, the suspect's statements, even a voluntary full confession, are inadmissible at trial as evidence of his guilt. *Harris* held that such statements are nevertheless admissible to impeach the defendant's testimony should he testify at his trial. That is, a defendant's incriminating statements, though obtained in violation of the *Miranda* rule, are admissible for the limited purpose of contradicting the defendant's testimony.[51] Chief Justice Burger, speaking for the *Harris* majority, explained that an impeachment exception is necessary to keep *Miranda* from becoming a "shield for perjury."

In *People v. Disbrow,* the California Supreme Court rejected the *Harris* rule for the state constitutional self-incrimination clause, Article 1, section 15.[52] Four arguments were offered against *Harris.* First, it was said to hearken back to the pre-*Miranda* approach to confessions, which had been rejected (in *Miranda*) because of the difficulties in applying it.[53] Second, a mere caution to juries from the trial judge to refrain from considering impeachment evidence as proof of guilt was said to be unlikely to be effective. Third, it was contended that *Harris* would reduce police incentives to comply with *Miranda* by creating an exception to the *Miranda* exclusionary rule. Finally, the *Disbrow* court reasoned that the integrity of the judiciary would be undermined by having to admit into a trial illegally obtained statements. Under the California Constitution, therefore, statements taken in violation of *Miranda* could not be used by the prosecutor at all, whether to prove guilt or to impeach the defendant's testimony.

Once again, as in the search and seizure and capital punishment areas, the California high court challenged the highest court in the land and, utilizing the state constitution, established expanded protections for the criminally accused. Once again, from a law enforcement perspective, the result was that the prosecution and conviction of criminals was rendered more difficult. A defendant could take the stand and lie, secure in the knowledge that the prosecutor could not rebut his testimony with any contradictory statements obtained by the police if they violated the *Miranda* rules.

THE CONSERVATIVE ASCENDANCY

The search and seizure and *Miranda* cases described above are illustrative but not exclusive. Indeed, they were part of a pattern of California Supreme Court cases that rejected U.S. Supreme Court doctrines on the basis of the state constitution.[54] And of course, all of the trial courts and all of the intermediate appeals courts throughout the state, in the many hundreds of thousands of cases before them, were duty-bound to follow the dictates of California's highest tribunal. Thus, the impact of these rulings on the criminal case law of the state can hardly be overestimated. In addition, the California Supreme Court made some lightning rod criminal law rulings that did not involve the state constitution.[55] One of the most controversial concerned the interpretation of a "use-a-gun, go-to-prison" law. In *People v. Tanner* the supreme court initially determined that the refusal of a trial judge to apply the law to an armed convenience store robber was a matter properly within the judge's discretion.[56] After a public outcry the court reconsidered the case and reversed its ruling.[57]

As they did with the death penalty, conservatives mobilized public opposition to these decisions, and in 1982 they succeeded in obtaining voter approval of an amendment to the state constitution, effectively reversing most of the California Supreme Court's ultraprotective search and seizure and *Miranda* rulings.

The California Constitution empowers voters to amend the fundamental law of the state by initiative, that is, by popular vote.[58] In 1978 this vehicle proved spectacularly successful when the Jarvis-Gann Initiative, Proposition 13, rolled back property taxes. (The California Supreme Court upheld Proposition 13 over a dissent by Chief Justice Bird, who found it violative of the state constitutional equal protection clause.[59]) The success of Proposition 13 gave great impetus to Proposition 8, the Victims' Bill of Rights.[60] First developed by state prosecutors and Republican legislators, the criminal justice reform measure appeared on the June 1982 primary election ballot. This had been preceded by a failed attempt to enact the package by ordinary legislation, and a successful court fight to ensure the initiative's place on the ballot.[61] On June 8, 1982, Proposition 8 was approved by 56.4 percent of those voting.[62]

Proposition 8 contained several provisions, collectively titled the "Victims' Bill of Rights."[63] The focus was entirely on criminal justice, covering such matters as the rights of victims, school safety, bail, and what was called "truth-in-evidence." The truth-in-evidence portion, which became Article 1, section 28(d), of the state constitution, is most relevant here. It reads as follows.

Except as provided by statute hereafter enacted by a two-thirds vote of the membership in each house of the Legislature, relevant evidence shall not be excluded in any criminal proceeding, including pretrial and post conviction motions and hearings, or in any trial or hearing of a juvenile for a criminal offense, whether heard in juvenile or adult court.

The operative words are "relevant evidence," for relevance here means relevance to the question of guilt or innocence. Evidence that was obtained illegally by the police is nonetheless "relevant" if it helps prove defendant's guilt. Thus, evidence excludable pursuant to the state constitution because of search and seizure or *Miranda* violations would be, as a result of this provision, admissible if relevant to guilt. (By contrast, evidence excludable under the *federal* Constitution would still be inadmissible because a state constitutional provision cannot subvert federal constitutional rules.[64]) In one bold stroke, as the state supreme court itself recognized, state constitutional exclusionary rules broader than the federal constitutional exclusionary rules were all eliminated.[65] Thus, although the California Constitution may impose greater restrictions than the U.S. Constitution on law enforcement personnel, the California courts may not enforce those restrictions by suppressing evidence beyond that required to be suppressed under the federal Constitution. Consequently, all of the search and seizure and *Miranda* cases discussed above — *Norman, Wimberly, Ruggles,* and *Disbrow* — are effectively nullified.[66] *Disbrow,* which had rejected the *Harris* rule, presents a clearcut example. In 1988, in *People v. May,* which raised the identical legal issue resolved in *Disbrow,* the state high court declared *Disbrow* "abrogated" and noted that the probable aim of Proposition 8 was "to dispense with exclusionary rules derived solely from the state Constitution."[67] Therefore, California now follows the federal rule and admits for impeachment purposes statements taken in violation of *Miranda.*

One study of Proposition 8 described its overall impact as follows:

Probably the single most startling statistic — at least to the authors — is that Proposition 8 succeeded in abrogating no fewer than twenty-seven leading cases of the Supreme Court of California. Those leading cases were of course relied upon in subsequent decisions by the supreme court and by lower courts in California. In total, there are well over one thousand appellate cases that were affected by Proposition 8 (and an undetermined number of superior court rulings). It is a rare piece of legislation or judicial decision that, in one stroke, accomplishes such a remarkable result.[68]

In 1986, four years after the approval of Proposition 8, a campaign was launched to unseat Chief Justice Rose Bird, mainly because of her record on criminal justice issues.[69] The Bird affair was outlined above in the section on the death penalty but some additional details should be considered. Under the California system, Bird and two associate justices, Grodin and Reynoso, had to run in a retention election.[70] Bird became a lightning rod for critics of the state court's liberalism, with special focus on criminal law.[71] The campaign against her was spearheaded by two organizations, Crime Victims for Court Reform, which included relatives of murder victims, and Californians to Defeat Rose Bird, which included tax crusaders Howard Jarvis and Paul Gann and former Los Angeles police chief Ed Davis.[72] Republican Governor George Deukmejian, campaigning (successfully) for reelection, and a coalition of prosecutors from around the state also opposed her.[73] Her supporters consisted of Democratic politicians, including former governor Pat Brown (Committee to Keep Politics out of the Courts), local bar associations, defense attorney organizations, environmentalists, and Bird's own Committee to Conserve the Courts.[74] Bird's campaign was outspent (by approximately $5.5 million expended by her opponents to roughly $2 million by the pro-Bird forces), and out-organized.[75] She amassed only 34 percent of the vote, with her two fellow Gerry Brown appointees scoring higher but still well short of the 50 percent required for affirmation.[76]

In the aftermath of the defeat of Bird and her two colleagues, Governor Deukmejian, who had already nominated two justices to the high court, got to make the three replacement appointments. By the time Deukmejian's second term ended in 1990, all but one of the Gerry Brown appointees had been replaced, and the one remaining retired right after the election of Deukmejian's successor, another Republican, Pete Wilson.[77]

The combination of the changes in personnel and Proposition 8 seems to have had a substantial impact upon the California Supreme Court. We have already shown the change with respect to the death penalty. From 1977 until Bird's rejection a decade later, the court disapproved fifty-eight capital convictions and upheld ten. From 1988 through 1993, the figures were 28 reversals and 132 approvals.[78] Another indicator of change are the criminal cases involving an interpretation of the California Constitution. Before Proposition 8 California Supreme Court cases rejected U.S. Supreme Court interpretations in favor of broader rights 83 percent of the time; after Proposition 8 that figure dropped to 47 percent.[79] Although these are imperfect indicators, omitting as they do civil cases and even some criminal law rulings, they strongly suggest a new direction for the court.

LIMITING THE INITIATIVE

In 1990, emboldened by their success, conservatives mounted a new campaign for yet another amendment to the state constitution. On June 5, 1990, the electorate approved Proposition 115, which among other things, sought to amend Article 1, section 24 of the state constitution. The proposed amendment declared that thirteen different state constitutional rights — virtually every provision affecting criminal justice in Article 1 of the California Constitution — "shall be construed by the courts of this state in a manner consistent with the Constitution of the United States." Presumably to cover any right not enumerated, the new proposition also added: "This Constitution shall not be construed by the courts to afford greater rights to criminal defendants than those afforded by the Constitution of the United States." The intent was to extend the Proposition 8 concept, which primarily affected police practices, to criminal procedure generally. Wherever criminal defendants had broader protections under the state constitution, Proposition 115 would eliminate them, leaving only the floor of federal constitutional protections.

The opposition to this wide-ranging provision came from an unexpected quarter: the newly reconstituted state supreme court. In *Raven v. Deukmejian*,[80] the court, with five Republican Deukmejian appointments sitting, invalidated part of Proposition 115. The amendment to Article 1, section 24, quoted above, was struck down on the grounds that it was "so far reaching as to amount to a constitutional revision beyond the scope of the initiative process." The court held that so sweeping a change in the state constitution would have to be accomplished by the more deliberative process of a constitutional convention or legislative approval, followed in either case by popular ratification. The initiative alone could not be used to effect such wide-reaching changes in the state constitution. The initiative power had been pushed too far.

What accounts for such an apparently prodefendant antiprosecution ruling by a relatively conservative court? The answer is that the court apparently saw this more as an anti*court* than an anticriminal measure, and there is nothing like institutional solidarity for transcending ideological divisions. Under section 24, the judiciary would be virtually barred from interpreting the state constitution differently from the federal in criminal cases. State judges, especially on the appellate courts, would lose a potent source of their authority. The state legislature and even trial courts could act without fear of reversal on state constitutional grounds. This was going too far — even for conservative supreme court justices. As the opinion in *Raven* put it, "In essence and practical effect, new article I, section 24, would vest all judicial interpretive power, as to fundamental criminal defense rights, in the United States Supreme Court. From a qualitative standpoint, the effect of Proposition 115 is devastating."[81]

CONCLUSION

There are some interesting lessons to be learned from this extraordinary and fascinating California experience. First and foremost, state constitutions may be used not only to broaden rights but also to restrict them. They are far easier to amend than the U. S. Constitution. Therefore, forces within a state dissatisfied with liberal court interpretations of the fundamental state law may, without nearly the same effort required on the federal level, undo those rulings. The 1972 amendment reinstating the death penalty and the 1982 amendment wiping out state exclusionary rules are potent examples.

They are, however, not the only examples. In Florida, within one-half year of the approval of Proposition 8, the voters adopted an amendment to the state constitutional search and seizure provision, requiring the provision to be "be construed in conformity with the 4th Amendment to the United States Constitution, as interpreted by the United States Supreme Court."[82] While differing from the California approach somewhat, the Florida "forced linkage" provision had the same goal: to compel the judiciary to curtail criminal defendant's rights.[83] It requires the Florida courts — which had also been quite liberal in establishing state constitutional rights — to adopt no broader rights than are granted by the U.S. Supreme Court. As in California, this amendment has proven effective. Before forced linkage, Florida Supreme Court cases rejected U.S. Supreme Court interpretations in favor of broader rights 80 percent of the time; after forced linkage the rejection rate dipped to 18 percent.[84] Thus, it is clear that state constitutions can be altered to support both conservative and liberal policies.

Second, the state judiciary must be careful not to unduly antagonize powerful state interests, especially on potentially inflammatory matters, such as capital punishment. Cases grounded on statutory construction or judicial rule-making are subject to legislative modification and therefore to political compromise, but decisions based on the state constitution are not so easily changed. If such decisions sufficiently provoke powerful state political forces, such as prosecutors and law enforcement groups, they will fight back. The state judiciary is vulnerable, accountable to the public in various ways, including limited terms of office and popular elections. The removal of Rose Bird and her two colleagues certainly proves the point.

On the other hand, at least until the 1980s, removing state judges was still a relatively rare phenomenon.[85] In Oregon in 1984, with circumstances comparable to the Bird situation, an attempt to unseat state supreme court justice Hans Linde failed dismally. As in California, Linde, the John Marshall of state constitutionalism, was opposed largely on the "law and order" issue, but his two primary opponents split the vote between them.[86] In 1992 Florida Chief Justice Ellen Barkett also survived an electoral attack on criminal procedure issues and abortion rights.[87] In that same year, however, Wyoming Supreme Court Justice Walter Urbigkit was defeated after he was targeted as being soft on criminals.[88]

Finally, lest those who would redirect a court get complacent, it should not be forgotten that the judges have potent weapons of their own. Constitutional amendments, even those designed to overturn court rulings, are themselves subject to judicial construction. The death penalty amendment did not totally eliminate judicial review of capital cases, and Proposition 115 was gutted by the high court's narrow construction of the referendum authority. The California Supreme Court has made quite clear that it is not going to yield its authority to interpret the state constitution without a fight. By and large, the American judiciary still retains the most powerful weapon of all: The public remains highly respectful of courts and ambivalent about tampering with their independence.

NOTES

    1.   U.S. Constitution, art. 2, sec. 2.

2.   U.S. Constitution, art. 3, sec. 1 established the "good behavior" rule. Recently, a national commission on judicial discipline and removal concluded that impeachment by the House of Representatives and removal by two-thirds of the Senate was the exclusive means of removing federal judges, although some scholars reject this view. See Maria Simon, "Note, Bribery and Other Not So 'Good Behavior': Criminal Prosecution as a Supplement to Impeachment of Federal Judges," *Columbia Law Review* 94 (June 1994): 1617–1673. The only Supreme Court justice to be impeached was Samuel Chase in 1804, and he was not removed. More recently, there was a failed attempt to impeach Justice William O. Douglas in 1970. See C. Herman Pritchett, *The American Constitution* (New York: McGraw-Hill, 1977), 104.

3.   Council of State Governments, *The Book of the States 1994–95* (Lexington, Ky.: Council of State Governments, 1994), 190–99.

4.   Janice C. May, "Constitutional Amendment and Revision Revisited," *Publius: The Journal of Federalism* 17 (Winter 1987): 162. Under the U.S. Constitution, Article 5, the typical amending procedure involves a proposed amendment by two-thirds of both houses of Congress followed by ratification by the legislatures of three-fourths of the states.

5.   May, "Constitutional Amendment," 157.

6.   Ibid., 158.

7.   Ibid., 162. These figures are conservative, as state constitutional amendments were proposed at a rate of over 250 per biennium for the period from 1986 to 1993. For each biennium during this same time period, the approval rate ranged from 63 percent to 74 percent. Janice C. May, "State Constitutions and Constitutional Revision, 1992–93," in *Book of the States*, Council of State Governments, 2.

8.   A computer search of a database consisting of all published California Supreme Court opinions since 1883 revealed a marked increase in state constitutional search and seizure litigation in the 1960s. From 1883 to 1959, a period of seventy-six years, only twelve cases citing the state constitutional search-and-seizure provision were found. From 1960 to the present, a thirty-two–year span, eighty-five such cases were decided. It should be kept in mind that throughout the states state constitutional litigation on criminal justice was "amazingly meager" in the last century, and what there was made little difference in the operation of the criminal justice system (Lawrence M. Friedman, "State Constitutions and Criminal Justice in the Late Nineteenth Century," *Albany Law Review* 53 [Winter 1989]: 267). State supreme courts spent 90 percent of their effort on noncriminal cases until the Warren years, when criminal matters leaped to 28 percent of their business (Robert A. Kagan, Bliss Cartwright, Lawrence M. Friedman, and Stanton Wheeler, "The Business of State Supreme Courts, 1870–1970," *Stanford Law Review* 30 [November 1977]: 121, 146).

9.   Earl Warren was chief justice of the United States from 1954 to 1969, during which time the Supreme Court generally expanded the federal constitutional rights of defendants and applied these rights to the states via the Fourteenth Amendment due process clause. Richard M. Nixon was elected president in 1968, after campaigning against the Warren Court, accusing it of hamstringing law enforcement. See James F. Simon, *In His Own Image: The Supreme Court in Richard Nixon's America* (New York: David McKay Co., 1973). President Nixon made four appointments to the Court: Chief Justice Warren E. Burger (1969), Associate Justices Harry A. Blackmun (1970), Lewis F. Powell, Jr. (1971), and William H. Rehnquist (1971). Alarmed liberals predicted dire consequences. See Alan M. Dershowitz and John Hart Ely, *"Harris v.*

New York: Some Anxious Observations on the Candor and Logic of the Emerging Nixon Majority," *Yale Law Journal* 80 (May 1971): 1198–1227. Political scientists offered more balanced analyses. See Richard Y. Funston, *Constitutional Counterrevolution?* (Cambridge, Mass.: Schenkman, 1977). In retrospect, it is more accurate to say of the Burger Court and its successor under Chief Justice Rehnquist (chief since 1986) that they did not narrow rights but rather declined to expand them further.

10.   The link between the change in the United States Supreme Court and the rise of the new judicial federalism is discussed in Barry Latzer, *State Constitutions and Criminal Justice* (Westport, Conn.: Greenwood Press, 1991), 2–4, 166.

11.   The Supreme Court has long acknowledged that it has no authority to review cases resting on "independent and adequate state grounds." When a state court upholds a right unambiguously on the basis of state law the grounds are considered "independent and adequate." *Michigan v. Long,* 463 U.S. 1032 (1983).

12.   From 1961 to 1980, the nation's homicide rate rose to its highest level in the twentieth century. U.S. Department of Justice, *Report to the Nation on Crime and Justice* (Washington, D.C.: Government Printing Office, 1988), 15.

13.   Preble Stolz, *Judging Judges* (New York: Free Press, 1981), 76–77. Traynor had been elevated to chief justice upon Gibson's retirement in 1964.

14.   Ibid., 76–80.

15.   *Mapp v. Ohio,* 367 U.S. 643 (1961) (holding that the Fourteenth Amendment due process clause requires the exclusion of illegally seized evidence in state courts); *People v. Cahan,* 44 Cal. 2d 434, 282 P.2d 905 (1955).

16.   *Gregg v. Georgia,* 428 U.S. 153 (1976). In *Gregg,* the Supreme Court upheld a bifurcated, or two-part, trial of capital cases in which guilt and sentence are separately determined, followed by review of all capital sentences by the state court of last resort.

17.   *Furman v. Georgia,* 408 U.S. 238 (1972). The three other justices in the majority took the position that capital sentencing was unconstitutionally administered, but not per se unconstitutional.

18.   *People v. Anderson,* 6 Cal. 3d 628, 493 P.2d 880, 100 Cal. Rptr. 152 (1972).

19.   *People v. Anderson,* 64 Cal. 2d 633, 414 P.2d 366, 51 Cal. Rptr. 238 (1966).

20.   *In re Anderson,* 69 Cal. 2d 613, 447 P.2d 117, 73 Cal. Rptr. 21 (1968). The court reversed on the grounds that a federal constitutional error had been committed when the jury was empaneled. It remanded the case for a new sentencing trial.

21.   The Supreme Court has no jurisdiction over cases resting on "independent and adequate state grounds." *Michigan v. Long,* 463 U.S. 1032 (1983). If a state court clearly bases a decision favorable to a criminal defendant on state law, the case cannot be reviewed by the Supreme Court.

22.   *People v. Anderson,* 493 P.2d 880 (1972) at 894 (footnote omitted).

23.   Stolz, *Judging Judges,* 82.

24.   California Constitution, art. 1, sec. 27, reads as follows:

All statutes of this state in effect on February 17, 1972, requiring, authorizing, imposing, or relating to the death penalty are in full force and effect, subject to legislative amendment or repeal by statute, initiative, or referendum.

    The death penalty provided for under those statutes shall not be deemed to be, or to constitute, the infliction of cruel or unusual punishments within the meaning of Article 1, Section 6 nor shall such punishment for such offenses be deemed to contravene any other provision of this constitution.

25. *People v. Frierson,* 25 Cal. 3d 142, 599 P.2d 587, 158 Cal. Rptr. 281 (1979).

26. *People v. Bean,* 46 Cal. 3d 919, 760 P.2d 996, 251 Cal. Rptr. 467 (1988).

27. *Rockwell v. Superior Court,* 18 Cal. 3d 420, 556 P.2d 1101, 134 Cal. Rptr. 650 (1976).

28. Proposition 7, approved in 1978, and implemented by death penalty legislation in that same year, altered and expanded the categories of murder in the first degree that were to be eligible for the death penalty.

29. See Table 7.2. Other commentators have offered different figures, but all support the same conclusion regarding the lack of success of death penalty cases before the California Supreme Court. See, for example, John H. Culver and John T. Wold, "Rose Bird and the Politics of Judicial Accountability in California," *Judicature* 70 (August–September 1986): 86, which reported that "[b]y May 1986, the court had overturned death sentences in all but three of the 56 capital cases it had decided, and no one on death row had been executed." (Footnote omitted.) J. Clark Kelso and Brigitte A. Bass, "The Victims' Bill of Rights: Where Did It Come From and How Much Did It Do?" *Pacific Law Journal* 23 (1992): 860, state that "the Supreme Court of California managed from 1977 until the passage of Proposition 8 in 1982 to reverse the imposition of the death penalty in twenty-two cases and affirm only two such convictions." (Footnote omitted.)

30. Culver and Wold, "Rose Bird," 86.

31. The one "holdover" was Justice Stanley Mosk, appointed to the court in 1964 by Gerry Bown's father, Governor Edmund G. ("Pat") Brown.

32. *People v. Cox,* 53 Cal. 3d 618, 809 P.2d 351, 385, 280 Cal. Rptr. 692 (1991).

33. *United States v. Leon,* 468 U.S. 897 (1984).

34. The evidence is "reliable" in the sense that there is little doubt that it helps to prove guilt, notwithstanding the legality of its acquisition. Much suppressed evidence consists of tangible contraband, such as illegal narcotics or firearms. There is debate however, about the extent of exclusion in criminal cases. See *Leon,* 468 U.S. at 907 n.6.

35. For a comparison of the text of Article 1, section 13, of the California Constitution with the Fourth Amendment, see Table 7.1.

36. The supremacy clause of the U.S. Constitution, Article 6, prohibits state courts from enforcing state rights that are narrower, or less protective, than applicable federal rights, but it permits enforcement of broader, more protective state rights.

37. *Chimel v. California,* 395 U.S. 752 (1969).

38. *United States v. Robinson,* 414 U.S. 218 (1973). Robinson had been stopped and arrested by a police officer who recognized him as someone whose driver's license had been revoked. A search of Robinson's pocket uncovered narcotics, leading to drug charges. Robinson sought to exclude the drugs on the grounds that the search that led to their discovery was an unlawful search incident to the traffic arrest. The Supreme Court rejected his claim and upheld the search.

39. Where an individual is stopped for a trivial offense, and especially where a full arrest is a matter of police discretion, critics contend that *Robinson* tempts police to conduct unlawful fishing expeditions to uncover evidence of crime before deciding whether to take the offender into custody. If the search turns up evidence of a more serious crime, such as a drug offense, a full arrest is likely. On the other hand, if the

search turns up nothing incriminating, the officer could simply issue a court appearance ticket for the minor transgression. Thus, instead of a warrantless search being justified by an arrest, the outcome of the search determines whether or not there will be an arrest. In effect, the arrest becomes an incident of the search, not the other way around.

40. *People v. Norman,* 14 Cal. 3d 929, 538 P.2d 237, 123 Cal. Rptr. 109 (1975). The *Norman* case relied on an earlier California Supreme Court decision, *People v. Brisendine,* 13 Cal. 3d 528, 531 P.2d 1099, 119 Cal. Rptr. 315 (1975), which had also held that under California law police may not make a full search of an arrested person's possessions as an incident of a lawful arrest.

41. The *Norman* court did approve a protective pat-down search (frisk) of an arrested person for weapons whenever he is to be transported in a patrol car. Apparently, however, this would not have justified a search of the pouch, as a discarded object would have posed no threat to the police officers.

42. Thus, under *Norman,* arrests for crimes that do not involve weapons, and for which, given the nature of the offense, there is no evidence to be found, cannot support a search-incident to arrest. Traffic offenses are a notable example. (Of course, police may not arrest at all for some traffic offenses. Where police may only issue a ticket, there can be no search-incident to arrest.)

43. The first Supreme Court case to establish an exception to the Fourth Amendment search warrant requirement for motor vehicles (the "automobile exception") was *Carroll v. United States,* 267 U.S. 132 (1925).

44. *Carroll v. United States,* 267 U.S. 132 (1925), relied on the mobility justification. The expectation of privacy rationale is commonly used in the more recent automobile search cases. See, for example, *California v. Carney,* 471 U.S. 386 (1985).

45. *United States v. Ross,* 456 U.S. 798 (1982).

46. *Wimberly v. Superior Court,* 16 Cal. 3d 557, 547 P.2d 417, 128 Cal. Rptr. 641 (1976).

47. *People v. Ruggles,* 39 Cal. 3d 1, 702 P.2d 170, 216 Cal. Rptr. 88 (1985).

48. The court would also have permitted a warrantless search of such closed containers if Ruggles had given consent to search or if there had been exigent circumstances, such as a reason to think that a weapon was inside. *Ruggles,* 702 P.2d at 176 n.6. The federal constitutional rule was not, at the time of *Ruggles,* as clear-cut as I have made it appear. *United States v. Ross,* 456 U.S. 798 (1982), established that a container recovered from an automobile could be searched without a warrant if there was probable cause to believe that evidence was concealed somewhere within the vehicle. But *Ross* required a warrant to open a container if police had reason to believe that evidence was stored in that particular container, as opposed to being stored in the vehicle generally. Eventually, the Supreme Court abandoned this complex rule and simply permitted warrantless searches of containers whether the probable cause related to the specific container or to the vehicle as a whole. *California v. Acevedo,* 500 U.S. 565 (1991). *Ruggles,* however, did not rely on the "specific container" exception to *Ross;* it demanded a warrant, consent, or exigency to justify the search of any container recovered during an automobile exception search.

49. *Miranda v. Arizona,* 384 U.S. 436 (1966).

50. *Harris v. New York,* 401 U.S. 222 (1971).

51. The accused may avoid the damage to his defense that this might cause by exercising his Fifth Amendment right not to testify. This tactic also has costs, however,

as the jury may wonder why the defendant refuses to proclaim his innocence; juries are routinely admonished to refrain from taking into account a defendant's failure to testify.

52.   *People v. Disbrow*, 16 Cal. 3d 101, 545 P.2d 272, 127 Cal. Rptr. 360 (1976).

53.   Before *Miranda,* confessions were admissible if they were "voluntary." *Miranda* cast doubt on the ability of courts to determine if statements were truly voluntary, in part, because of the difficulty of knowing what goes on in the police station. In the post-*Miranda* era, the admissibility of confessions has been dominated by inquiries into the administration of *Miranda* warnings rather than the voluntariness of confessions. The *Harris* decision, which created an exception to *Miranda*'s exclusionary rule, implied that statements used to impeach would still have to meet the voluntariness standard.

54.   Prior to 1982, the California Supreme Court interpreted the state constitution differently from then-prevailing federal law in numerous cases, including the following: *People v. Laiwa,* 34 Cal. 3d 711, 668 P.2d 697, 195 Cal. Rptr. 390 (1983) (search after arrest); *People v. Chavers,* 33 Cal. 3d 462, 658 P.2d 96, 189 Cal. Rptr. 169 (1983) (automobile exception); *De Lancie v. Superior Court,* 31 Cal. 3d 865, 647 P.2d 142, 183 Cal. Rptr. 866 (1982) (surreptitious surveillance); *People v. Bustamonte,* 30 Cal. 3d 88, 634 P.2d 927, 177 Cal. Rptr. 573 (1981) (lineups); *People v. Kurland,* 28 Cal. 3d 376, 618 P.2d 213, 168 Cal. Rptr. 667 (1980) (challenges to search warrants); *People v. Blair,* 25 Cal. 3d 640, 602 P.2d 738, 159 Cal. Rptr. 818 (1979) (seizure of credit card records); *People v. Ramirez,* 25 Cal. 3d 260, 599 P.2d 622, 158 Cal. Rptr. 316 (1979) (rights of prisoners); *Barber v. Municipal Court,* 24 Cal. 3d 742, 598 P.2d 818, 157 Cal. Rptr. 658 (1979) (interference with right to counsel); *People v. Zelinski,* 24 Cal. 3d 357, 594 P.2d 1000, 155 Cal. Rptr. 575 (1979) (limiting search and seizure by private security); *People v. Barraza,* 23 Cal. 3d 675, 591 P.2d 947, 153 Cal. Rptr. 459 (1979) (entrapment); *Hawkins v. Superior Court,* 22 Cal. 3d 584, 586 P.2d 916, 150 Cal. Rptr. 435 (1978) (right to preliminary hearing); *People v. Wheeler,* 22 Cal. 3d 258, 583 P.2d 748, 148 Cal. Rptr. 890 (1978) (racially motivated peremptory challenges of jurors); *People v. Cook,* 22 Cal. 3d 67, 583 P.2d 130, 148 Cal. Rptr. 605 (1978) (challenges to search warrants); *People v. Pettingill,* 21 Cal. 3d 231, 578 P.2d 108, 145 Cal. Rptr. 861 (1978) (repeated interrogations); *People v. Jiminez,* 21 Cal. 3d 595, 580 P.2d 672, 147 Cal. Rptr. 172 (proof of voluntariness of confession); *People v. Hannon,* 19 Cal. 3d 1203, 564 P.2d 1203, 138 Cal. Rptr. 885 (1977) (speedy trial); *Allen v. Superior Court,* 18 Cal. 3d 520, 557 P.2d 65, 134 Cal. Rptr. 650 (1976) (defense disclosures); *Wimberly v. Superior Court,* 16 Cal. 3d 557, 547 P.2d 417, 128 Cal. Rptr. 641 (1976) (automobile exception); *People v. Disbrow,* 16 Cal. 3d 101, 545 P.2d 272, 127 Cal. Rptr. 360 (1976) (*Miranda* impeachment exception); *People v. Longwill,* 14 Cal. 3d 943, 538 P.2d 753, 123 Cal. Rptr 297 (1975) (search incident to arrest); *People v. Norman,* 14 Cal. 3d 929, 538 P.2d 237, 123 Cal. Rptr. 109 (1975) (search-incident to arrest); *White v. Davis,* 13 Cal. 3d 757, 533 P.2d 222, 120 Cal. Rptr. 94 (1975) (surreptitious surveillance); *Burrows v. Superior Court,* 13 Cal. 3d 238, 529 P.2d 590, 118 Cal. Rptr. 166 (1974) (seizure of credit card records); *Reynolds v. Superior Court,* 12 Cal. 3d 834, 528 P.2d 45, 117 Cal. Rptr. 437 (1974) (defense disclosures); *Mills v. Municipal Court,* 10 Cal. 3d 288, 515 P.2d 273, 110 Cal. Rptr. 329 (1973) (trial by jury); *People v. Anderson,* 6 Cal. 3d 628, 493 P.2d 880, 100 Cal. Rptr. 152 (1972) (death penalty); *People v. Krivda,* 5 Cal. 3d 357, 486 P.2d 1262, 96 Cal. Rptr. 62 (1971) (searches of trash); *In re Johnson,* 62 Cal. 2d 325, 398 P.2d 420, 42 Cal. Rptr. 228 (1965) (right to counsel).

55. See Kelso and Bass, "Victims' Bill of Rights," 857–858; Culver and Wold, "Rose Bird," 85–86.

56. *People v. Tanner,* 23 Cal. 3d 16, 587 P.2d 1112, 151 Cal. Rptr. 299 (1978), *vacated,* 24 Cal. 3d 514, 596 P.2d 328, 156 Cal. Rptr. 450 (1979).

57. Kelso and Bass, "Victims' Bill of Rights," 857–858; Culver and Wold, "Rose Bird," 85.

58. California Constitution, art. 18, sec. 3.

59. *Amador Valley Joint Union High School District v. State Board of Equalization,* 22 Cal. 3d 208, 583 P.2d 1281, 149 Cal. Rptr. 239 (1978).

60. Kelso and Bass, "Victims' Bill of Rights," 862–863.

61. Ibid., 863–864. In an interesting preliminary bout, Proposition 8 was almost kept off the ballot. State law required that the signatures on the petitions to place an initiative measure on the ballot be validated either individually or by statistical sample. If the sampling method was used, state law required 110 percent of the minimum number of signatures for approval. Proposition 8 garnered 108.76 percent of the minimum. Proponents of the measure then obtained from the state legislature a this-time-only change in the law allowing Proposition 8 to appear on the ballot with 105 percent of the requisite number of signatures. Without fully discussing the validation process, the California Supreme Court allowed Proposition 8 to come before the electorate. *Brosnahan v. Eu,* 31 Cal. 3d 1, 641 P.2d 200, 181 Cal. Rptr. 100 (1982).

62. Kelso and Bass, "Victims' Bill of Rights," 865.

63. For the full text and the analysis presented in the ballot pamphlet see *Brosnahan v. Brown,* 32 Cal. 3d 236, 651 P.2d 274, 186 Cal. Rptr. 30 (1982).

64. To put the matter differently, Proposition 8 could not constitutionally provide for the admission of evidence, relevant or not, which must be excluded pursuant to *Mapp v. Ohio,* 367 U.S. 643 (1961). *Mapp* held that the Fourteenth Amendment due process clause required state courts to exclude evidence seized in violation of the Fourth Amendment.

65. *In re Lance,* 37 Cal. 3d 873, 694 P.2d 744, 210 Cal. Rptr. 631 (1985).

66. To be safe, we should say "probably nullified," because in some cases the issue has not arisen in the California Supreme Court since Proposition 8 went into effect, so the court has not had an opportunity to rule on the vitality of some of its pre–Proposition 8 holdings. In other cases, because the crimes occurred before Proposition 8 went into effect, the state supreme court applied the law that was in force prior to Proposition 8. An example of this is *People v. Ruggles,* 39 Cal. 3d 1, 702 P.2d 170, 216 Cal. Rptr. 88 (1985), discussed above. A state intermediate appeals court has since acknowledged that *Ruggles* was superseded by Proposition 8 as to searches conducted after June 8, 1982. *People v. Rodrigues-Fernandez,* 286 Cal. Rptr. 700, 703 n.2 (Cal. Ct. App. 1991).

67. *People v. May,* 44 Cal. 3d 309, 748 P.2d 307, 243 Cal. Rptr. 369 (1988).

68. Kelso and Bass, "Victims' Bill of Rights," 865–866 (footnote omitted).

69. See Robert S. Thompson, "Judicial Retention Elections and Judicial Method: A Retrospective on the California Retention Election of 1986," *Southern California Law Review* 61 (September 1988): 2007–2064; Gerald F. Uelman, "Supreme Court Retention Elections in California," *Santa Clara Law Review* 28 (Spring 1988): 333–355.

70. The California Supreme Court consists of a chief justice of the state and six associate justices. The term of office is twelve years, but the appointee's term does not

begin until his predecessor's has ended, so the period of service could be much longer if the predecessor's term is aborted. Justices are nominated by the governor, after consultation with the state bar, followed by confirmation by a commission on judicial appointments, consisting of the chief justice, the state attorney general and the senior presiding justice of the intermediate appellate courts. After nomination by the governor and confirmation by the commission, the appointee is immediately sworn in but then subject to voter retention in the next gubernatorial election. Since governors are elected to four-year terms, an appointee could serve on the court for up to four years without public endorsement. Once the predecessor's term (if any remains) expires, the replacement must again face the public in a gubernatorial election year to qualify for his or her own term. Judicial appointees run unopposed on a nonpartisan ballot, the public voting "yes" or "no" on retention; a majority vote is required for election. Rose Bird was first appointed chief justice in 1977, by Governor Edmund G. ("Gerry") Brown, and was retained in the 1978 gubernatorial election. This entitled her to serve through 1986, the remainder of her predecessor's term. In 1986 she ran for her own term and was defeated, resigning on January 5, 1987.

71.   Culver and Wold, "Rose Bird," 87.

72.   Ibid., 87–88.

73.   John T. Wold and John H. Culver, "The Defeat of the California Justices: The Campaign, The Electorate, and the Issue of Judicial Accountability," *Judicature* 70 (April–May 1987): 349.

74.   Ibid., 349–350.

75.   Ibid.

76.   Ibid., 351. Reynoso garnered 40 percent of the vote; Grodin captured 43 percent.

77.   The only Democrat still left, Stanley Mosk, the dean of California judges, was appointed by Gerry Brown's father, Pat Brown.

78.   See Table 7.2.

79.   Latzer, *State Constitutions*, 163.

80.   *Raven v. Deukmejian,* 52 Cal. 3d 336, 801 P.2d 1077, 276 Cal. Rptr. 326 (1990).

81.   *Raven,* 801 P.2d at 1087 (emphasis omitted).

82.   Florida Constitution, art. 1, sec. 12, amended in November 1992, effective January 3, 1983. See Christopher Slobogin, "State Adoption of Federal Law: Exploring the Limits of Florida's 'Forced Linkage' Amendment," *University of Florida Law Review* 39 (Summer 1987): 653–732; Paul R. Joseph, "No Different Drummer: The Effect of the 1983 Amendment to Article I, § 12 of the Florida Constitution," *St. Thomas Law Review* 5 (Fall 1992): 101–130.

83.   Unlike Proposition 8, the Florida amendment applies only to search and seizure law, and does not affect other state exclusionary rules. Secondly, it purports to change the interpretation of the substantive search and seizure right, not just the exclusionary remedy.

84.   Latzer, *State Constitutions,* 163.

85.   Susan B. Carbon, "Judicial Retention Elections: Are They Serving Their Intended Purpose?" *Judicature* 64 (November 1980): 221–223, reports that from 1934 to 1980 only thirty-three judges were not retained.

86.   See Ronald K. L. Collins, "Hans Linde and His 1984 Judicial Election: The Primary," *Oregon Law Review* 70 (Winter 1991): 747–791.

87.   Andrew Blum, "Jurists, Initiatives on Ballot," *National Law Journal*, 16 November 1992, 1.

88.   Ibid.

8

School Finance and Inequality in New Jersey

Russell S. Harrison and G. Alan Tarr

In *Robinson v. Cahill* (1973), the New Jersey Supreme Court ruled that the state's system of school finance, largely funded by local property taxes, violated the state constitution's requirement that the state provide to all children a "thorough and efficient education."[1] The New Jersey court's decision came at a particularly propitious time for school-finance reformers. Thirteen days earlier, in *San Antonio Independent School District v. Rodriguez* (1973), the U.S. Supreme Court had rejected a challenge under the federal equal protection clause to Texas's very similar system of school finance.[2] *Rodriguez* had seemed to preclude constitutional attacks on school finance, but *Robinson* redirected and reinvigorated the litigation campaign for school-finance reform. The ruling reminded potential litigants — and government officials — that state systems of school finance had to satisfy state, as well as federal, constitutional requirements. In addition, it underscored the obligations imposed on state governments by distinctive state constitutional provisions. There is, for example, no federal analogue to New Jersey's "thorough and efficient" clause or to several other state constitutional requirements. Finally, *Robinson* demonstrated that state courts might be more receptive to school-finance challenges than the federal courts had been.[3]

In the two decades since *Robinson* was decided, twenty-two state supreme courts have considered state constitutional challenges to state systems of school finance. Twelve courts rejected the challenges, typically according the state legislature broad discretion in structuring the state's system of school finance.[4] But ten courts, finding that existing systems of school finance violated constitutional mandates, required that they be replaced.[5] Since 1989 the supreme courts of Kentucky, Montana, Texas, and (once again) New Jersey have all invalidated school-finance programs.

School finance thus represents one of the most important areas of constitutional policymaking by state courts in recent decades. However, researchers have not systematically examined the consequences of the state courts' involvement in school-finance reform.[6] This is surprising, because research on the impact of federal judicial rulings suggests that court decisions do not always achieve their intended goals and may have unanticipated consequences. This study helps to fill that research gap by analyzing the impact of judicially mandated school-finance reform in New Jersey. In addition to their substantive interest, our findings should also be helpful in assessing the usefulness of insights derived from the study of federal judicial impact in understanding state courts' role in state constitutional politics.

THE "DYNAMIC COURT" VERSUS THE "CONSTRAINED COURT"

Models of Judicial Effectiveness

Sympathetic commentators have viewed state judicial rulings as crucial in achieving educational equity. Mark Jaffe and Kenneth Kersch, for example, have called *Robinson* a "paradigmatic example of a state court using its state constitution to spur significant social reform."[7] Kern Alexander, attorney for the plaintiffs in school-finance litigation in Kentucky, has argued that "state legislatures in most circumstances are unlikely to provide equal educational opportunities without judicial intervention."[8] But judicial rulings can, according to Christopher Edley, break "the virtual death-grip of inertia in our political and educational institutions" and "open up a new world of possibilities."[9] Thus, the willingness of state judges to intervene aggressively has led Charles Benson to conclude that "the future of court action in helping to create systems of education that are both equitable and economically efficient looks far brighter than it did just twenty years ago."[10]

Underlying these claims is a view of state courts' capacity to institute social change that Gerald Rosenberg has identified as the "dynamic court" model.[11] According to this model, courts can initiate social reform because they are free from the electoral constraints and institutional arrangements that prevent change. Because judges are not electorally accountable, they can afford to take unpopular stands. Unlike legislators, they are not constrained by entrenched interests, which are strategically situated to block reforms. Moreover, access to the courts does not depend on political or economic resources but simply the ability to advance legal arguments. Finally, judicial decisions are determined by the quality of those arguments rather than by political power, so even groups that are weak and unpopular can prevail in the courts.

Contrasted to this dynamic court model is what Rosenberg has called the "constrained court" model, which suggests that courts seldom serve as effective agents of social change.[12] According to the constrained court model, it is often difficult to frame arguments for social change in terms of legal rights, given existing constitutional and statutory law. Even when such arguments can be advanced, attachment to legal precedent and fear of political repercussions make courts reluctant to venture too far outside the political mainstream. Most important, as the literature on judicial impact shows, there is often a sizable gap between the intended and actual effects of judicial action.[13]

Early impact studies found that states and localities were able to resist or blunt the mandates of the U.S. Supreme Court and of lower federal courts on a wide range of issues, such as school desegregation, school prayer, and the rights of defendants.[14] Even when states and localities introduced policy changes in response to judicial mandates, the anticipated payoffs often did not materialize. For example, several studies found that state legislative reapportionment failed to increase the influence of center cities, as anticipated by partisans of judicial intervention.[15] Taken together, studies of the impact of federal judicial policies reveal that the effects of court rulings are often multiple and diffuse, some anticipated and some not, with the implementation and impacts of specific court decisions mediated by a wide range of intervening variables.

Constrained or Dynamic Courts?

Which is more accurate, the dynamic court model or the constrained court model? According to Rosenberg, courts can effectively promote social reform only when the various constraints identified in the constrained court model are overcome.[16] Because this happens only rarely, in general the constrained court model better describes the capacity of the courts to promote policy innovation. Nevertheless, Rosenberg suggests that courts can promote social change when there are:

1. ample legal precedent supporting the desired change;
2. support from the executive and from substantial numbers in the legislature for the change;
3. support for the change from some citizens or at least low levels of opposition from all citizens; and
4. incentives offered to induce compliance, costs imposed for noncompliance, market mechanisms for implementation, or a willingness on the part of officials to act, using court orders to leverage additional resources or provide protection for their actions.

Rosenberg's research offers a useful framework for analyzing the policymaking effectiveness of state courts, and we shall employ it in this study. Nevertheless, because Rosenberg's research focused exclusively on federal courts, the question arises as to whether his conclusions likewise apply to state court policymaking. To address this, we consider the New Jersey Supreme Court's rulings on public-school finance.

SCHOOL-FINANCE LITIGATION IN NEW JERSEY

The *Robinson* Odyssey

Robinson v. Cahill is a classic example of agenda-setting policy-making: The New Jersey Supreme Court invalidated the state's system of school finance without endorsing an alternative system, thereby obliging state officials to devise their own remedy for the constitutional violation.[17] In *Robinson* I the New Jersey Supreme Court unanimously held that the state's system of school finance failed to meet the New Jersey Constitution's requirement of a "thorough and efficient education" for all children.[18] The justices interpreted this constitutional mandate to "embrace that educational opportunity which is needed in the contemporary setting to equip a child for his role as a citizen and as a competitor in the labor market."[19] Although the court did not mandate equal expenditures for all students, it assumed that there was a strong correlation between per pupil expenditures and quality of education. Continued heavy reliance on the local property tax to fund education was no longer permissible, the court held, because it resulted in unconstitutional inequalities. In *Robinson* II the court gave the legislature until the end of 1974 to establish a constitutionally adequate system of school finance.[20]

Initially, when the legislature failed to meet the court-imposed deadline, the justices acquiesced, extending the deadline to October 1.[21] Four months later, however, in the face of continuing legislative inaction, the court reversed course, threatening to redistribute school aid itself unless the legislature developed a new system of school finance for the 1976–1977 school year.[22] This threat produced begrudging legislative action: One day before the court's deadline, legislators enacted the Public School Education Act of 1975, which at least in part met the court's requirements. In *Robinson* V a divided court held the Act constitutional as long as it was fully funded for the 1976-1977 school year.[23]

Enactment of the Public School Education Act, however, did not resolve the controversy. The legislature refused to fund the act for over eight months, prompting the New Jersey Supreme Court to issue an injunction forbidding the operation of an unconstitutional school system after July 1, 1976.[24] This injunction put enormous pressure on the legislature to act, and nine days after the injunction went into effect, legislators adopted a 2 percent gross income tax to fund the new school finance act. In *Robinson* VII the Court ended the confrontation by lifting the injunction.[25]

From *Robinson* to *Abbott*

Resolution of *Robinson v. Cahill* brought only a temporary respite in school-finance litigation in New Jersey. In 1981 litigants filed suit once again, claiming that the new system of school finance did not ensure a "thorough and efficient" education for all students and particularly for indigent students in poor urban districts. In 1990 the New Jersey Supreme Court in *Abbott v. Burke* (*Abbott* II) partially agreed, "hold[ing] the Act unconstitutional as applied to poorer urban districts."[26] To remedy this situation, the justices held, the state must ensure that per pupil funding in poorer urban school districts was at least equivalent to funding in the state's wealthiest districts. The justices gave the state five years to devise and implement a remedy that would achieve that result.

Even before the court had decided *Abbott*, Governor James Florio, anticipating the court's ruling, had proposed a new state aid plan, labeled the Quality Education Act.[27] This plan involved a $1.4 billion increase in income taxes dedicated to education aid and property tax relief. Enacted without a single Republican vote by the New Jersey legislature, the

Quality Education Act proved extremely unpopular, contributing to the election of veto-proof Republican majorities in both houses of the state legislature in 1991 and to Florio's defeat when he ran for reelection in 1993. Responding to citizen outrage, the legislature in 1991 amended the Quality Education Act to divert $360 million from school aid to property tax relief. This, however, angered the litigants in *Abbott*, who believed that it deprived inner-city schools of funds to which they were entitled under the supreme court's decision. In 1994 their suit to require additional state funding was again before the New Jersey Supreme Court.

Applying Rosenberg's Models to State Constitutional Policymaking

Because Rosenberg's models were developed in analyzing the effects of policy initiatives of the United States Supreme Court and other federal courts, they must be modified to reflect the distinctive institutional and legal context of state constitutional policymaking. These changes, however, do not appear to involve critical elements of Rosenberg's theory. Certainly, they had no effect on state court policymaking regarding school finance.

The dynamic court model stresses the importance of judicial independence in promoting activism. However, state court judges are more accountable than their federal counterparts, because in almost half the states they are elected and in only one are they granted life tenure upon elevation to the bench. If this connection between lack of accountability and activism were crucial, one might expect that state judges who were more accountable would be less inclined to initiate major policy changes. At least with regard to school finance, however, this expectation is not borne out. Mode of judicial selection did not determine judicial receptivity to school-finance challenges. Focusing on those courts that heard challenges to school-finance programs, one finds that for courts selected by partisan election, three out of four invalidated the programs; for those selected by nonpartisan election, three out of ten; for those selected by gubernatorial or legislative appointment, two out of three; and for those selected by merit selection, two out of six.[28] Put differently, of those courts that heard challenges to school-finance programs, 43 percent of the courts on which judges were elected invalidated the programs compared with 44 percent of the courts on which judges were appointed.

Length of judicial term is likewise an indicator of judicial independence. Thus, if judicial independence were decisive in promoting activism, one might expect that state judges with longer terms of office would be more likely to invalidate school-finance programs than would those serving shorter terms. Our data, however, do not support this expectation.[29] Looking once again solely at courts that heard challenges to school-finance programs, one finds that 50 percent of the courts whose judges served less than ten-year terms (eight out of sixteen) invalidated the challenged school-finance programs. In contrast, only 28.6 percent of the courts whose judges served ten-year terms or longer (two out of seven) invalidated the programs. Thus, length of judicial term was not positively related to willingness to strike down state systems of school finance.

Constitutional Guarantees and Intervention

The constrained court model suggests that enlisting courts in social change is made more difficult by the absence of positive rights guarantees on which to base legal arguments. As Rosenberg put it, "there are no constitutional rights to decent housing, adequate levels of welfare, or clean air."[30] However, this is only true if one restricts one's attention to the federal Constitution. Some state constitutions do protect such rights — the New York Constitution, for example, guarantees the needy a right to public assistance, and the Illinois Constitution affirms a right to a healthy environment.[31] Even more important, some state constitutions impose obligations on state government to meet certain substantive goals, such as a "thorough and efficient education" for all children, and litigants can base arguments for social change on such provisions.[32]

If the availability of such provisions is crucial for activism, one would expect that courts whose state constitutions offered greater support for education would be more likely to invalidate school-finance systems. In fact, differences among state constitutions do not account for state courts' disparate rulings on school finance; rather, courts have reached opposite results interpreting virtually identical constitutional provisions. For example, while the Kentucky, New Jersey, and Washington Supreme Courts concluded that the education articles of their state constitutions required invalidation of existing school-finance programs, the Colorado and New York Supreme Courts upheld comparable programs in their states on the basis of very similar provisions. Moreover, while the Arkansas and California Supreme Courts ruled that the systems of school finance in their states violated state constitutional guarantees of equality, the Michigan, Ohio, and Oregon Supreme Courts — looking at similar provisions — reached the opposite conclusion.

Were the Conditions Present in New Jersey for Successful Judicial Policymaking?

We turn now to a consideration of the school-finance litigation in New Jersey in light of the conditions identified by Rosenberg as necessary for successful judicial policymaking. Two conclusions emerge from our analysis. First, not all the conditions Rosenberg identified appear necessary for state court policymaking. In particular, the availability of ample legal precedent does not appear decisive. Second, insofar as Rosenberg's conditions do apply, those conditions were better met in the *Robinson* litigation than in the *Abbott* litigation. Thus, one would expect the New Jersey Supreme Court's initial intervention in school finance to be more successful than its later effort. Exactly how successful the court was, of course, remains to be seen.

Ample Legal Precedent

Among the factors Rosenberg identified as necessary for effective judicial policymaking was ample legal precedent. "Unless litigators can find strong precedents on which to base their claims," he argued, "cases demanding significant social reform will be losers."[33] Thus, this condition relates not to the effects of the court's mandates but to the court's willingness to rule in favor of those seeking social change. In fact, however, the New Jersey Supreme Court's initiatives on school finance seem to belie this claim. Prior to *Robinson v. Cahill*, only the California Supreme Court had invalidated a school-finance plan, and the precedential value of its ruling — based on the equal protection clause of the federal Constitution — was undermined by the U.S. Supreme Court's ruling in *San Antonio Independent Board of Education v. Rodriguez*.[34] Moreover, the New Jersey Constitution's "thorough and efficient" clause, on which the New Jersey court ultimately based its decision, had never previously been interpreted as a major restraint on legislation regarding education.[35] Indeed, what is striking about the opinion of the court in *Robinson* I is the paucity of precedent cited in support of the ruling.

Instead of the extent of supportive precedent, what seems determinative for state courts is the institutional identity of the court. Prior to *Robinson*, the New Jersey Supreme Court was already accustomed to playing a vigorous policy role and had established its reputation as an activist court.[36] It had intervened aggressively to ensure reapportionment of the state legislature and had pioneered changes in tort law. In contrast to their colleagues on other courts, the New Jersey justices forthrightly identified themselves as "policymakers."[37] As one former justice put it, "no thicket [is] too political for us."[38] Thus, the court's willingness to intervene in the school-finance dispute was prepared by the court's previous involvement in controversial political issues.

Conversely, it should be noted that in school-finance litigation the existence of ample precedent did not necessarily promote judicial intervention. From 1980 to 1987, seven state supreme courts considered challenges to state systems of school finance. In several instances, plaintiffs based their arguments on state constitutional provisions announcing a strong state commitment to education, together with rulings in other states interpreting similar provisions as requiring the invalidation of school-finance programs based on property taxes. None-theless, in six of these cases the courts upheld the challenged programs. Thus, ample precedent was neither a necessary nor a sufficient condition for state court invalidation of school-finance programs.

Support from the Executive and from the Legislature

Rosenberg argued that courts could promote social change only if they enjoyed support from the executive and from substantial segments of the legislature. The condition of executive support was met during both the *Robinson* and *Abbott* eras. Indeed, up to 1993 New Jersey's governors provided consistent, if not always effective, support for the New Jersey Supreme Court's school-finance rulings. Governor William Cahill, the nominal defendant in *Robinson*, had earned a reputation as an "education governor" even before the court's ruling, and he immediately proposed enactment of an income tax to provide the state funding mandated by the court. However, he was defeated for renomination in the Republican primary, in part because of his support for an income tax and, as a lame duck, was unable to exercise effective leadership. His successor, Governor Brendan Byrne, likewise endorsed the court's ruling. His proposals formed the basis for the Public School Education Act of 1976, and in order to ensure funding for the Act, he supported the court's injunction prohibiting the operation of the schools under the previous funding plan. Finally, as noted previously, Governor James Florio introduced his own school-finance reforms even before *Abbott* was announced, and his Quality Education Act went even further than the court mandated.

Legislative support for the court's rulings, on the other hand, has been inconsistent and at times begrudging. In the immediate aftermath of *Robinson*, legislators voiced cautious support, although emphasizing difficulties of implementation.[39] Subsequently, legislative majorities enacted and ultimately funded the Public School Education Act of 1976 and the Quality Education Act of 1990. However, the legislature's support for the Public School Education Act was unenthusiastic and long delayed, and the enactment of the Quality Education Act was quickly followed by funding cuts in 1991 and by the election of a Republican-dominated legislature opposed to the act.

The election of Republican majorities in both houses of the state legislature, followed two years later by the election of Governor Christine Whitman, signaled reduced support for the fiscal approach outlined by the New Jersey Supreme Court. In sum, insofar as gubernatorial and legislative support are necessary for effective judicial intervention, one can conclude that such support was present to a greater extent in the aftermath of *Robinson* than in the aftermath of *Abbott* and will be even less likely should the New Jersey court again require revision of the state's system of school finance.

Support — or Absence of Intense Opposition — from the Citizenry

While New Jerseyites generally endorsed the aim of school-finance reform following both *Robinson* and *Abbott*, they were not enthusiastic about paying increased taxes to support such reform. Nonetheless, greater support for the court's ruling was evident after *Robinson*. In the aftermath of *Robinson v. Cahill*, an overwhelming majority (73 percent to 22 percent) favored an increase in state aid to local schools.[40] Although Governor Cahill was not renominated by the Republican party largely because of his support for an income tax, his successor as governor, Brendan Byrne, was supported by both parties when he proposed an income tax to meet the court's requirements. Moreover, he was renominated by his party and won reelection.

In contrast, in the aftermath of *Abbott v. Burke*, the popular support — or absence of intense opposition — needed for effective judicial policymaking did not appear to be present. A poll conducted after the court's ruling revealed sharp divisions on school finance among the citizenry.[41] Seventy percent of those questioned had heard of the court's decision, and of those respondents 54 percent agreed with the court's ruling while 38 percent disagreed. However, the ruling clearly polarized the citizenry. Almost one-third of respondents strongly agreed with the court's ruling while almost one-fourth strongly disagreed. Moreover, a majority of respondents (54 percent to 35 percent) opposed the Quality Education Act, proposed by Governor Florio in anticipation of the court's mandates, and most (59 percent to 30 percent) doubted that it would improve the quality of public education.

Even more striking were the political consequences of the passage of Governor Florio's Quality Education Act and of the income tax increases he proposed to finance it. A major antitax movement, Hands Across New Jersey, emerged to protest Florio's tax increases. Republicans, who were in the minority in both houses of the state legislature, captured more than two-thirds majorities in each in 1991; and Christine Todd Whitman, despite a generally lackluster campaign, defeated Florio in 1993 by attacking his tax increases and pledging to reduce income taxes.

Factors Promoting Implementation

Rosenberg identified four factors conducive to effective implementation: (1) incentives to induce compliance, (2) market mechanisms for implementation, (3) costs imposed for noncompliance, and (4) the willingness of governmental officials to act, using judicial rulings to leverage additional resources or provide protection for their actions. Neither of the first two factors was applicable to New Jersey's school-finance litigation. The New Jersey Supreme Court offered no incentives for compliance, except for the cessation of judicial supervision, and market mechanisms were not available for implementing the court's mandates.

However, the third and fourth factors promoting effective implementation were present in the New Jersey litigation. After initially granting a delay for implementation of *Robinson*, the court made clear its willingness to impose costs for noncompliance. It threatened to redistribute school aid in the absence of legislative action, closed the state's schools when the legislature failed to fund its reform program, and demonstrated that it would continue to strike down inadequate state responses through its decision in *Abbott* II and its willingness to entertain a challenge to the legislative response to *Abbott*.

Furthermore, state officials and other important political actors demonstrated a willingness to act in support of the court's mandates. Governors Cahill, Byrne, and Florio favored funding equalization and the imposition of new taxes to promote equalization, and they actively sought to meet the court's mandates. (In fact, the court's rulings may have enabled them to pursue a course they would have pursued in any event.) They were supported in this by elements in the legislature, which enacted school-finance reforms in response to the court's rulings, as well as by major publications such as the *New York Times* and leading New Jersey papers and by powerful pressure groups such as the New Jersey

Education Association. Equally important, school officials in urban districts strongly supported the court's rulings and were eager to implement them as well as to pressure the legislature to deliver the resources that the court's rulings seemed to require. These districts were not only the main beneficiaries of *Robinson* and *Abbott* but also their instigator: In fact, it was school officials in Jersey City who initiated the *Robinson* case. Thus, under Rosenberg's theory, the conditions favoring effective implementation were present after both *Robinson* and *Abbott*.

Our analysis has suggested that of the four factors identified by Rosenberg as crucial for successful judicial intervention, only three are pertinent for state judicial policymaking. It has further suggested that the factors favoring successful judicial intervention were present to a greater degree following *Robinson v. Cahill* than following *Abbott v. Burke*. Thus, *Robinson* can be seen as an important test of the dynamic court model, and the court's success or failure in *Robinson* may indicate the prospects for *Abbott* as well. Thus, it is appropriate to consider in detail the consequences of the court's intervention in *Robinson*.

TESTING THE EFFECTS OF JUDICIAL INTERVENTION

Level of State Expenditures

Approach

According to the New Jersey Supreme Court in *Robinson*, the state constitution established the provision of "thorough and efficient" education as a state responsibility. Historically, New Jersey had relied on local school districts to fund elementary and secondary education — through the 1940s, Trenton's contribution to local school budgets was between 3 percent and 6 percent.[42] The court held, however, that this delegation to local school districts did not absolve the state of its responsibility. Because the system of school finance challenged in *Robinson* failed to meet this constitutional obligation, the state was obliged to increase its funding of education. Thus, one aim of the New Jersey court was increased state funding for elementary and secondary education.

To assess whether the court's rulings achieved this aim, we have utilized an "interrupted times series" analysis.[43] That is, we have measured the percentage of education funding provided by the state before and after *Robinson v. Cahill*, as well as changes in the state percentage over time, in order to ascertain the impact of the court's decisions, relative to preexisting trends.

Findings

On initial inspection, *Robinson* may appear to have achieved its objective of promoting substantially greater state funding for education. According to one account, between the 1975–1976 and 1976–1977 school years, state aid per pupil increased over 40 percent.[44] Yet this figure substantially overestimates the effects of *Robinson*. For one thing, the increase in state funding for education in New Jersey was part of a national trend, occurring both in states with successful challenges to school-finance programs and in those without such challenges. According to the National Center for Education Statistics, nationally the percentage of school revenues from state government climbed 7 percent from 1970 to 1980, at the same time that current expenditures per pupil rose 35 percent.[45] Moreover, within New Jersey itself, state aid to local school districts was increasing steadily even before Robinson was decided and funding to meet its mandates was provided. From 1965–1966 to 1974–1975, state aid increased at a mean annual rate of 14.7 percent.[46] Comparing the projected state aid without *Robinson* with the aid actually provided after the adoption and funding of the Public School Education Act, Richard Lehne concluded that "credit for a modest increase of about 7 percent in state assistance to local school districts can be attributed to *Robinson*.[47]

It is also noteworthy that after the initial infusion of funds following *Robinson*, state aid as a percentage of local districts' revenues did not continue its dramatic increase. Rather, state aid as a percentage of total school district revenues tended to stabilize. In the 1977–1978 period, state aid represented 40.0 percent of district revenues, and three years later, in the 1980–1981 period, the percentage remained roughly the same (39.4 percent).[48] By 1984–1985, during a period of economic prosperity, the state contribution had increased to 42.8 percent, but by 1987–1988 it had shrunk to 42.0 percent.

Implications

When the New Jersey Supreme Court in *Robinson* required the state to increase its aid to elementary and secondary education, it did not promote a new policy. Rather, it continued and somewhat accelerated a trend toward greater state funding that already existed in the state and that paralleled developments occurring nationwide. At least in terms of overall level of state aid, the modest independent effect of the court's ruling hardly justifies claims of a judicially mandated revolution in school finance.

Interdistrict Distribution of Education Funds

Approach

One major aim of the New Jersey Supreme Court in *Robinson* was to reduce the disparities in expenditures for education among school districts. To assess the effects of the New Jersey Supreme Court's intervention on the distribution of educational funds, we again have employed an interrupted times series analysis.[49] We have measured the direction and extent of change in interdistrict funding disparities both before and after *Robinson v. Cahill* and, by comparing the two trends, ascertained the impact of the court's decisions, relative to preexisting trends. More specifically, we have based our comparison on per student expenditures for all school districts in New Jersey from 1961 through 1991, using alternate year data.[50]

A preliminary analysis revealed that certain public school systems — vocational schools; special district schools for the physically and mentally challenged; and "sending districts," which taught few if any of their own students — were highly deviant from the rest. Therefore, these were excluded in order to focus on more directly comparable school systems. The school systems that remained included three types of systems: (1) comprehensive systems serving students from kindergarten through twelfth grade; (2) systems providing only grammar schools; and (3) systems serving only post–grammar school students (i.e., those in middle school or high school). The grammar school districts largely coincided with municipal boundaries, while the high school districts were almost exclusively regional systems serving several municipalities. The comprehensive districts were typically, though not always, coterminous with one of New Jersey's 567 municipalities.

We then rank-ordered all school systems in New Jersey on the basis of school expenditures. Comparison of the expenditures of the top and bottom districts in the state might skew our results, because these districts might enroll very few students and exhibit wide fluctuations in annual per student expenditures. We therefore decided to compare the ratios of expenditures by those systems at the ninetieth percentile to those at the tenth percentile. That is, we compared the ratio of expenditures by those that were 10 percent (or one decile) from the top as well as those that were 10 percent (or one decile) from the bottom, assuming that these were more representative of typical districts throughout the state. We also computed the ratio of expenditures of those systems at the seventy-fifth and twenty-fifth percentiles (the third and first quartiles). These measures enable us to compare interdistrict spending disparities between typical high expenditure school systems and typical low expenditure school systems. Presumably if every district spent the same amount, the ratio of expenditures from the high to the low districts would be one to one, for a value of one. The greater the disparity in expenditures, the higher the ratio.

Findings

Figure 8.1 portrays the results of our comparison of per pupil expenditures by school systems throughout New Jersey for every other year from 1961 through 1991. It shows that in 1961 the typical district at the ninetieth percentile spent almost 2.4 times as much as the typical district at the tenth percentile. In the same year the typical district at the seventy-fifth percentile (or third quartile) spent about 1.5 times as much

FIGURE 8.1
Trends in Inequality of Per Pupil Expenditures
among New Jersey School Systems

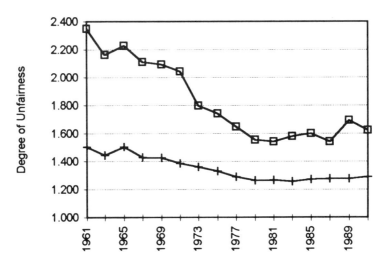

☐ Ratio of ninetieth to tenth percentiles (Ninth/First Decile)
+ Ratio of seventy-fifth to twenty-fifth percentiles (Third/First Quartile)

as the typical district at the twenty-fifth percentile (or first quartile). For the entire period from 1961 through 1991, the average ratios of inequality were less than 2 to 1. That is, typical districts at the top echelons spent less than twice the dollars per student committed by typical school systems at the bottom ranks. Overall, then, there was considerably less interdistrict inequality than a focus on top and bottom districts might have led one to expect.

More important, our data reveal surprising findings about the pattern of interdistrict inequalities over time. They show a clear and persistent decline in interdistrict funding disparities from 1961 through 1973. This means that these inequalities were decreasing, not increasing, prior to the New Jersey Supreme Court's intervention in *Robinson*. During the period of litigation prior to the eventual adoption of the new funding formula (1973–1976), these inequalities continued to decrease at roughly the same rate.

After the enactment of the new funding formula and the conclusion of the litigation in 1976, the same trend of decreasing inequalities continued for a few years. However, despite the judicial intervention, the rate of decrease actually lessened. Moreover, after about the 1981–1983 period a new trend emerged of increased interdistrict inequalities. These changes helped stimulate the *Abbott v. Burke* round of litigation.

Implications

Summarizing the findings of earlier judicial-impact studies, Charles Johnson and Bradley Canon concluded that federal courts are more likely to be legitimizers of ongoing trends than progenitors of radical new developments.[51] Our findings with regard to both state support for education and interdistrict disparities in educational expenditures seem to suggest that the same is true for state courts. Long before 1977 inequality in New Jersey school finances was declining.

Thus, both federal and state courts seem most likely to act when they in effect simply ratify a pattern of widespread social reform that has already begun and in fact has extended over many years, rather than to intervene to reverse a trend. Even when they do act, the ability of courts to change complex social, economic, and political interactions is relatively limited. As Gerald Rosenberg has suggested, "perhaps only when political, social, and economic forces have already pushed society far along the road to reform will courts have any independent effect. Even then their decisions may be more a reflection of significant social reform already occurring than an independent, important contribution to it."[52]

Other Aspects of Judicial Effectiveness

Our analysis thus far has focused on the level of state aid to local school districts and on interdistrict inequalities in expenditures. These, however, do not exhaust the issues pertinent to school-finance reform in New Jersey and elsewhere. Although space constraints preclude dealing with them in depth, at least two of these issues deserve mention, as topics for future research.

Equalization of Funding and Educational Performance

The New Jersey Supreme Court's insistence on equalizing funding among school districts is based on the assumption that there is a direct connection between level of funding and educational outcomes. Thus, in *Robinson* the court asserted that "there is a significant connection between the sums expended and the quality of the educational opportunity."[53] The justices reiterated this "conventional wisdom" in *Abbott* II. After all, the court reasoned, "if factors [such as teacher ratios, experience, and educational background and salary] are not related to the quality of education, why are the richer districts willing to spend so much for them?"[54]

The court's focus on fiscal factors reflects, at least in part, the way in which the parties in *Robinson* and *Abbott* defined the dispute. The plaintiffs in both cases chose to focus primarily on fiscal solutions to the state's educational problems, rather than exploring more controversial structural changes. Their choice tied the hands of the judges, who could neither address issues unless the parties bring them before the court nor, typically, conduct their own research to search for alternative solutions or even to analyze past, present, or future trends.[55] The justices in *Abbott* recognized this difficulty, asserting that "[o]ur power to require a thorough and efficient education is not limited to a money remedy."[56] However, they also tied imposition of a nonmonetary remedy to litigation specifically requesting such relief.

The problem with the court's focus on fiscal factors is that they may not be determinative for educational success. Indeed, many social scientists dispute the court's — and plaintiffs' — assumption that there is a connection between the level of inputs and the quality of educational outputs. Other social scientists, however, disagree, and an extensive and sophisticated body of literature has developed debating the question of whether and to what extent money matters.[57] The importance of this question can scarcely be exaggerated. The effectiveness of the New

Jersey Supreme Court's — and other courts' — rulings on school finance depends on whether they accurately identified the factors that promote effective education. Insofar as those skeptical of the educational importance of funding levels are correct, even if the courts' rulings had equalized per pupil spending among school districts, they would not necessarily have ensured a "thorough and efficient" education for all students. Only through an analysis of "output measures," of the effect of changes in resource levels on student performance over time, could one ultimately determine the success of the New Jersey Supreme Court's intervention.

Equalization of Funding and Efficiency

The New Jersey Constitution requires that the state establish a system of education that is both thorough and efficient. However, in evaluating the New Jersey system of public school finance according to these criteria, the New Jersey Supreme Court has emphasized "thoroughness," defined in terms of educational equity, but paid scant attention to "efficiency." Thus, it has rejected the state's efforts to focus on how efficiently educational resources were employed in poorer districts and on whether more cost-effective use of existing resources, rather than increasing resources, would improve education in those districts. Although recognizing that some mismanagement had occurred, the justices flatly denied in *Abbott* that it was "a significant factor in the general failure to achieve a thorough and efficient education in poorer urban districts."[58] Moreover, even if additional funding "will not enable the poorer urban districts to satisfy the thorough and efficient test," the court maintained, "they are entitled to pass or fail with at least the same amount of money as their competitors."[59]

Yet this claim seems dubious. If a more cost-effective means were available that ensured a thorough and efficient education, then it seems unlikely that the New Jersey Constitution would preclude its adoption because differences in expenditures remained. The New Jersey court's failure to address the constitutional requirement of an "efficient education" suggests the desirability of research aimed at explicating the meaning and implications of the phrase. More important, this requirement suggests the propriety of exploring alternative approaches to providing a "thorough and efficient" education for the children of New Jersey and thereby satisfying the constitutional mandate.

CONCLUSION

For over two decades, school-finance reformers have attributed the educational plight of the urban poor to interdistrict inequalities in school funding and have called on courts to remedy the situation. During this same period, judicial-impact scholars have repeatedly warned against expecting judicial mandates to promote fundamental social change. Our analysis of judicial involvement in school-finance reform in New Jersey confirms the wisdom of those warnings. When the New Jersey Supreme Court announced its decision in *Robinson v. Cahill*, the ruling was hailed as inaugurating a revolution in education. Yet the actual effects of *Robinson* were hardly revolutionary. The level of state funding for education rose, but it had already been rising. The level of interdistrict inequality declined, at least temporarily, but it had already been declining. Thus, the court's mandates gave further impetus to preexisting trends rather than initiating fundamental change. Moreover, as the renewal of litigation in *Abbott* suggests, the changes that the court's rulings produced did not substantially improve the quality of education provided to students in poor school districts.

The failure of *Robinson* to promote fundamental social change is striking because that ruling and its progeny in large measure exemplified the conditions identified by Rosenberg as necessary for the operation of the dynamic court model. The New Jersey Supreme Court enjoyed support from Governors Cahill and Byrne and, ultimately, from the legislature as well. While the state's citizenry did not welcome the tax increase necessary to fund the court's mandates, opposition was for the most part muted and unorganized. Indeed, most New Jerseyites favored greater state aid to public education. The New Jersey court ensured compliance through its continued involvement in school finance and its willingness to threaten (and temporarily impose) unacceptable costs for noncompliance. Finally, the court throughout the *Robinson* litigation enjoyed the support of statewide elites and of local officials strategically situated to ensure implementation of its mandates.

The failure of the dynamic court model to predict the effects of *Robinson*, even in circumstances in which it seemed applicable, suggests that judicial initiatives in constitutional policymaking may be even less promising than Rosenberg had assumed. In particular, it underscores the crucial importance of judicial understanding of "social facts," that is, "the recurrent patterns of behavior on which policy must be based."[60] For judges to achieve their policy ends, they must obtain accurate information about the situations they intend to affect and about the likely efficacy of various means they might use to alter those situations. However, as Donald Horowitz has noted, the structure of litigation and the backgrounds of judges typically interfere with their obtaining and utilizing such information.[61]

With respect to school-finance litigation in New Jersey in particular, our findings caution against expecting too much from the *Abbott* round of litigation, for in contrast to *Robinson*, the factors that presumably promote effective judicial intervention seem to be absent. If the New Jersey Supreme Court's invalidation of school funding in *Abbott* paved the way for the Quality Education Act and a massive increase in state tax rates, these in turn prompted an electoral revolt that swept from office both Democratic legislators who had supported Governor Florio's tax increase and ultimately the governor himself. Governor Whitman campaigned on a platform of reductions in governmental expenditures and taxes, and few of those making up the Republican legislative majorities represent the districts that most benefit from *Abbott*. By mid-1995, with school finance again before the courts, the potential for a confrontation between the court and the political branches may have increased, but the prospects for a successful judicial attack on inadequate education have not.

NOTES

1. *Robinson v. Cahill*, 303 A.2d 273 (N.J. 1973). The pertinent constitutional provision is New Jersey Constitution, art. 8, sec. 14, para. 1.

2. *San Antonio Independent School District v. Rodriguez*, 411 U.S. 1 (1973).

3. The analysis in this paragraph follows that in G. Alan Tarr, *Judicial Process and Judicial Policymaking* (St. Paul, Minn.: West, 1994), 371.

4. Unsuccessful challenges to state systems of school finance include: *Lujan v. State Board of Education*, 649 P.2d 1005 (Colo. 1982); *Thompson v. McDaniels*, 285 S.E.2d 156 (Ga. 1981); *Thompson v. Engleking*, 557 P.2d 635 (Idaho 1975); *Hornbeck v. Somerset County Board of Education*, 458 A.2d 758 (Md. 1983); *Milliken v. Green*, 203 N.W.2d 457 (Mich. 1972); *Woodahl v. Straub*, 520 P.2d 776 (Mont. 1974); *Board of Education v. Nyquist*, 439 N.E.2d 359 (N.Y. 1982); *Board of Education v. Walter*, 390 N.E.2d 813 (Ohio 1979); *Fair School Finance Council of Oklahoma, Inc. v. State*, 746 P.2d 1135 (Okla. 1987); *Olsen v. Oregon*, 554 P.2d 139 (Or. 1976); *Danson v. Casey*, 399 A.2d 476 (Pa. 1978); *Richland County v. Campbell*, 364 S.E.2d 470 (S.C. 1988); and *Kukor v. Grover*, 436 N.W.2d 568 (Wis. 1989). It should be noted that the Montana court reversed its position in *Woodahl* fifteen years thereafter, in *Helena Elementary School District No. 1 v. State* 769 P.2d 684 (Mont. 1989).

5. In addition to *Robinson v. Cahill*, successful challenges to state systems of school finance include: *DuPree v. Alma School District No. 651*, 651 S.W.2d 90 (Ark. 1983); *Serrano v. Priest* [*Serrano* II], 557 P.2d 929 (Cal. 1976); *Horton v. Meskill*, 376 A.2d 359 (Conn. 1977); *Rose v. Council for Better Education*, 790 S.W.2d 186 (Ky.

1989); *Helena Elementary School District No. 1 v. State*, 769 P.2d 684 (Mont. 1989); *Abbott v. Burke*, 575 A.2d 359 (N.J. 1990); *Seattle School District No. 1 v. State*, 585 P.2d 71 (Wash. 1978); *Pauley v. Kelly*, 255 S.E.2d 859 (W. Va. 1979); and *Washakie County School District No. 1 v. Herschler*, 606 P.2d 310 (Wyo. 1980). It is noteworthy that *Abbott v. Burke* represents a second successful challenge to the system of school finance in New Jersey.

6.   Earlier studies that have to a limited extent attempted to do so include: Julie Underwood and Deborah Verstegen, eds., *The Impacts of Litigation and Legislation on Public School Finance: Adequacy, Equity, and Excellence* (New York: Harper & Row, 1990); and Allan R. Odden, ed., *Rethinking School Finance: An Agenda for the 1990s* (San Francisco: Jossey-Bass, 1992).

7.   Mark Jaffe and Kenneth Kersch, "Guaranteeing a State Right to Quality Education: The Judicial-Political Dialogue in New Jersey," *Journal of Law & Education* 20 (Summer 1991): 271. For a more skeptical assessment, see John Dayton, "The Judicial-Political Dialogue: A Comment on Jaffe and Kersche's 'Guaranteeing a State Right to a Quality Education,'" *Journal of Law & Education* 22 (Summer 1993): 323–334.

8.   Kern Alexander, "The Common School Ideal and the Limits of Legislative Authority: The Kentucky Case," *Harvard Journal on Legislation* 28 (Summer 1991): 343.

9.   Christopher F. Edley, Jr., "Introduction: Lawyers and Education Reform," *Harvard Journal on Legislation* 28 (Summer 1991): 302.

10.   Charles S. Benson, "Definitions of Equity in School Finance in Texas, New Jersey, and Kentucky," *Harvard Journal on Legislation* 28 (Summer 1991): 421.

11.   Gerald N. Rosenberg, *The Hollow Hope; Can Courts Bring About Social Change?* (Chicago: University of Chicago Press, 1991), 21–25.

12.   Ibid., 10–21.

13.   Overviews of this literature include Stephen Wasby, *The Impact of the United States Supreme Court: Some Perspectives* (Homewood, Ill.: Dorsey Press, 1970); and Charles A. Johnson and Bradley C. Canon, *Judicial Policies: Implementation and Impact* (Washington, D.C.: CQ Press, 1984).

14.   Pertinent studies include Jack Peltason, *Fifty-Eight Lonely Men: Southern Judges and School Desegregation* (New York: Harcourt, Brace and World, 1961); Richard Johnson, *The Dynamics of Compliance* (Evanston, Ill.: Northwestern University Press, 1967); G. Alan Tarr, *Judicial Impact and State Supreme Courts* (Lexington, Mass.: Lexington Books, 1977); and Neal A. Milner, *The Court and Local Law Enforcement* (Beverly Hills, Calif.: Sage, 1971).

15.   See, for example, Robert S. Erikson, "The Partisan Impact of State Legislative Reapportionment," *Midwest Journal of Political Science* 15 (1971): 57–71; and Rosenberg, *The Hollow Hope*, 296–302, together with the sources cited in the latter account.

16.   Rosenberg, *The Hollow Hope*, 30–36.

17.   For discussion of this concept, see Mary Cornelia Porter and G. Alan Tarr, "Editors' Introduction," in *State Supreme Courts: Policymakers in the Federal System*, ed. Mary Cornelia Porter and G. Alan Tarr (Westport, Conn.: Greenwood Press, 1982), xvii.

18.   *Robinson v. Cahill*, 303 A.2d 273 (N.J. 1973). Our account of the *Robinson* litigation and its political aftermath relies primarily on Richard Lehne, *The Quest for*

Justice: The Politics of School Finance Reform (New York: Longman, 1978), and on Jaffe and Kersch, "Guaranteeing a State Right to a Quality Education."

19.   303 A.2d 273, 295.

20.   *Robinson v. Cahill* (*Robinson* II), 306 A.2d 65 (N.J. 1973).

21.   *Robinson v. Cahill* (*Robinson* III), 335 A.2d 6 (N.J. 1975).

22.   *Robinson v. Cahill* (*Robinson* IV), 351 A.2d 713 (N.J. 1975).

23.   *Robinson v. Cahill* (*Robinson* V), 355 A.2d 129 (N.J. 1976).

24.   *Robinson v. Cahill* (*Robinson* VI), 358 A.2d 457 (N.J. 1976).

25.   *Robinson v. Cahill* (*Robinson* VII), 360 A.2d 400 (N.J. 1976).

26.   *Abbott v. Burke* (*Abbott* II), 575 A.2d 359, 363 (N.J. 1990). In *Abbott* I, 495 A.2d 376 (N.J. 1985), the New Jersey Supreme Court remanded the case to an administrative law proceeding.

27.   This paragraph draws on the excellent discussion in Barbara G. Salmore and Stephen A. Salmore, *New Jersey Government and Politics: Suburban Politics Comes of Age* (Lincoln: University of Nebraska Press, 1993), chap. 15, as well as on Jaffe and Kersch, "Guaranteeing a State Right to a Quality Education."

28.   Partisan election states: Arkansas, Pennsylvania, Texas, and West Virginia; nonpartisan election states: Arizona, Georgia, Idaho, Kentucky, Montana, Ohio, Oregon, Washington, and Wisconsin; gubernatorial appointment states: California and New Jersey; legislative appointment state: South Carolina; and merit selection states: Colorado, Connecticut, Maryland, New York, Oklahoma, and Wyoming. Our information on modes of judicial selection is drawn from *Book of the States, 1990–91* (Lexington, Ky.: Council of State Governments, 1990), 210–212, table 4.4.

29.   Our data on length of judicial terms is drawn from *Book of the States, 1990–91*, 204–205, table 4.1.

30.   Rosenberg, *The Hollow Hope*, 11.

31.   The right to public assistance is guaranteed in the New York Constitution, Article 17, section 1. For discussion, see Peter J. Galie, *The New York State Constitution: A Reference Guide* (Westport, Conn.: Greenwood Press, 1991), 262–263. State constitutional rights to a clean environment are discussed in A. E. Dick Howard, "State Constitutions and the Environment," *Virginia Law Review* 58 (1972): 193–229.

32.   On the advantages of using state education provisions rather than equality guarantees in school-finance litigation, see Molly McUsic, "The Use of Education Clauses in School Finance Reform Litigation," *Harvard Journal on Legislation* 28 (Summer 1991): 307–340.

33.   Rosenberg, *The Hollow Hope*, 31.

34.   The California Supreme Court's ruling is *Serrano v. Priest* (*Serrano* I), 487 P.2d 1241 (Cal. 1971). Eventually, the California court found that the state's system of school finance violated the state constitution; see *Serrano v. Priest* (*Serrano* II), 557 P.2d 929 (Cal. 1976).

35.   See Robert F. Williams, *The New Jersey Constitution: A Reference Guide* (Westport, Conn.: Greenwood Press, 197), 120–121.

36.   This account of the New Jersey Supreme Court relies on G. Alan Tarr and Mary Cornelia Aldis Porter, *State Supreme Courts in State and Nation* (New Haven, Conn.: Yale University Press, 1988), chap. 5.

37.   See Henry R. Glick, *Supreme Courts in State Politics: An Investigation of the Judicial Role* (New York: Basic Books, 1971); and Kenneth N. Vines, "The Judicial

Rôle in the American States: An Exploration," in *Frontiers of Judicial Research*, ed. Joel B. Grossman and Joseph Tanenhaus (New York: John Wiley and Sons, 1969).

38.	Quoted in Lehne, *The Quest for Justice*, 43.

39.	Lehne, *The Quest for Justice*, 68.

40.	The survey data reported in this paragraph are drawn from the Eagleton Poll, a survey of New Jersey residents, conducted in July 1977.

41.	The poll data analyzed in this paragraph are from the *Star-Ledger*/Eagleton Poll, conducted by telephone from July 2–10, 1990.

42.	Salmore and Salmore, *New Jersey Government and Politics*, 259.

43.	For a discussion of this methodology and its use in policy evaluation research, see Thomas D. Cook and Donald T. Campbell, eds., *Quasi-Experimentation* (Chicago: Rand McNally, 1979); and Peter H. Rossi and Howard Freeman, *Evaluation*, 3d ed. (Beverly Hills, Calif.: Sage, 1985).

44.	James Gordon Ward, "Implementation and Monitoring of Judicial Mandates: An Interpretive Analysis," in *The Impacts of Litigation and Legislation on Public School Finance: Adequacy, Equity, and Excellence*, ed. Underwood and Verstegen (New York: Ballinger, 1990), 241.

45.	These data are reported in Allan R. Odden, "School Finance and Education Reform: An Overview," in *Rethinking School Finance*, ed. Odden, 5, table 1.1; 10, table 1.2.

46.	These data are reported in Lehne, *The Quest for Justice*, 169.

47.	Lehne, *The Quest for Justice*, 170.

48.	Data on state appropriations as a percentage of total school district revenues are drawn from New Jersey State Department of Education, *Annual Report* (Trenton, N.J.: Department of Education, various years).

49.	For a review of techniques useful to supplement the visual comparison of trends before and after a key policy intervention, see Thomas D. Cook and Donald T. Campbell, "Quasi-Experiments: Interrupted Time-Series Designs," 207–232; Leslie J. McCain and Richard McCleary, "The Statistical Analysis of the Simple Interrupted Time-Series Quasi-Experiment," 233–294; and Donald T. Campbell, "The Regression-Discontinuity Design," in *Quasi-Experimentation*, ed. Cook and Campbell, 137–146.

All these strategies assume the validity of one tail of a frequency distribution of actual research efforts that range from (1) the extreme pure-science experimental laboratory methods advocated by Campbell, (2) the middle-ground pragmatic methods favored by Rossi, and (3) the combination of "art-form" and "intuitive wisdom" strategies favored by Lee Cronbach or by E. G. Guba and Y. S. Lincoln. See Rossi and Freeman, *Evaluation*, 34–38, and for classic examples of interrupted time-series studies, 304–309.

The visual approach used in the present research emphasizes the utility of visual comparison of trends charted by LOTUS 1-2-3, Harvard Graphics, or other easily understandable programs.

50.	Annual expenditure data for every New Jersey school system from 1961 to 1991 were compiled and evaluated for this analysis. These data were collected by Russell S. Harrison and reported in his "Patterns of Inequality in New Jersey Public School Finance: Implications for Court Intervention, Implementation, and Impact," (paper presented at the annual meeting of the New Jersey Political Science Association, Trenton, N.J., March 1993). Sources that were useful in the collection of these data include, for the period 1961 to 1977, *Report of the Commissioner of Education*

(Trenton: New Jersey Department of Education, 1978), and for the period 1977 to 1991, *Legislative District Data Book* (New Brunswick, N.J.: Bureau of Government Affairs, 1992).

51. Johnson and Canon, *Judicial Policies*, 268.

52. Rosenberg, *The Hollow Hope*, 5–6.

53. *Robinson v. Cahill*, 303 A.2d 273, 277 (N.J. 1973).

54. 575 A.2d 359, 397, 406.

55. See the classic discussion in Donald L. Horowitz, *The Courts and Social Policy* (Washington, D.C.: Brookings Institution, 1977), chap. 2.

56. 575 A.2d 359, 388.

57. For recent contributions to the debate, which also provide a bibliography, see Eric A. Hanushek, "When School Finance 'Reform' May Not Be Good Policy," Richard J. Murnane, "Interpreting the Evidence on 'Does Money Matter?'" and Ronald F. Ferguson, "Paying for Public Education: New Evidence on How and Why Money Matters," *Harvard Journal of Legislation* 28 (Summer 1991): 423–498. The court in *Abbott* noted this dispute (at 575 A.2d 359, 403–408) but dismissed the research as inconclusive.

58. 575 A.2d 359, 406.

59. 575 A.2d 359, 403.

60. Horowitz, *Courts and Social Policy*, 45. For a summary of Horowitz's critique and a consideration of its applicability to state constitutional policymaking, see G. Alan Tarr and Russell S. Harrison, "Legitimacy and Capacity in State Supreme Court Policymaking: The New Jersey Supreme Court and Exclusionary Zoning," *Rutgers Law Journal* 15 (1984): 542–556.

61. Horowitz, *Courts and Social Policy*, chap. 2.

Bibliographic Essay

PRIMARY SOURCES

State constitutional conventions represent one of the most important sources for students of state constitutional politics. Fortunately, verbatim transcripts of several recent conventions, as well as records of many earlier ones, are available on microfiche. Listings of convention records and other pertinent materials are found in Cynthia E. Browne, *State Constitutional Conventions from Independence to the Completion of the Present Union, 1776–1959* (Westport, Conn.: Greenwood Press, 1973); and in Susan Rice Yarger, *State Constitutional Conventions, 1959–1975* (Westport, Conn.: Greenwood Press, 1976).

Likewise pertinent, of course, are the state constitutions themselves. Multivolume collections of state constitutions include Francis N. Thorpe, *The Federal and State Constitutions* (Washington, D.C.: Government Printing Office, 1909); and William F. Swindler, *Sources and Documents of United States Constitutions* (Dobbs Ferry, N.Y.: Oceana, 1982–). Greenwood Press is presently publishing a fifty-two-volume series titled *Reference Guides to the State Constitutions of the United States*, of which twenty-one volumes are in print. Each volume presents a constitutional history of a single state, together with a clause-by-clause commentary on the state's current constitution and a bibliography for the constitutional history and constitutional law of the state.

SECONDARY SOURCES

Historical Patterns

Several excellent studies of state constitutional politics in the eighteenth and nineteenth centuries are available. The development of state constitutions during the nation's early decades is chronicled in Donald S. Lutz, *Popular Consent and Popular Control: Whig Political Theory in the Early State Constitutions* (Baton Rouge: Louisiana State University Press, 1980); Elisha P. Douglass, *Rebels and Democrats: The Struggle for Equal Political Rights and Majority Rule during the American Revolution* (Chapel Hill: University of North Carolina Press, 1955); Jackson Turner Main, *The Sovereign States, 1775–1783* (New York: Franklin, Watts, 1973); and Gordon S. Wood, *The Creation of the American Republic, 1776–1787* (New York: W. W. Norton, 1969). Important regional and single-state studies include Fletcher M. Green, *Constitutional Development in the South Atlantic States, 1776–1860: A Study in the Evolution of Democracy* (Chapel Hill: University of North Carolina Press, 1930); Joan Wells Coward, *Kentucky in the New Republic: The Process of Constitution Making* (Lexington: University Press of Kentucky, 1979); Ronald M. Peters, Jr., *The Massachusetts Constitution of 1780: A Social Compact* (Amherst: University of Massachusetts Press, 1978); Charles Erdman, Jr., *The New Jersey Constitution of 1776* (Princeton, N.J.: Princeton University Press, 1929); and J. Paul Selsam, *The Pennsylvania Constitution of 1776: A Study in Revolutionary Democracy* (Philadelphia: University of Pennsylvania Press, 1930).

Overviews of state constitutional politics during the nineteenth century are provided by Willard Hurst, *The Growth of American Law: The Lawmakers* (Boston: Little, Brown, 1950); James Q. Dealey, *Growth of American State Constitutions* (New York: Da Capo Press, 1972); Albert L. Sturm, "The Development of American State Constitutions," *Publius: The Journal of Federalism* 12 (Winter 1982): 57–98; and Kermit L. Hall, "Mostly Anchor and Little Sail: The Evolution of American State Constitutions," in *Toward a Usable Past: Liberty under State Constitutions*, ed. Paul Finkelman and Stephen E. Gottleib (Athens: University of Georgia Press, 1991), 388–417. The interplay between economic development and state constitutional politics is explored in Herbert Hovenkamp, *Enterprise and American Law, 1836–1937* (Cambridge, Mass.: Harvard University Press, 1991); Tony Freyer, *Producers versus Capitalists: Constitutional Conflict in Antebellum America* (Charlottesville: University Press of Virginia, 1994); L. Roy Gunn, *The Decline of Authority: Public Economic Policy and Political Development in New York, 1800–1860* (Ithaca, N.Y.: Cornell University Press, 1988); and A. James Heins, *Constitutional Restrictions against State Debt* (Madison: University of Wisconsin Press, 1963). State constitutional conflicts over suffrage are detailed in James A. Henretta, "The Rise and Decline of 'Democratic-Republicanism': Political Rights in New York and the Several States, 1800–1915," in *Toward a Usable Past*, ed. Finkelman and Gottleib, 50–90; and in Chilton Williamson, *American Suffrage: From Property to Democracy, 1760–1860* (Princeton, N.J.: Princeton University Press, 1960). The classic convention debates over suffrage and representation in Virginia, Massachusetts, and New York are collected in Merrill D. Peterson, ed., *Democracy, Liberty, and Property: The State Constitutional Conventions of the 1820s* (Indianapolis, Ind.: Bobbs-Merrill, 1966). The Rhode Island rebellion sparked by failure to revise the state constitution is recounted in Marvin E. Gettleman, *The Dorr Rebellion: A Study in American Radicalism, 1833–1849* (New York: Random House, 1973).

An introduction to state constitutional developments in the latter half of the nineteenth century is provided by Morton Keller, *Affairs of State: Public Life in Nineteenth Century America* (Cambridge, Mass.: Belknap Press, 1977). Several studies have focused on constitutional developments in the West, including Gordon Morris Bakken, *Rocky Mountain Constitution Making, 1850–1912* (Westport, Conn.: Greenwood Press, 1987); David A. Johnson, *Founding the Far West: California, Oregon, and Nevada, 1840–1890* (Berkeley: University of California Press, 1992); Christian G. Fritz, "The American Constitutional Tradition Revisited: Preliminary Observations on State Constitution-Making in the Nineteenth-Century West," *Rutgers Law Journal* 25 (Summer 1994): 945–998; and Dennis C. Colson, *Idaho's Constitution: The Tie That Binds* (Moscow: University of Idaho Press, 1991). Southern efforts to reconstitutionalize white supremacy in the aftermath of Reconstruction are examined in J. Morgan Kousser, *The Shaping of Southern Politics: Suffrage Restrictions and the Establishment of the One-Party South, 1880–1910* (New Haven, Conn.: Yale University Press, 1974); and Ralph Chipman McDaniel, *The Virginia Constitutional Convention of 1901–1902* (Baltimore, Md.: Johns Hopkins University Press, 1928).

The vigorous debate during the late nineteenth century over the scope of powers to be exercised by state constitutional conventions is reflected in John Alexander Jameson, *A Treatise on Constitutional Conventions* (New York: Da Capo, 1972); and Walter F. Dodd, *The Revision and Amendment of State Constitutions* (Baltimore, Md.: Johns Hopkins University Press, 1910).

During the twentieth century, three political movements have dominated state constitutional politics. The first movement, led by elite reformers, involved the effort to replace nineteenth-century state constitutions with more streamlined and "modern" state charters. The document developed by reformers to advance their goal was the *Model State Constitution*, 6th ed. (New York: National Municipal League, 1963). Standard reform critiques of state constitutions include W. Brooke Graves, ed., *Major Problems in State Constitutional Revision* (Chicago: Public Administration Service, 1960); and John P. Wheeler, Jr., *Salient Issues of Constitutional Reform* (New York: National Municipal League, 1961). Developments during the period of greatest reform activity are surveyed in Albert L. Sturm, *Thirty Years of State Constitution-Making: 1938–1968* (New York: National Municipal League, 1970). The political conflicts at the conventions that proposed new state constitutions during this period are analyzed in Elmer E. Cornwell, Jr., Jay S. Goodman, and Wayne R. Swanson, *State Constitutional Conventions* (New York: Praeger, 1975). An overview of the use of constitutional conventions in the states is provided by Kermit L. Hall, Harold M. Hyman, and Leon V. Sigal, eds., *The Constitutional Convention as an Amending Device* (Washington, D.C.: American Historical Association and American Political Science Association, 1981). A thorough analysis of one failed reform effort is John P. Wheeler, *Magnificent Failure: The Maryland Constitutional Convention of 1967–1968* (New York: National Municipal League, 1972).

The second movement in state constitutional politics has been the effort to reinvigorate state declarations of rights as protections of individual rights. The voluminous legal literature on this "new judicial federalism" is surveyed in Earl M. Maltz, Robert F. Williams, and Michael Araten, "Selected Bibliography on State Constitutional Law, 1980–1989," *Rutgers Law Journal* 20 (Summer 1989): 1093–1113. *Rutgers Law Journal* also publishes a yearly survey of developments in state constitutional law. Useful collections of articles include Stanley H. Friedelbaum, ed., *Human Rights in the States: New Directions in Constitutional Policymaking* (Westport, Conn.: Greenwood Press, 1988); and "Special Issue: New Developments in State Constitutional Law,"

Publius: The Journal of Federalism 17 (Winter 1987): 1–179. Efforts to put the new judicial federalism into political context include Mary Cornelia Porter, "State Supreme Courts and the Legacy of the Warren Court: Some Old Inquiries for a New Situation," in *State Supreme Courts: Policymakers in the Federal System*, ed. Mary Cornelia Porter and G. Alan Tarr (Westport, Conn.: Greenwood Press, 1982); G. Alan Tarr and Mary Cornelia Aldis Porter, *State Supreme Courts in State and Nation* (New Haven, Conn.: Yale University Press, 1988); G. Alan Tarr, "The Past and Future of the New Judicial Federalism," *Publius: The Journal of Federalism* 24 (Spring 1994): 63–79; and John Kincaid, "The New Federalism Context of the New Judicial Federalism," *Rutgers Law Journal* (forthcoming).

The third major movement in state constitutional politics has been the use of the constitutional initiative to circumvent established political channels and promote fundamental change. Analyses of the politics of constitutional populism are found in David B. Magelby, *Direct Legislation: Voting on Ballot Propositions in the United States* (Baltimore, Md.: Johns Hopkins University Press, 1984); and Thomas E. Cronin, *Direct Democracy: The Politics of Initiative, Referendum, and Reform* (Cambridge, Mass.: Harvard University Press, 1989). Scholars have vehemently debated the effects of amendment via constitutional initiative; representative accounts include: Donald E. Wilkes, "First Things Last: Amendomania and State Bills of Rights," *Mississippi Law Journal* 54 (1984): 223–259; James M. Fischer, "Ballot Propositions: The Challenge of Direct Democracy to State Constitutional Jurisprudence," *Hastings Constitutional Law Quarterly* 11 (Fall 1983): 43–89; and Janice C. May, "Constitutional Amendment and Revision Revisited," *Publius: The Journal of Federalism* 17 (Winter 1987): 153–179.

Contemporary Controversies

Four contemporary controversies have attracted particular attention in recent years. The first is the constitutional politics of school-finance reform. Accounts of early reform efforts are included in Kern Alexander and K. Forbis Jordan, eds., *Constitutional Reform of School Finance* (Lexington, Mass.: Lexington Books, 1973). Later developments and the effects of reform efforts are considered in "Symposium: Investing in Our Children's Future: School Finance Reform in the '90s," *Harvard Journal on Legislation* 28 (Summer 1991): 293–568; and Julie Underwood and Deborah Verstegen, eds., *The Impacts of Litigation and Legislation on*

Public School Finance: Adequacy, Equity, and Excellence (New York: Harper & Row, 1990). For studies of school-finance reform in New Jersey, see Richard Lehne, *The Quest for Justice: The Politics of School Finance Reform* (New York: Longman, 1978); and Mark Jaffe and Kenneth Kersch, "Guaranteeing a State Right to Quality Education: The Judicial-Political Dialogue in New Jersey," *Journal of Law and Education* 20 (Summer 1991): 271–300. The Texas battle over school-finance reform is ably summarized in Janice C. May, "Financing Public Schools in Texas: A Protracted Imbroglio," *State Constitutional Commentaries and Notes* 2 (Fall 1980): 7–13.

A second major issue involves the role of state courts in extending the rights of defendants under state constitutions. Arguments for state judicial activism are presented in William J. Brennan, "State Constitutions and the Protection of Individual Rights," *Harvard Law Review* 90 (1977): 489–504; and Shirley Abrahamson, "Criminal Law and State Constitutions: The Emergence of State Constitutional Law," *Texas Law Review* 63 (March–April 1985): 1141–1193. Arguments against such activism are presented in Earl M. Maltz, "The Dark Side of State Court Activism," *Texas Law Review* 63 (March–April 1985): 995–1023; and Earl M. Maltz, "Lockstep Analysis and the Concept of Federalism," *Annals of the American Academy of Political and Social Science* 496 (March 1988): 98–106. The best overview of state rulings on the rights of defendants is Barry Latzer, *State Constitutions and Criminal Justice* (Westport, Conn.: Greenwood Press, 1991). The broader context of the dispute over expansion of defendants' rights is supplied by Stuart Scheingold, *The Politics of Street Crime* (Philadelphia, Pa.: Temple University Press, 1991). For an account of one effort to limit state judicial activism by constitutional amendment, see Christopher Slobogin, "State Adoption of Federal Law: Exploring the Limits of Florida's 'Forced Linkage' Amendment," *University of Florida Law Review* 39 (Summer 1987): 653–732.

Another major controversy has involved direct efforts to unseat state judges who have expansively interpreted state rights guarantees. The prime example is in California, where in 1986 Chief Justice Rose Bird and two associate justices lost their bids for reelection. The early political travails of Chief Justice Bird and the California Supreme Court are recounted in Preble Stolz, *Judging Judges* (New York: Free Press, 1981). The controversy over defendants' rights in California is described in Candace McCoy, *Politics and Plea Bargaining: Victims' Rights in California* (Philadelphia: University of Pennsylvania Press, 1994). The campaign that led to Bird's defeat is chronicled in John H. Culver and

John T. Wold, "Rose Bird and the Politics of Judicial Accountability in California," *Judicature* 70 (August–September 1986): 81–89; and John T. Wold and John H. Culver, "The Defeat of the California Justices: The Campaign, the Electorate, and the Issue of Judicial Accountability," *Judicature* 70 (April–May 1987): 348–355. The implications of the justices' defeat for state constitutional politics are assessed in Robert S. Thompson, "Judicial Retention Elections and Judicial Method: A Retrospective on the California Retention Election of 1986," *Southern California Law Review* 61 (September 1988): 2007–2064. The perspective of one of the defeated justices is presented in Joseph R. Grodin, *In Pursuit of Justice: Reflections of a State Supreme Court Justice* (Berkeley: University of California Press, 1989).

The fourth current controversy involves the movement to impose term limitations on state legislators, a movement that has had national ramifications. In this still-developing area, basic sources include: Bernard Grofman, ed., *Legislative Term Limits: Public Choice Perspectives* (Boston: Kluwer-Hijhoff, forthcoming); Gerald Benjamin and Michael J. Malbin, eds., *Limiting Legislative Terms* (Washington, D.C.: Congressional Quarterly Press, 1992); and David M. Mason, ed., *Term Limits: Sweeping the States?* (Washington, D.C.: The Heritage Foundation, 1992).

Index

Proposition 115 (California), 167, 168, 169
Proposition 131 (California), 121
Proposition 140 (California), 121
Public Records Law (Florida), 96n19; privacy and, 83, 84, 85
Public School Education Act (1975), 186, 190; enactment of, 182, 187
Punishment: cruel and unusual, 156; ideological war over, 141-42
Purdy, Tim, term limits and, 118, 119

Quality Education Act (1990), 182, 186, 197; opposition to, 183, 187-88

Rasmussen v. South Florida Blood Service (1987), privacy and, 90
Rausch, John David, Jr., on term limits, xvii-xviii
Raven v. Deukmejian (1990), 167, 168
Reagan, Ronald, 88, 116, 156, 157; crime issue and, 132
Reapportionment, xvi, 7
Referendum, 11, 44, 47, 50-51, 65; changes by, 50 (table); constitutional lawmaking through, 141-42; crime and, 129; national, 124
Rehnquist, William H.: appointment of, 170n9; rights and, 74, 171n9
Rehnquist Court, 154; search and seizure and, 159, 162
Restitution, 135, 138, 139
Restore Our American Rights (ROAR), 117
Retention elections, 88
Revision 1 Basic Document (Florida), 79-80, 93; opponents of, 81-82; privacy and, 92
Revision 2 Basic Document (Florida), 80; opposition to, 82, 92
Revisions, 28; amendments and, 27
Reynolds v. Sims (1964), 7
Reynoso, Cruz: death penalty reversals and, 157; retention election for, 166; Victims' Bill of Rights and, xviii
Rights: amendments concerning, 64-65; expanding, 74; legal doctrine concerning, xiv; positive, 65; protection of, xiii, xx

Right-to-die/refuse-treatment cases, privacy amendment and, 90
Robinson v. Cahill (1973), 160, 161, 172-73n39, 181-82, 185, 186, 187, 193, 194, 197; impact of, 179, 189-90, 191, 196; implementation of, 188, 189; judicial intervention and, 189; school finance and, 178, 182
Roe v. Wade (1973), 86
"Roll-off" phenomenon, 88
Rosenberg, Gerald: dynamic court model and, 180; on effective implementation, 188; judicial policymaking and, xix, 185; on rights, 184; on social reform, 181, 186, 193
Ross, Steven, term limits and, 117
Rules and Calendar Committee (Florida), SJR 935 and, 84

Sadowski, Bill, joint resolution by, 83
St. John, Ron, term limits and, 118
Salokar, Rebecca Mae, on amendment proposals, xvii
San Antonio Independent School District v. Rodriguez (1973), 185; equal protection and, 178
Scalia, Antonin, 144n17
Schabarum, Pete, term limits and, 122
Scheingold, Stuart, on criminal process, 130
Schimmiger, Robin, amendments by, 59
School expenditures: per student, 191-93, 192 (table); interdistrict distribution of, 191-93
School-finance litigation, 178, 197; legislative support for, 186; in New Jersey, 181-89
School-finance reform, xix; judicial effectiveness and, 194, 196; judicially mandated, 179; support for, 187
School funding, 48, 178; challenging, 179, 183, 184; equalization of, 194, 195, 196; performance and, 194
Search and seizure, 145n27, 151, 154-55; automobiles and, 161; in California, 159-63, 170n8; in Florida, 176n83; violations of, 165

About the Contributors

GERALD BENJAMIN is Professor of Political Science at the State University of New York at New Paltz and Director of the Center for New York State and Local Government Studies at SUNY's Rockefeller Institute of Government in Albany. From 1993 to 1995, he served as Research Director of New York's Temporary State Commission on Constitutional Revision. He has written or edited, alone or with others, twelve books and numerous government reports and articles, most of them dealing with state and local government in New York.

MELISSA CUSA is Assistant to the Director of the Center for New York State and Local Government Studies at the Nelson A. Rockefeller Institute of Government in Albany. She helped author several chapters of *The New York State Constitution: A Briefing Book* for New York's Temporary Commission on Constitutional Revision and was involved in every stage of the editing and production of that document.

RUSSELL S. HARRISON is Associate Professor of Political Science at Rutgers University (Camden) and holds a joint appointment in the Graduate Department of Public Administration and Public Policy. He is the author of *Inequality in Public School Finance: Validated Policies for*

Reform (1976) and has directed numerous studies involving policy evaluation research and economic development impact analysis, primarily in New Jersey.

BARRY LATZER is Professor of Government at the John Jay College of Criminal Justice and a member of the faculty of the doctoral program in Criminal Justice of the Graduate School of the City University of New York. He is the author of *State Constitutional Criminal Law* (1995) and of *State Constitutions and Criminal Justice* (Greenwood, 1991), as well as of numerous articles on constitutional criminal procedure and state courts.

DONALD S. LUTZ is Professor of Political Science at the University of Houston. He is an expert in early American political thought and the author of numerous books and articles, including *Popular Consent and Popular Control: Whig Political Theory in the Early State Constitutions* (1980) and *The Origins of American Constitutionalism* (1988).

CANDACE MCCOY is Assistant Professor of Criminal Justice at the Graduate School of Criminal Justice, Rutgers University (Newark). She is the author of *Politics and Plea Bargaining: Victims' Rights in California* (1994) and is currently working on a book about the impact of litigation on police practices.

JOHN DAVID RAUSCH, JR., is Assistant Professor of Political Science at Fairmont State College in West Virginia. He has published articles on term limits in *Oklahoma Politics*, the *National Civic Review*, and *Comparative State Politics*. His other research interests include legislative studies and direct democracy.

REBECCA MAE SALOKAR is Associate Professor of Political Science at Florida International University. She is the author of *The Solicitor General: The Politics of Law* (1992), as well as of several articles and chapters on the role of legal counsels for both the legislative and executive branches. Her current research focuses on the state constitutional right to privacy.

G. ALAN TARR is Professor of Political Science at Rutgers University (Camden). He is the author or coauthor of several books in judicial politics, including *State Supreme Courts in State and Nation* (1988), *Judicial Process and Judicial Policymaking* (1994), and *State Supreme*

Courts: Policymakers in the Federal System (Greenwood, 1982). He also serves as series editor of *Reference Guides to the State Constitutions of the United States*, published by Greenwood Press.

ISBN 0-313-28523-3

HARDCOVER BAR CODE